Editor
Martin A. Conway
The University of Leeds, UK

Associate Editors

Donna Rose Addis **Susan E. Gathercole** **Lia Kvavilashvili**
Patricia J. Bauer **J. Richard Hanley** **Michelle Moulds**
Karl-Heinz Bäuml **Joni Holmes** **Katherine Rawson**
Steve Dewhurst **Reed Hunt** **Jefferson A. Singer**

Consulting Editors

Alan D. Baddeley **Fergus I. M. Craik** **Henry L. Roediger III** **Daniel Schacter**

Aims and Scope of *Memory*

Memory publishes high quality research in all areas of memory research. This includes experimental studies of memory (including laboratory-based research, everyday memory studies and applied memory research), developmental, educational, neuropsychological, clinical and social research on memory. By representing all significant areas of memory research, the journal cuts across the traditional distinctions of psychological research. *Memory* therefore provides a unique venue for memory researchers to communicate their findings and ideas both to peers within their own research tradition in the study of memory, and also to the wider range of research communities with direct interest in human memory.

Memory is covered by the following abstracting, indexing and citation services: Current Contents/Social and Behavioral Sciences; Elsevier Science B.V.; Ergonomics Abstracts; European Reference Index for the Humanities (ERIH); Focus on Cognitive Psychology; MEDLINE; PsycBITE; PsycINFO; Research Alerts; SCOPUS; Social Sciences Citation Index; Sociological Abstracts.

Copyright: It is a condition of publication that authors assign copyright or license the publication rights in their articles, including abstracts, to Taylor & Francis. This enables us to ensure full copyright protection and to disseminate the article, and of course the journal, to the widest possible readership in print and electronic formats as appropriate. Authors retain many rights under the Taylor & Francis rights policies, which can be found at http://journalauthors.tandf.co.uk/preparation/copyright.asp. Authors are themselves responsible for obtaining permission to reproduce copyright material from other sources.

First published 2011 by Psychology Press

Published 2020 by Routledge
2 Park Square, Milton Park, Abingdon, Oxon OX14 4RN
52 Vanderbilt Avenue, New York, NY 10017

Routledge is an imprint of the Taylor & Francis Group, an informa business

Copyright © 2011 Taylor & Francis

All rights reserved. No part of this book may be reprinted or reproduced or utilised in any form or by any electronic, mechanical, or other means, now known or hereafter invented, including photocopying and recording, or in any information storage or retrieval system, without permission in writing from the publishers.

Notice:
Product or corporate names may be trademarks or registered trademarks, and are used only for identification and explanation without intent to infringe.

Typeset by Datapage (India) Private Limited, Chennai, India

ISBN 13: 978-1-84872-753-3 (pbk)
ISBN 13: 978-1-138-45170-4 (hbk)

AF739151

MEMORY, 2011, 19 (7), 685–696

Psychology Press
Taylor & Francis Group

SenseCam: A wearable camera that stimulates and rehabilitates autobiographical memory

Steve Hodges, Emma Berry, and Ken Wood

Microsoft Research Ltd, Cambridge, UK

SenseCam is a wearable digital camera that captures an electronic record of the wearer's day. It does this by automatically recording a series of still images through its wide-angle lens, and simultaneously capturing a log of data from a number of built-in electronic sensors. Subsequently reviewing a sequence of images appears to provide a powerful autobiographical memory cue. A preliminary evaluation of SenseCam with a patient diagnosed with severe memory impairment was extremely positive; periodic review of images of events recorded by SenseCam resulted in significant recall of those events. Following this, a great deal of work has been undertaken to explore this phenomenon and there are early indications that SenseCam technology may be beneficial to a variety of patients with physical and mental health problems, and is valuable as a tool for investigating normal memory through behavioural and neuroimaging means. Elsewhere, it is becoming clear that judicious use of SenseCam could significantly impact the study of human behaviour. Meanwhile, research and development of the technology itself continues with the aim of providing robust hardware and software tools to meet the needs of clinicians, patients, carers, and researchers. In this paper we describe the history of SenseCam, and the design and operation of the SenseCam device and the associated viewing software, and we discuss some of the ongoing research questions being addressed with the help of SenseCam.

Keywords: SenseCam; Wearable camera; Autobiographical memory.

SenseCam is a small digital camera designed to take photographs automatically, without user intervention, while it is being worn (Hodges et al., 2006; Microsoft Corporation, 2011). Unlike a regular digital camera or a cameraphone, it does not have a viewfinder or a display that can be used to frame photos. Instead it is fitted with a wide-angle (fish-eye) lens that maximises its field-of-view. This means that nearly everything in view of the wearer is captured by the camera. See Figure 1 and 2.

A number of electronic sensors are built into SenseCam. These sensors are monitored by the camera's microprocessor, and changes in sensor readings can be used to automatically trigger a photograph to be taken. For example, a significant change in light level or the detection of a person in front of the camera can be used as triggers. In addition, by default an internal timer is used to automatically trigger a photograph every 30 seconds. SenseCam also has a manual trigger button that lets the wearer take pictures in the more traditional fashion, a privacy button that causes the camera to stop taking photos for 4 minutes at a time, and an on-off button. Three LED lights and an internal sounder are used to give the wearer feedback.

The device is called SenseCam because two of the main components of its operation are sensing the environment and using its camera to

Address correspondence to: Steve Hodges, Microsoft Research, 7 JJ Thomson Avenue, Cambridge, CB3 0FB, UK. E-mail: steve.hodges@microsoft.com

© 2011 Psychology Press, an imprint of the Taylor & Francis Group, an Informa business
http://www.psypress.com/memory http://dx.doi.org/10.1080/09658211.2011.605591

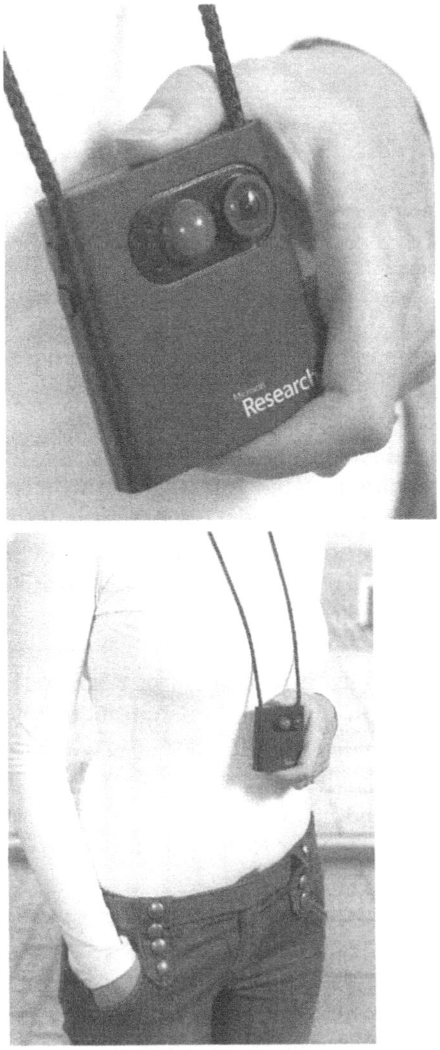

Figure 1. The SenseCam shown close-up and as typically worn, using an adjustable lanyard. The two side buttons are visible on the left, and there is an additional on-off button on the top of the device. There are three LED lights to indicate various aspects of operation. To view this figure in colour, please see the online issue of the journal.

record images. The images captured and stored by SenseCam during the course of an event may subsequently be uploaded onto a desktop or laptop computer via a USB connection. A custom SenseCam Image Importer application facilitates the transfer of images in this way. The images can then be viewed either one by one or in an animated sequence using a SenseCam Image Viewer application. This animation technique is rather like watching a movie of the event, but because the sequence of images can be displayed much more rapidly than they were captured, it's far quicker and easier than reviewing a video of the day.

A BRIEF HISTORY OF THE SENSECAM PROJECT

The SenseCam device has undergone a number of iterations since its inception in 2003. The original motivation for SenseCam was the idea of a "human black box recorder" (Wood, Fleck, & Williams, 2004) like the devices used in aeroplanes and some cars that continually record information from a variety of sensors in case it is useful subsequently. In 2003 such a notion was becoming a practical possibility for the first time, as the cost, size, and power consumption of the relevant electronic components continued to reduce, and the first SenseCam prototype incorporating a digital camera along with various other electronic sensors was made viable.

On a visit to Microsoft Research Cambridge towards the end of 2003, Narinder Kapur, Consultant Clinical Neuropsychologist at Addenbrooke's Hospital in Cambridge was shown a SenseCam prototype and he saw its potential to alleviate severe memory impairment in his patients. The following year Microsoft Research and Addenbrooke's Hospital initiated a clinical trial of SenseCam with a patient with severe memory impairment following a brain infection, whom we refer to as Mrs B (Berry et al., 2007; Hodges et al., 2006). This trial lasted many months, and as it went on it became increasingly clear that the use of SenseCam to capture digital images of events, coupled with the subsequent periodic review of these images, had a powerful effect on Mrs B's ability to recall the same events. It appeared that Mrs B had true autobiographical recollection of events that had occurred weeks and months earlier. She described thoughts, feelings, and happenings that were not depicted in the images themselves. What's more, even when the images were taken away from Mrs B so that she was unable to view them, she was still able to describe the events many months later. Therefore SenseCam images may provide such a powerful cue that reviewing them is sufficient to reinforce consolidation of the episode into a retrievable long-term memory store. By contrast, a written diary does not appear to provide powerful enough cues to overcome the hippocampal deficit (Berry et al., 2009).

On the basis of these preliminary clinical data from the Mrs B trial, in 2005 Microsoft Research

Figure 2. Example images captured by SenseCam. To view this figure in colour, please see the online issue of the journal.

started to design a more refined SenseCam prototype known as the v2.3 device (Hodges et al., 2006), described in detail later. The v2.3 SenseCam research prototype enabled further trials in Cambridge to be started and was also made available to the research community thereby seeding a network of collaborations across the world (Laursen, 2009). In the years that followed, Microsoft Research continued to produce SenseCam devices to the same v2.3 research prototype design, and disseminated around 300 of these to researchers and clinicians interested both in the technology itself and in a wide range of potential applications. Microsoft Research was also able to fund a number of collaborative projects in two tranches, first in 2005 and then another in 2007. An annual meeting for those working with SenseCam was initiated to facilitate the sharing of ideas, experiences and results. The first of these, held in the summer of 2007, was quite small, but by 2009 the "Annual SenseCam Symposium" was attracting an international attendance. The ever-growing interest in SenseCam in an increasing number of application areas has also enabled the commercialisation of SenseCam. The first product, the Vicon Revue (available from http://viconrevue.com/), is based on the v2.3 SenseCam research prototype. A brief history of SenseCam can be found in Table 1.

THE SENSECAM DEVICE

SenseCam design requirements

Experience with early prototypes showed that the form factor of SenseCam—its size and shape—is important. It must be convenient to put on and take off, and reasonably small and light so that it is comfortable while being worn. In work to date, users have almost exclusively worn the camera on a lanyard around their neck, which appears to meet these two criteria for most people, most types of clothing, and in most conditions. Our experience shows that ideally the camera should be worn reasonably high up, as this reduces unwanted movement and is closer to the eye-line.

In addition to the form factor of the device, other important practical issues include battery lifetime, storage capacity, and ease of use. It was critical that the device could operate for an entire day (i.e., around 12 hours of continuous operation), and ideally for 2 to 3 days in case the patient forgets to recharge it or does not have a charger with them. A related requirement is enough storage for at least 1 day's worth of data, and ideally in excess of 1 week. With enough on-board storage, it is possible to travel without needing a computer to upload the images to every evening.

SenseCam electronics

The "brain" of the SenseCam is an embedded microcontroller, which communicates with and controls a number of external sensors. The images and sensor data are stored on a standard 1GB SD card. Unlike most consumer digital cameras, the SD is not designed to be removed by the user—it is hidden within the device. Instead, a USB connection is used to copy data from the camera. The 0.3 megapixel (VGA resolution) images recorded by SenseCam are stored as compressed JPEG files on the internal SD memory card. The typical image size (around 30k bytes) allows for around 30,000 images to be stored on a 1GB SD card. Although digital stills cameras with very much higher resolutions are commonplace today, at the time the v2.3 SenseCam was designed it was much easier to use a lower-resolution off-the-shelf image capture module. The low resolution also has the side-effect of requiring less power when storing images.

In addition to image data, the memory card is used to store a log file which records the data

TABLE 1
A brief history of SenseCam

2003	SenseCam was born. The notion of a "black box" accident recorder motivated the first prototype.
	Addenbrooke's Hospital expresses interest.
2004	Initiation of trial with first amnesia patient, Mrs B.
2005	Initial results from Mrs B are very encouraging.
	New v2.3 SenseCam hardware developed.
	Microsoft Research initiates collaborations with academia.
2006	Interest grows as the Mrs B trial becomes more widely known.
	Trials with Alzheimer's patients initiated in Cambridge, UK.
2007	Several more collaborations between Microsoft Research and academics and clinicians initiated.
	First meeting of SenseCam collaborators in Cambridge, UK.
2008	Second SenseCam collaborators meeting, again in Cambridge, UK.
2009	First annual "SenseCam Symposium" in Chicago, US attracts an international audience.
	Vicon announce commercial version of SenseCam, the Vicon Revue.
2010	Vicon Revue becomes available.
	Over 50 research institutions and labs worldwide are using SenseCam in their research.

from the sensors every few seconds. The log file also records the reason for taking each photograph (e.g., manual shutter press, timed capture, or significant change in sensor readings, see next section). The SenseCam has a built-in real-time clock that ensures the timestamps of all files on the storage card are accurate.

The main components in SenseCam are listed in Table 2, along with a summary of their technical specifications. Figure 3 depicts the front and the back of the SenseCam circuit board and the main hardware components.

SenseCam is powered from a 980mAh 3.7V lithium-ion rechargeable battery, a similar size and capacity to those commonly used in mobile phones. This battery is recharged from a PC or from a mains power adapter over the USB connection, typically taking around 3 hours from "flat" to "fully charged". The battery lifetime of SenseCam depends on how frequently images are taken; the most power is consumed by capturing images and saving them to memory. The graph in Figure 4 shows that capturing images at the maximum rate of one approximately every 5 seconds can yield a battery life just below 12 hours. Typically SenseCam captures images every 30 seconds or so, giving a battery life close to 24 hours of continuous operation. SenseCam will maintain its real-time clock for up to 9 months without use.

SenseCam operation

The SenseCam device uses a very simple algorithm to trigger its camera: a photo will be taken every 30 seconds by default (this interval is configurable), and an extra photo will be taken every time the ambient light level changes significantly. In addition, if the camera is stationary and the passive infra red (PIR) sensor detects a person passing in front of the camera, a photo will be taken. Finally, an image may be captured manually at any time by pressing the "shutter" button on the device. In the case of manual capture SenseCam makes an audible "beep" to indicate that a photo has been taken successfully, but in all other cases it is silent in operation. A yellow light on the top of the device illuminates whenever a photo is being recorded.

TABLE 2
The main components in SenseCam in addition to the microcontroller, with a summary of their specification

Component	*Specification*
Flash memory	Standard SD card up to 2GB.
Camera module and wide-angle lens	VGA (640 $\times$ 480 pixel) resolution with 119° diagonal wide-angle lens.
Accelerometer	Tri-axis, range $\pm$ 2g.
Temperature	Range –5 to +125°C, $\pm$ 2°C.
Light level	Independent measurement of red, green, and blue intensity.
Passive infra red (PIR) body heat detector	Miniature form factor, low-power operation, wide-angle detection.
Push buttons	Three in total, configurable operation.
Sounder/buzzer	Simple tones for feedback to wearer.

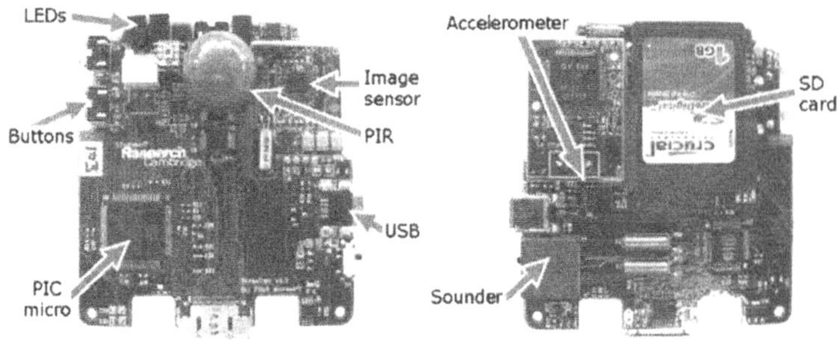

Figure 3. The front (left) and back (right) of the SenseCam circuit board. To view this figure in colour, please see the online issue of the journal.

It is also possible to temporarily stop taking pictures for a period of about 4 minutes by pressing the "privacy" button. When this button has been pressed, a red light comes on and the camera suspends operation; a beep sounds 15 seconds before the camera automatically starts taking pictures again. In order to extend the pause for another 4 minutes, the privacy button can be pressed again. On the other hand, pressing the manual shutter button at any time when the camera is suspended will cause the camera to resume taking photographs.

The aim of SenseCam is to capture enough images to record the significant elements of an event, without capturing an excessive number. In theory it would be possible for SenseCam to simply capture images as quickly as possible and then to select the best ones from these at a later time. However, there are a number of disadvantages to this approach: it would use significantly more power and memory, and would place an onus on the wearer or researcher to look through a great many more images than would otherwise be the case. Also, a device that captures snapshots every 30 seconds may arouse less concern than a device that captures images much more frequently.

The sensors can be individually enabled or disabled through the use of a configuration file on the SD memory card. It is also possible to configure many other aspects of the SenseCam device operation, such as what effect each push button has and how frequently photos are captured by default. Not only does this configurability aid testing and development, it also enables researchers, clinicians, and patients to tune device operation for specific needs.

SenseCam software

While the SenseCam device provides a convenient way of recording images and sensor data relating to an event, it provides no way of reviewing or analysing this information and only provides a relatively limited storage capacity (suitable for a few weeks of daily use). These limitations are overcome by connecting SenseCam to a computer via a USB cable. The images can be viewed on a PC-based SenseCam Image

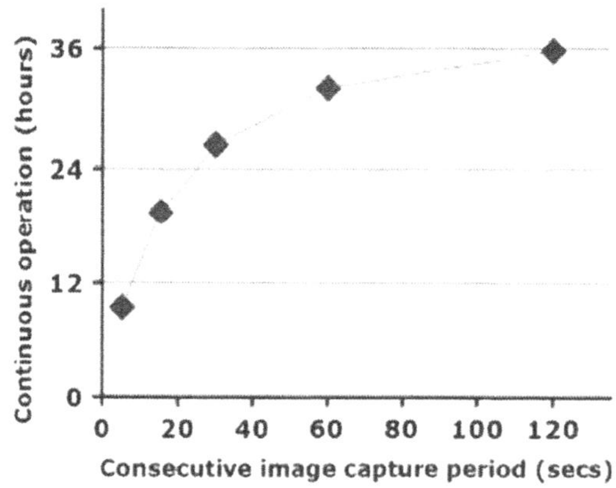

Figure 4. Graph showing how battery life is affected by frequency of image capture. Note that these data were collected from a SenseCam that had the latest, lowest-power version of the camera module fitted; some SenseCam devices have earlier versions that seem to be more power hungry. Battery capacity and hence battery lifetime will also decrease as the battery ages.

Viewer application we have developed that displays individual images and also replays image sequences and displays sensor data captured by the device. Figure 5 gives an example screenshot of the version of the Viewer application, which has been used most extensively in clinical trials to date.

The basis of the SenseCam Image Viewer, which is designed to be straightforward for people with no experience of computers to use, is a window in which images are displayed and a simple VCR-type control that allows an image sequence to be played slowly (around 2 images/second), quickly (around 12 images/second), rewound and paused. The animated sequence of images displayed in the "quick" mode creates a kind of "flip-book" movie effect and has been referred to previously as rapid-serial-visual presentation (RSVP; Spence, 2001). It turns out to be a quick but very effective way of reviewing a large number of images captured from the first-person perspective.

The viewer allows the user to delete images and to correct for the "fish-eye" lens effect. With long sequences of images it can be useful to associate named "bookmarks" with individual images or sequences. Once created, bookmarks can be used to help navigate a long image sequence—clicking on the thumbnail of a bookmark automatically advances or rewinds to that particular image in the sequence.

There are several viewer options. It is possible to display an analogue clock to indicate at what time of day the image displayed was originally taken and to load and display the raw sensor data associated with an image sequence; an example of this is shown inset in Figure 5.

THE FUTURE OF SENSECAM TECHNOLOGY

The camera

Although the device has proven to be well suited for research into a wide range of applications, there are many ways in which SenseCam could be improved. One of the most visible improvements that could be made to the SenseCam would be a size reduction. Given the improvements in electronic device technology over the 5 years since the original design, this is a very realistic proposition. The SenseCam research prototype includes an expansion port, which exposes various electrical signals to allow additional sensors to be connected, and the firmware to be modified. To date, two external sensors have been prototyped: an external image sensor and a digital compass. The external image sensor connects to the SenseCam via a flying lead and can be used in place of the built-in camera—so that the SenseCam unit itself can be worn inside a pocket for example, to protect it from rain. Alternatively, the external camera may be used as a second image-capture device, to generate a larger field of view. The design of a plug-in digital compass was motivated by the observation that it's beneficial to capture as many images as possible. If a wearer turns to face a new direction resulting in a new vista for themselves and the SenseCam, this is readily sensed by the compass since the SenseCam will rotate too (Budvytis, Scott, & Butler, 2008).

Many other sensors are natural choices for integration with SenseCam. One example is a GPS location tracker, which would allow the SenseCam to record its location when worn and "geo-tag"

Figure 5. The SenseCam Image Viewer application, allowing playback and review of SenseCam images and (inset) associated sensor readings. To view this figure in colour, please see the online issue of the journal.

captured images accordingly. Another idea is to record physiological data from the wearer, such as heart rate and galvanic skin response. Although we have used separate, standalone GPS and physiological data loggers in conjunction with SenseCam, and synchronised the time-stamped data subsequently, we have not designed a more integrated hardware solution. It is possible that future commercially available incarnations of SenseCam will do this.

Companion devices

SenseCam is designed to be small, low-powered, and unobtrusive in use, and therefore does not include any kind of display for reviewing captured images or sensor data. However, it would be useful to review images without the need for a PC and one can imagine a purpose-built plug-in companion device to do this. It would also be possible to build an interface into SenseCam for transferring images to a mobile phone, either via a cable or wirelessly via Bluetooth, so that a simple image viewer application on the phone could be used. Finally, another idea that has been suggested is a dedicated SenseCam "docking station" which makes the uploading of SenseCam data and recharging of the device even easier than it is using a USB connection to a computer. While we have no concrete plans for such devices, we see no technical impediment to building them given suitable demand.

SENSECAM RESEARCH: MEMORY AND BEYOND

Why are SenseCam images such a powerful cue for recall?

We do not yet know why SenseCam images cue recall of events so powerfully. Anecdotally, both healthy users and memory-impaired patients have experienced so-called "Proustian" moments of recall when viewing SenseCam images of personally experienced events. Particular images often

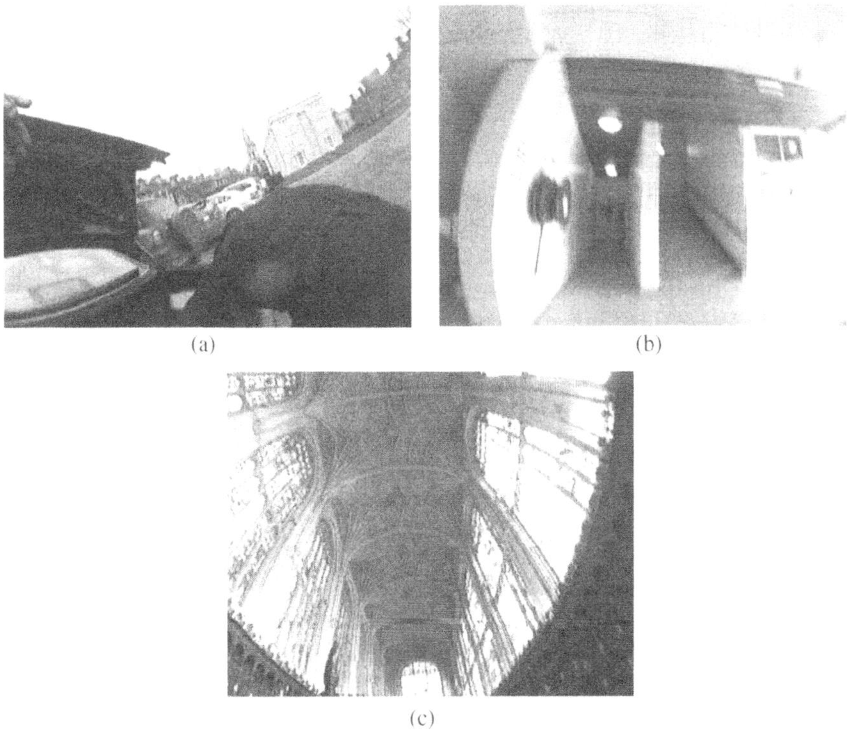

Figure 6. Example SenseCam images that led to autobiographical recall in different patients. (a) The mix of new, pale stonework and old, dirty stonework in the set of buildings in the background led a patient with moderate Alzheimer's disease to ponder the incongruence; a private thought at the time which she subsequently recalled. (b) Despite the extremely low image quality, a TBI patient remembered having to go up a flight of stairs to use the lavatory, and this triggered recall of subsequent events. (c). An image of the vaulted roof in King's College chapel, Cambridge. On viewing this image a patient with Alzheimer's disease remembered what he had thought at the time he was there: "This should be one of the Seven Wonders of the World!". To view this figure in colour, please see the online issue of the journal.

trigger an autobiographical recollection, where the thoughts, feelings, and emotions at the time the event was experienced come "flooding back". Researchers experimenting with SenseCam themselves, healthy people, and memory-impaired patients have consistently reported this effect; they state that something in the image—often the apparently mundane or trivial—triggers a memory for a private thought or feeling they had at the time, and this seems to enable access to the rest of the memory for the event. We therefore propose that one of the secrets of SenseCam is quite simple: it takes hundreds of images and at least one of these images is likely to have captured a moment when encoding of a memory took place. When the patient subsequently views that image, taken from their viewpoint at the time of encoding, recall of the event is triggered. This has important implications for rehabilitation because it suggests that, in order for the patient to gain maximum benefit from the device, he or she should have the opportunity to view all of their images. Figure 6 shows some example images which have triggered recall in patients the authors have worked with; on the face of it, none of these images is an obvious candidate for cueing detailed and vivid recall.

Another theory of why SenseCam images cue recall so powerfully is that the sequences closely resemble normal autobiographical memories (Brewer, 1986; Conway, 2005). Properties of SenseCam images that may be similar to episodic memory images are that they represent short time slices of experience, they are temporally ordered, they are visual, but samples rather than continuous, they are not taken intentionally (i.e., they are formed outside awareness), they have a field or viewer's perspective, and they are triggered by sensory changes that may correspond to event boundaries. That is, episodic memories may be formed at goal junctions of action sequences when there is major change in the predominating goal. It is possible therefore that the detection of changes in the wearer's activity and in their environment through onboard sensors could cause the SenseCam to trigger at junctions of goal processing. For these reasons it could well be possible that SenseCam produces images that are close in nature to visual autobiographical memories. This quality of the images along with the frequency of image capture may combine to provide a strong stimulus for recall.

Not only does the review of SenseCam images seem to cue recall more effectively than other approaches, such as the review of a written diary, but it also appears to be more enjoyable for the patient. Both anecdotal feedback and more formal assessment indicate that patients feel more confident, less stressed, and more able to cope with their impairment when using SenseCam compared to keeping and reviewing a written diary or using no intervention at all (Berry et al., 2007).

Neurological implications of SenseCam image review

Since the initial study with Mrs B was undertaken (Hodges et al., 2006; Wood et al., 2004) we have carried out a functional magnetic resonance imaging (fMRI) study, which shows that when Mrs B views SenseCam images she has recently reviewed it causes activation in parts of her brain associated with normal autobiographical remembering (Berry et al., 2009). Other authors have found similar results with memory-impaired patients (Loveday & Conway, 2011). Moreover there is evidence that the hippocampus activates in healthy controls when they are either viewing SenseCam images or when they are remembering events that they have rehearsed with SenseCam (St. Jacques, Conway, Lowder, & Cabeza, 2011).

A tentative hypothesis arising from these studies is that, if it is true that SenseCam causes increased activation of regions of the brain associated with autobiographical memory, then stimulating these brain regions through the use of SenseCam may lead to improved memory and cognition more generally in healthy and impaired populations. This hypothesis has yet to be empirically tested but is nevertheless an exciting possibility. The evidence from these studies and others also suggests that SenseCam may be valuable as a tool for investigating normal memory through behavioural and neuroimaging means.

Combining SenseCam images with physiological data

Some of our collaborators have investigated the use of physiological measures in conjunction with SenseCam images (Bridnley, Bateman, & Gracey, 2010). In the clinical setting doing so can enhance the ability of brain-injured patients to develop awareness of, and therefore improve, emotional regulation. Improvement in emotional regulation is especially important to participation in everyday life after a brain injury; it may facilitate the return to social and professional activities thereby reducing the likelihood of contact with mental health services and the criminal justice system.

Work to date has focused on collaboratively reviewing SenseCam image sequences and related biometric information with the patient, and identifying emotional trigger situations. However, practical difficulties such as a lack of clinician time and the technical challenges of combining images and sensor data have made it difficult to develop these potential applications further. We hypothesise that the development of a robust, easy to use software application that combines SenseCam images with physiological markers such as heart-rate, galvanic skin response, and skin temperature data will allow clinicians and researchers to quickly identify in a valid and reliable way the triggers or events that lead to emotional arousal.

Moreover, it has been suggested that combining SenseCam imagery with physiological measures could be used within standard cognitive behavioural therapy settings to treat a range of psychological disorders such as depression, anxiety, and psychosis. For example, SenseCam images might help in the treatment of depressed patients, by enhancing therapeutic interventions that aim to alter negative bias by helping patients to remember and elaborate positive events.

Exploiting SenseCam image content

The SenseCam Image Importer and Viewer software (described earlier) provides the basic image-handling functionality required for much of the current clinical work. However, there is also research underway using more sophisticated image-processing techniques to expand and improve the range of research applications of SenseCam.

One of our collaborators has worn a SenseCam every day since June 2006, amassing in excess of 5 million images in that time (Doherty, Pauly-Takacs, Gurrin, Moulin, & Smeaton, 2009). These images have been used as part of an even larger data set for developing and testing algorithms that allow image content to be categorised automatically, thereby inferring the activity of the wearer (Byrne, Doherty, Snoek, Jones, & Smeaton, 2008; Doherty, O'Conaire, Blighe, Smeaton, & O'Connor, 2008). Examples of activities that may be established in this way include socialising, eating (and what types of food), travel behaviours, the environments that people experience (urban or rural), whether they are working at a desk or computer, and the movement of the user (whether they are walking, standing, or sitting). The combination of SenseCam as an automatic data collection tool that requires no conscious input from the wearer, with the subsequent automatic analysis of the images, provides a light-weight, continuous way of collecting data relating to many aspects of daily life. The applications to outcome measurements in medical and other settings are potentially numerous.

Work has also been carried out to explore ways of automatically detecting unusual and pertinent images from large data sets (Doherty, 2009). Given people's natural tendency to forget the routine or mundane, a way of detecting images that fall broadly into that category is likely to be valuable, whether it's used to hide those images (since they may be less relevant to the user) or to promote them (since they are less likely to be memorable). The categorisation and prioritisation of recorded images can be used to alter the way in which images and sequences are presented to the user (Lee et al., 2008), an area of research that will become increasingly important as the size of SenseCam images collections continues to grow. A final area of research highlighted here is work that uses information relating to the names of geographical places and iconic landmarks gathered from the Internet to provide additional context when viewing SenseCam image sequences (Doherty, 2009).

Further applications

In addition to its value as a memory aid, many other applications have been proposed for SenseCam technology. The authors have noted that experience with SenseCam in one domain has a tendency to generate enthusiasm for its application in many others. For example, there is interest in using SenseCam as a tool to assist in the assessment of physical and mental health problems such as autism, learning disabilities, and neurological conditions. Examples include assessing how much physical activity a patient undertakes or monitoring the number of face-to-face interactions a patient has in a typical week. This type of assessment can be continued for months or even years after an intervention to determine long-term outcomes.

Monitoring travel behaviour and exercise with SenseCam is also likely to be beneficial in programmes designed to improve fitness and/or reduce the weight of patients. Using standard techniques such as questionnaires, accurately monitoring the extent and nature of exercise that people partake in throughout the day is difficult. SenseCam provides a way to unobtrusively monitor daily activities (Kelly & Foster, 2010), and ultimately the computer vision and machine learning techniques outlined earlier may be able to categorise these automatically. A related use of SenseCam is monitoring the type, amount, and frequency of food, drink, or medication intake. SenseCam provides ground truth data that is otherwise difficult to obtain, and in the longer term we hope that manual analysis of the data will be replaced by automated image analysis techniques.

SenseCam may be useful in emergency settings. It has been suggested that this approach could be useful in a variety of scenarios, including use by the ambulance service for correlating the speed and nature of treatment at the scene of a road traffic accident with long-term patient outcome, and deployment in natural disaster situations such as the recent earthquake in Haiti where SenseCam was trialled during a search and rescue mission. Law enforcement, military, and security organisations have suggested that SenseCam might be useful both as a tool for documenting situations in the field and as a way of eliciting vivid recall by personnel during subsequent debriefing.

SenseCam has been used in innovative ways to get a first-hand account of the lives of certain groups of people for whom this would otherwise be difficult. For example research is underway in which children with autism and people with learning disabilities wear the device during the course of a day. The images are reviewed by their carers to better understand how they experience daily life (Buchanan, Frith, & Conboyhill, 2009; Marcu & Hayes, 2010). Similar research has been suggested for other situations, for example as a way to understand how both doctors and patients experience their time in Accident and Emergency departments.

Researchers have used SenseCam as a tool for ethnography since it provides a way of unobtrusively recording behaviour both of the wearer and people with whom the wearer interacts (Byrne et al., 2008). In education settings SenseCam provides a way for teachers to enhance the reflective practice techniques sometimes used during on-the-job development (Fleck & Fitzpatrick, 2006). Research into the obvious questions surrounding the privacy implications of SenseCam and other recording devices has also been published (Nguyen et al., 2009).

Finally, since its inception SenseCam technology has been associated with the burgeoning field of life-logging, first mooted over 60 years ago (Bush, 1945) and now a practical possibility (Bell & Gemmell, 2007). The prime tenet of life-logging is that advances in technology will allow us to record every aspect of our daily lives and the minutiae of our interactions with others, and that this will greatly improve our lives by freeing us from the constraints and fallibilities of human memory. But there is also considerable scepticism about the feasibility of this ideal and about its desirability (Mayer-Schönberger, 2009). Our research both informs and sidesteps this debate by demonstrating clear value of a specific life-logging technology to a number of important applications.

Remaining questions

Despite the wide range of research already undertaken, there are still a great many outstanding questions about SenseCam and its role in cognition. These include: "How often and at what interval are patients required to view images in order for the memories to become consolidated?", "Is mass practice as effective as spaced rehearsal?", "For how long are memories retained?", "How do different classes of patient or injury respond differently to the images, or is the effect highly heterogeneous, even among patient types?", "What is the importance of first-person image capture?", "Do only 'important' images need to be viewed or is it necessary that these images are contained within their temporally ordered sequence?", "Does audio or annotation improve memory recall and retention?", "What is the effect of improved autobiographical recollection on a patient's well-being?", "Can SenseCam be used effectively to improve semantic memory, prospective memory or executive functioning?"

and "Are the sensors important and if so, how and why?"

Work with SenseCam in research laboratories and clinics around the world is beginning to address many of these questions, and we encourage people to participate in the SenseCam research community, both online (SenseCam wiki) and via the Annual SenseCam Symposium.

CONCLUSIONS

SenseCam is a small digital camera designed to take photographs regularly and passively without user intervention, while being worn. The photos can subsequently be uploaded via USB onto a PC and viewed using a simple interface. Preliminary research indicates that SenseCam aids the recall of episodic memories in patients with severe memory impairment and that early repeated viewing of SenseCam images may reinforce consolidation of the episode into a long-term memory store. Neuroimaging studies indicate that viewing SenseCam images of personally experienced events activates parts of the brain involved in normal autobiographical memory in both healthy and impaired populations.

It appears that SenseCam is particularly suited to people with memory or cognitive impairment because it captures images autonomously, enabling patients to record their experiences without conscious thought, meaning that the wearer can truly participate in an event without having to pause to capture the moment. SenseCam also appears to be less burdensome than the use of a regular camera or written diary.

A great many research questions remain. We do not yet know why SenseCam is such a powerful memory aid: it may be that the sheer volume of images means that even in severely impaired patients one of the images is bound to cue recall, or that the first-person viewpoint of the images stimulates recollection because they are similar to normal episodic memory.

New research in the computer science domain applies computer vision techniques to the content of the images, thereby enabling the activity of the wearer to be inferred. Work to automatically label, segment, and present pertinent images and image sequences is also underway and is likely to enable numerous additional applications for SenseCam in both clinical and non-clinical areas. Worldwide, research continues into the potential of this simple yet intriguing device.

REFERENCES

Bell, G., & Gemmell, J. (2007). A digital life. *Scientific American*, March.

Berry, E., Hampshire, A., Rowe, J., Hodges, S., Kapur, N., Watson, P., et al. (2009). The neural basis of effective memory therapy in a patient with limbic encephalitis. *Journal of Neurology, Neurosurgery, and Psychiatry with Practical Neurology, 80*, 1202–1205.

Berry, E., Kapur, N., Williams, L., Hodges, S., Watson, P., Smyth, G., et al. (2007). The use of a wearable camera, SenseCam, as a pictorial diary to improve autobiographical memory in a patient with limbic encephalitis. [Special issue, "Encephalitis: Assessment and Rehabilitation Across the Lifespan"]. *Neuropsychological Rehabilitation, 17*(4/5), 582–681.

Brewer, W. F. (1986). What is autobiographical memory? In D. Rubin (Ed.), *Autobiographical memory* (pp. 25–49). Cambridge, UK: Cambridge University Press.

Brindley, R., Bateman, A., & Gracey, F. (2011). Exploration of use of SenseCam to support autobiographical memory retrieval within a cognitive-behavioural therapeutic intervention following acquired brain injury. *Memory, 19*(7), 745–757.

Buchanan, M., Frith, H., & Conboyhill, S. (2009). *Towards utilizing SenseCam and positive psychology to increase subjective wellbeing in adults with learning disabilities.* SenseCam 2009 Symposium at the 39th Annual Meeting of the Society for Neuroscience: Neuroscience 2009, Chicago, USA, 16–17 October.

Budvytis, I., Scott, J., & Butler, A. (2008, May). Compass-based automatic picture taking using SenseCam. In *Adjunct Proceedings of Pervasive 2008, the Sixth International Conference on Pervasive Computing, May 2008, Sydney, Australia* (pp. 41–44). Berlin, Germany: Springer-Verlag.

Bush, V. (1945). As we may think. *Life Magazine*, September.

Byrne, D., Doherty, A., Smeaton, A. F., Jones, G., Kumpulainen, S., & Jarvelin, K. (2008). *The SenseCam as a tool for task observation.* HCI 2008, 22nd BCS HCI Group Conference, Liverpool, UK, 1–5 September.

Byrne, D., Doherty, A. R., Snoek, C. G. M., Jones, G. F., & Smeaton, A. F. (2008). *Validating the detection of everyday concepts in visual lifelogs.* SAMT 2008 – 3rd International Conference on Semantic and Digital Media Technologies, Koblenz, Germany, 3–5 December.

Conway, M. A. (2005). Memory and the self. *Journal of Memory and Language, 53*, 594–628.

Doherty, A., Pauly-Takacs, K., Gurrin, C., Moulin, C., & Smeaton, A. F. (2009). *Three years of SenseCam images – Observations on cued recall.* Invited speech at SenseCam 2009, Symposium at the 39th Annual

Meeting of the Society for Neuroscience: Neuroscience 2009, Chicago, USA, 16–17 October.

Doherty, A. R. (2009). *Providing effective memory retrieval cues through automatic structuring and augmentation of a lifelog of images* (PhD thesis). Dublin City University, Dublin, Ireland.

Doherty, A. R., Ó Conaire, C., Blighe, M., Smeaton, A. F., & O'Connor, N. (2008). *Combining image descriptors to effectively retrieve events from visual lifelogs.* MIR 2008 – ACM International Conference on Multimedia Information Retrieval, Vancouver, Canada, 30–31 October.

Fleck, R., & Fitzpatrick, G. (2006). Supporting reflection with passive image capture. Paper presented at the 7th International Conference on the Design of Cooperative Systems, May 9–12, 2006, Carry-le-Rouet, Provence, France.

Hodges, S., Williams, L., Berry, E., Izadi, S., Srinivasan, J., Butler, A., et al. (2006). SenseCam: A retrospective memory aid. In P. Dourish & A. Friday (Eds.), *Ubicomp 2006, the 8th International Conference on Ubiquitous Computing, Lecture Notes in Computer Science LNCS 4206* (pp. 177–193). Berlin, Germany: Springer-Verlag.

Kelly, P., & Foster, C. (2010). *A new technology for measuring our journeys: Results from a pilot study.* Early Career Investigator Prize. 2010 Annual Conference of the International Society of Behavioral Nutrition and Physical Activity, Minneapolis, 9–12 June.

Laursen, L. (2009). A memorable device. *Science, 323*, 1422–1423.

Lee, H., Smeaton, A. F., O'Connor, N., Jones, G., Blighe, M., Byrne, D., et al. (2008). Constructing a SenseCam visual diary as a media process [Special issue "Canonical processes of media production"]. *Multimedia Systems Journal, 14*(6), 341–349.

Loveday, C., & Conway, M. A. (2011). Using SenseCam with an amnesic patient: Accessing inaccessible everyday memories. *Memory, 19*(7), 697–704.

Marcu, G., & Hayes, G. R. (2010). Use of SenseCam in therapeutic interventions for children with autism. In G. R. Hayes & D. S. Tan (Eds.), *Proceedings of the Workshop on Interactive Systems in Healthcare (WISH)* (pp. 113–116). Atlanta, GA: Dealer Analysis Group.

Mayer-Schönberger, V. (2009). *Delete: The virtue of forgetting in the digital age.* Princeton, NJ: Princeton University Press.

Microsoft Corporation (2011). Microsoft Research SenseCam website. Retrieved from: http://research.microsoft.com/sensecam.

Spence, R. (2001). *Rapid, serial and visual: A presentation technique with potential. Information visualisation* (pp. 13–19). Harlow, UK: Addison Wesley.

Nguyen, D. H., Marcu, G., Hayes, G. R., Truong, K. N., Scott, J., Langheinrich, M., et al. (2009). Encountering SenseCam: Personal recording technologies in everyday life. In S. Helal, H. Gellersen, & S. Consolvo (Eds.), *Proceedings of Ubicomp 2009: The 11th International Conference on Ubiquitous Computing* (pp. 165–174). New York, NY: ACM Press.

SenseCam Wiki (n.d.). In *Wikipedia*. Retrieved September 2, 2011, from http://www.clarity-centre.org/sensecamwiki.

St. Jacques, P. L., Conway, M. A., Lowder, M., & Cabeza, R. (2011). Watching my mind unfold vs. yours: An fMRI study using a novel camera technology to examine neural differences in self-projection of self versus other perspectives. *Journal of Cognitive Neuroscience, 23*(6), 1275–1284.

Wood, K., Fleck, R., & Williams, L. (2004). Playing with SenseCam. In *Proceedings of Playing with Sensors: Exploring the boundaries of sensing for playful ubiquitous computing, Workshop at Ubicomp 2004, the 6th International Conference on Ubiquitous Computing.* Retrieved from http://www.sussex.ac.uk/Users/rmmf20/SenseCamPlay.pdf.

MEMORY, 2011, 19 (7), 697–704

Psychology Press
Taylor & Francis Group

Using SenseCam with an amnesic patient: Accessing inaccessible everyday memories

Catherine Loveday[1] and Martin A. Conway[2]

[1]Department of Psychology, University of Westminster, London, UK
[2]Institute of Psychological Sciences, University of Leeds, Leeds, UK

Forgetting is a normal and everyday occurrence that may sometimes reflect a complete loss of the mnemonic record or a failure to encode it in the first place. However, on many occasions with the help of cues we can eventually or suddenly recall a memory that seemed to be lost, thus highlighting the probability that many instances of "forgetting" may in fact reflect inaccessibility rather than true loss. We report here on our amnesic patient CR who presents an extreme example of this normal everyday forgetting. For 4 weeks, CR recorded regular personal autobiographical events both on a SenseCam (henceforth SC) and in a written diary form. Subjective and objective aspects of recall were measured each weekend both without any cues and then with either a SC or diary cue. We show that the SC enabled CR to recall significantly more detailed episodic memories than reading the diary and importantly we observed that the qualitative nature of these memories was different. We comment on the considerable potential of SC for therapeutic purposes.

Keywords: Amnesia; Memory access; SenseCam; Forgetting; Proust.

Every day, people form memories that they later cannot access (Williams, Conway, & Baddeley, 2008). In a series of studies people recalled all the events of a day at the end of a day, or at various delays up to 2 weeks (Loveday & Conway, 2010). Failure to recall increased with each day's delay and at a 5-day delay recall was radically reduced. There seem a number of possibilities here. One might be that many memories formed during the day are simply forgotten, i.e., permanently removed from long-term memory. Perhaps they are over-written or one of the other accounts about forgetting applies. However, in some cases people remember an event they thought they had "forgotten" and this suggests the problem is not generally one of a permanent removal or deletion from long-term memory but rather a lowering or loss of accessibility. Our hypothesis is that if an event becomes represented in long-term memory it is never lost until the neural networks in which it is represented themselves decay and become dysfunctional. It follows from this that the forgetting of everyday events, which have been represented in memories in long-term memory, is mainly the product of a loss of access and, in particular, an inability to find or generate an effective cue that could access a "forgotten" memory. In the present study we show how images from SC often present such cues and, when they do, "forgotten" memories come to mind in what we have termed "Proustian moments" of remembering.

A "Proustian moment" (PM) is a moment of intense recollection when images of the past flood into consciousness, and the rememberer has a powerful experience of recollection. Such moments have an almost "aha!" quality to them and may often feature the recall of highly specific

Address for correspondence: Catherine Loveday, Department of Psychology, University of Westminster, 309 Regent Street, London, W1B 2UW, UK. E-mail: c.loveday@westminster.ac.uk

© 2011 Psychology Press, an imprint of the Taylor & Francis Group, an Informa business
http://www.psypress.com/memory http://dx.doi.org/10.1080/09658211.2011.610803

details that were not available previously and, in some cases, were not previously known. According to our account of autobiographical remembering, PMs occur when highly specific episodic memories become part of an autobiographical construction and enter conscious awareness (Conway, 2005, 2009). An autobiographical memory is a mental construction in which conceptual autobiographical knowledge and episodic memories are activated together. According to this account, autobiographical memories are patterns of activation over conceptual knowledge structures that can index specific episodic memories. Such patterns of activation are triggered and shaped by successively generated cues which in turn are elaborated by executive control processes (for an extended account of this model see Conway, 2005, 2009). Critical to this process is the eventual creation of a cue that can access episodic memories. Without such a cue a specific memory cannot be constructed and the representation remains at the conceptual level—something like this appears to occur in some clinically depressed patients (Williams et al., 2007), and in some brain-damaged patients (Baddeley & Wilson, 1986). We suggest, however, that it a fairly normal and common occurrence and that we often have conceptual knowledge of past events without being able to recall episodic details. For example, a person might know that 5 days ago they were at work, but recall nothing else. In contrast, a person who has a relevant cue may recall an episode in detail. Consider another example: A colleague who viewed SC photographs taken at an academic meeting of his walk into the university where the meeting was held, recognised the street, he "knew" he had walked down it, but then quite suddenly and unexpectedly recalled the song that had being playing on his iPod at this point in his walk. Note that this was after a 3-month retention interval. We will see that such PMs are far from unusual when viewing SC photographs.

Our amnesic patient CR, with a large right hemisphere lesion in the medial temporal lobe, presents an extreme example of this normal, everyday, forgetting and is thus an ideal case study in which to investigate the potential for SC cues in promoting the retrieval of otherwise unrecovered specific episodic details. An increasing number of studies offer good evidence that SC cues can significantly enhance recall in both healthy and memory-impaired populations (see e.g., Browne, Berry, Kapur, et al., 2011). Probably the most well-known and earliest published example is the case of Mrs B, a lady with a severe memory impairment described by Berry et al. (2007). Mrs B showed notable and long-term improvement in recall of personally experienced events that had been recorded and reviewed on SC. The following study was designed to extend and develop the current understanding of how and why SC may promote remembering, in particular by assessing the qualitative nature of SC-cued recall. Specifically, the following study investigates the differential effects of SC and written diaries on subjective and objective measures of remembering in CR.

THE CASE OF CR

CR is a 47-year-old woman who, at the age of 44, suffered a severe case of herpes simplex viral encephalitis, leaving her with significant damage to the right side of her brain, including a large portion of the medial temporal lobe extending to the fusiform gyrus, basal ganglia, the insula, and the inferior frontal lobe. CR has a profound amnesia for her 20s, 30s, and early 40s, to the extent that she is unable to recall any episodic details about the birth or development of any of her children. In addition she demonstrates a lesser but still significant level of amnesia for her childhood and adolescence. Formal assessment using the Autobiographical Memory Interview (AMI; Kopelman, Wilson, & Baddeley, 1989) reveals a relatively intact personal semantic memory for all periods but significantly impaired memory for specific autobiographical/episodic memories at all ages. It appears that while CR is able to recall some specific autobiographical memories, these are drawn from a small library of well-learned stories, not unlike the case of patient SS (Cermak & O'Connor, 1983). Those that do have the qualities of a more genuine autobiographical memory tend not to be generated spontaneously or in response to general cues but rather are prompted by highly specific cues. CR's family describe her autobiographical memory as a locked vault that can be opened but only through prompting with very specific triggers. Further testing with the Autobiographical Memory Test (AMT; Williams & Broadbent, 1986) supported these findings, with CR showing a strong tendency to respond with very generalised memories. Some specific memories were produced but only two of these were more than a few days old and once again these appeared to be well-learned stories that were repeated on a number of times throughout our visits. In summary, in terms of autobiographical memory functioning CR showed a very unreliable and inconsistent memory for anything that was more than 3 days old.

In terms of her current neuropsychological functioning, formal testing reveals that CR is of high average intelligence, with good short-term and working memory, and with executive functioning that lies within the normal range. However, she shows some impairment on any recall that extends to 30 minutes or more and has a tendency to produce intrusions and repetition errors.

METHOD

Following an initial brief neuropsychological assessment (reported above), CR was asked to record one discrete event per weekday on the SC for a period of 4 weeks, and to write a brief diary-style account as soon as possible after the event, as part of a larger ongoing study. Each written account was recorded with a date and CR was also asked to give each event a nominal title (e.g., "visit to Red Cross show"), which she was asked to record on a separate sheet. A discrete event was defined as anything that had a clear beginning and end, for example a shopping trip or lunch with a friend. Typically these were between 1 and 2 hours long. CR was also assured that she should not worry if she was unable to record an event on any particular day or for whatever reason preferred not to.

Throughout this 4-week period CR's husband (a highly qualified and practising medic) carried out a recall session each weekend to assess memory for each of the events that had been recorded in the preceding week. These sessions were carried out at their convenience on either the Saturday or the Sunday but always as a single session with occasional short breaks. The date was recorded so that the time lag between the event and the recall could be determined and later used in the analysis. CR was asked to initially recall as much as possible about the first event of the week. The only cue she was given at this stage was the nominal title that she had assigned to that event at the time of recording. She was asked to report anything at all she could remember about the event, giving as much detail as possible and was not given any other prompts. When she could remember no more she was provided with SC or diary cues and was again asked to recall as much as possible, particularly anything specific. When looking at SC images she was allowed to review at her own rate and because of her profound prosopagnosia she was also allowed to ask her husband the identity of people that appeared in the images. At the post-cue review stage, details could therefore either be recognised (old) or recalled (new). The type of cue given was counterbalanced across days (Monday—SC, Tuesday diary, or so forth) and CR did not know in advance which events would be tested with which cues. After completing initial and cued recall of the first event the same recall procedure was repeated with the remaining events from that week. All recall sessions were recorded on a digital Dictaphone and were later transcribed and coded. In addition, for both the initial recall and cued recall sessions she was asked to rate the memories for vividness using a 5-point scale where "1" was not at all vivid, "3" was usual level of vividness, and "5" was extremely vivid.

For a sample of the memories (6 days), the qualitative content of each memory was analysed by categorising every detail along three dimensions: (1) whether it related to an action, a place, people, a sensory-perceptive detail, an affect, a cognition, or a time sign; (2) whether it was old (a recognised element of the cue itself) or new (produced without a cue *or* as an additional detail not present in the cue itself); (3) whether it was episodic in nature, autobiographical knowledge, or a qualified memory or something that appeared to have been worked out from the cues, e.g., "I suppose I might have ..." or "I think I must have ...". In addition we noted the extent of self-reference by counting the number of times "I" or "me" was quoted. Finally, we counted the number PMs that occurred. Of these memories, 20% were independently scored by a second rater and inter-rater reliability was shown to be high for all measures ($r > 0.95$).

RESULTS

The data provided the opportunity to examine the effects of diary and SC cues on both subjective and objective measures of memory. The subjective experience was assessed by analysing vividness ratings while the effects on more objective measures of memory were determined by examining how much CR was able to remember and what the precise nature of the memories were.

Subjective measures

Vividness ratings were taken from the full 4-week period and were examined in a number of ways. First, a correlational analysis examined the relationship between retention interval (1–7 days) and the vividness ratings given by CR after her first recall attempt. This showed an expected significant negative correlation such that vividness ratings improved with shorter retention interval ($r = -0.527$; $p < .05$). The same analysis was repeated to examine the relationship between retention interval and the vividness ratings given after cues (SC or diary) and this revealed a significant but smaller negative correlation ($r = -0.340$; $p < .05$), suggesting that the use of cues in general reduced the correlation between retention interval and vividness ratings.

The second analysis directly compared the effects of retention interval on perceived vividness for the initial recall attempt and the second recall attempt, i.e., after cueing with the SC or diary. In keeping with the reduced correlation reported above, Figure 1 shows that the post-cue vividness ratings appeared to be more resilient to increased retention interval than initial vividness ratings, however a two-way ANOVA showed that while there was an overall increase in vividness, $F(1, 18) = 7.08$; $p < .05$, there was no effect of cue type, $F(1, 18) = 0.18$; $p > .05$ (see Figure 2) and no interaction between retention interval and the pre- and post-cue conditions, $F(1, 18) = 0.38$; $p > .05$.

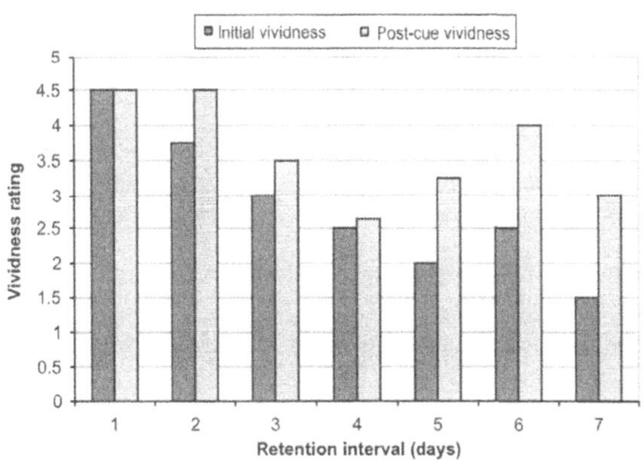

Figure 1. The effect of retention interval on perceived vividness ratings before and after cueing.

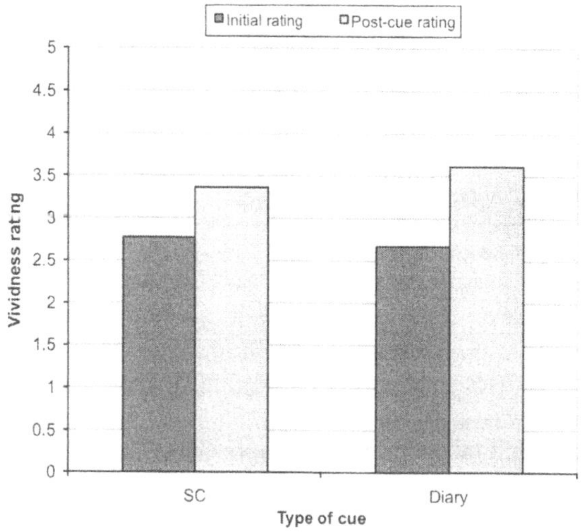

Figure 2. The effects of SenseCam and diary cues on perceived vividness ratings.

Objective measures

Memories from the first week were subjected to a detailed qualitative analysis. Of these recall attempts, three were subsequently cued with CR's diary entry and two with SC. Initial recall attempts were analysed in terms of whether each part of the memory could be described as an episodic detail, a piece of general knowledge or something that was assumed or guessed. In the latter case this was coded as a "qualified" memory, e.g., "I was probably feeling OK". Table 1 shows that the nature and extent of initial recall (pre-cue) was equivalent for the initial knowledge and qualified memories of the two conditions but the number of episodic details were higher in the condition that was later recalled with the SC cue. A chi-squared analysis showed that this was a small but significant effect, $\chi^2(1) = 6.43$; $p < .05$.

The post-cue memories, i.e., the second attempts at recall with support from diary or SC cue, were also subjected to a detailed qualitative analysis. As with initial recall, a distinction was made as to whether each part of the memory could be described as an episodic detail, a piece of general knowledge, or something that was assumed or guessed. The number of qualified memories and PMs was also recorded. Second, each part of the memory was coded in terms of whether or not it was already present in the cue. Where the information was present in the cue, this was categorised as "recognised" but where it was not present it was categorised as "new recall". Table 2 shows the categorisation of the

TABLE 1
Comparison of total number of episodic details, "qualified" memory, and items of knowledge at initial recall (i.e., before cueing)

	Condition	
Aspect of memory	*Diary*	*SenseCam*
Episodic detail	250	329
Qualified memory	30	37
Knowledge	87	73

memories in this way, according to whether the cue was a diary cue or a SC cue. In terms of recognition memory there appears to be a slightly higher number of memories produced in both the episodic and semantic domains in response to the SC cue and a chi-squared analysis supports this finding, $\chi^2(1) = 23.10$; $p < .001$. However for new recall there was a much more dramatic difference between the memories cued by SC and those cued with the diary, with a particularly big increase in the number of episodic details. Again, this is borne out by a chi-squared analysis, which showed a very large effect of cue, $\chi^2(1) = 684.62$; $p < .001$. In addition it can see that there are a much larger number of self-references and five times as many PMs after the SC cues.

Table 3 shows the results of a further analysis, which sought to further investigate the nature of the episodic details produced. Here it can be seen that the content of the episodic memories was influenced by the type of cue they were given such that there was a greater percentage of cognitions and sensory-perceptive details after the SC cues and less focus on specific actions.

DISCUSSION

The findings clearly show that SC cues powerfully facilitate CR's recall of episodic memories and allow her autobiographical memories to become specific and detailed. Interestingly this was not reflected in her subjective ratings of the vividness of her memories, which were highly vivid at short retention intervals. In our view this occurs because when CR manages to recall anything specific for her that is a vivid moment. Thus the subjective experience is not correlated with the amount and specificity of what is recalled. However, Table 2 and 3 strikingly show that CR recalls much more episodic detail to SC than diary cues. Moreover, these are new highly specific episodic details *not* depicted in the SC photographs that nonetheless cue the memories. In addition to this, CR has more PMs to SC cues then to diary cues. Indeed, in our larger study (in preparation) we have collected many PMs from CR who has continued to use the SC continuously over a period of about 18 months. A PM is a particularly interesting experience for CR and occurs quite unexpectedly eliciting an exclamation from her as a flood of details comes to mind and she experiences intense recollection. She herself referred to her PMs as being moments of "reliving".

Why might SC photographs have this striking effect in accessing otherwise inaccessible memories? We believe there are several reasons. One is that SC photographs are highly cognitively compatible with human memory with which they share the following features: they are visual, represent short time slices of experience, they are time compressed and fragmentary, they

TABLE 2
Comparison of frequency of episodic details, "qualified" memory items, and items of knowledge after cueing with SC or diary

		Condition	
	Aspect of memory	*Diary*	*SenseCam*
Recognition (information present in cue & recognised)	Episodic detail	80	96
	Qualified memory	3	20
	Knowledge	4	47
New recall (new information not present in cue)	Episodic detail	76	419
	Qualified memory	7	46
	Knowledge	0	40
Self-references		33	137
Number of "Proustian moments"		2	10

TABLE 3
Percentage of each type of episodic detail recalled, as a function of cue

	Condition	
Type of episodic detail recalled	*Diary*	*SenseCam*
Actions	46.1	36.7
Places	6.6	9.7
People	11.8	10.4
Sensory-perceptive	7.9	12.1
Affect	5.3	4.0
Cognition	15.8	19.7
Time sign	6.6	7.3

are formed outside intentional awareness, they preserve the perspective of the individual at the time of the event, and they are temporally ordered. These features that overlap at least in part with features of episodic memory (Conway, 2005), make SC images highly compatible with human episodic memory and because of this may increase the probability of containing an effective cue with which to stimulate memories. A second is that each SC photograph contains a great deal of visual information and series of such photographs, a SC "movie", typically containing 150+ photographs represents a wide range of related but changing visual cues. The probability of encountering an effective cue in such an informationally rich record of an event is obviously increased relative to other cues, e.g., a written diary record.

A third, and the final, possibility considered here relates to the nature of CR's brain injury. The lesion site is in the right hemisphere (RH) encompassing much of the right temporal lobe, much of the right fusiform gyrus (hence her prosopagnosia), and extending into the posterior part of the frontal lobe. It has long been thought that neural networks in the right hemisphere, especially the right frontal lobe, may be differentially involved in memory retrieval whereas, and in contrast, networks in the left hemisphere are more directly involved in memory encoding, the so-called hemispheric encoding/retrieval asymmetry model (HERA; see Nyberg, Cabeza, & Tulving, 1996; Tulving, Kapur, Craik, Moscovitch, & Houle, 1994). Given that CR's lesion is in the RH, this could explain her amnesia, her ability to form new memories, and then her impaired ability to access those memories. Essentially CR's RH retrieval networks no longer function, so memories cannot be retrieved but the intact LH encoding continues to form memories. As CR can retrieve these recent memories we might further assume that, possibly through some process of consolidation, retrieval of or access to recently formed memories gradually transfers to RH networks and in the process is lost from LH encoding networks.

The above reasoning provides a good account of the pattern of CR's amnesia but it fails to provide any account of her retrieval of memories to SC cues. Indeed, it now seems that the HERA model may itself be something of a simplification of the underlying encoding and retrieval networks that appear more complex and task sensitive than previously thought—see Velanova et al. (2003) and also Cabeza and St. Jacques (2007) for an overview of the bilateral complex of networks involved in the construction of autobiographical memories. It now seems that some LH prefrontal cortex (PFC) networks may be involved in transient aspects of retrieval whereas RH PFC networks may mediated more sustained aspects of retrieval. To tentatively translate this into our current thinking about autobiographical memory we suggest that LH networks, which play in an important role in memory encoding, also modulate cue selection and elaboration. Such cues are used to probe, access, and activate more posterior networks where episodic memories are stored. This is an iterative process and the initial cue is elaborated semantically as the posterior networks are repeatedly accessed (Conway & Pleydell-Pearce, 2000). In this account we further suggest that the role of RH PFC networks is to maintain a stable pattern of activation in posterior networks once a memory has been formed.

According to this latter account, CR's problem lies in part in maintaining coherent and stable patterns of activation in posterior networks and also in elaborating effective cues with which to probe posterior networks. (Indeed this might suggest the interesting possibility that processing in RH and LH retrieval networks is at least partly linked.) However, the LH retrieval networks remain functional and if an appropriate cue arises then episodic memories can be directly accessed hence the effects of SC cues in CR. One prediction of this view is that activation in CR's posterior, episodic, networks when it occurs would be largely unconstrained, assuming that RH retrieval networks that would normally control construction, perhaps by channelling it in various ways, no longer function. Interestingly, at the behavioural level, when CR has a PM it is characterised by a "flood" of episodic details into conscious awareness. The same appears true of non-brain-damaged individuals when they have PMs to SC cues but it is more pronounced in CR. Related to this, in a recent fMRI study of CR recalling SC movies she has viewed prior to going in the scanner, strikingly intense and widespread activation was observed in the occipital lobes and posterior parietal regions (study in preparation). Thus, paradoxically, when CR can access episodic memories she recalls many highly specific details and occasionally more than intact controls.

Finally, and briefly, we want to consider the therapeutic benefits CR has gained by routinely using SC. The first and most obvious is that she can now often remember everyday events such as lunch with a friend, a trip out, shopping, a day with her children, and so on. This simply was not possible before. One perplexing issue worth noting is that CR still suffers from a very dense prosopagnosia and recognises virtually no one in her SC photographs, but these nonetheless still cue moments of remembering and when these occur she is able to infer who the individuals in the photographs are. This remains a perplexing aspect of CR's response to SC cues. A second and less-obvious benefit of the SC cues has been to restore some of CR's confidence when in social interactions. Clearly, to undertake social interactions with people one does not recognise and with whom one cannot recall sharing experiences is powerfully disabling. CR has found that by reviewing SC movies of events in which she interacted with people, people she is about meet again, she can recall and share memories with them. This has had a very positive effect on CR and markedly improved her interactions with others.

SC is proving to be a remarkable tool for studying memory of everyday events. It provides a degree of control that memory researchers have not had before both in the collection of photographs and their later presentation as memory cues. SC has great potential, and there are many more questions it raises that now become tractable. One in particular, which we consider important, is: what makes an effective SC cue? On the other hand, given that SC does increase access to memories (there will be boundaries on this and we assume that there are some patient groups in which SC will be ineffective), it is an effective memory prosthesis for the experiences of a person's life, and we believe that there is a potential benefit for most people with impaired memories. Perhaps the most important group here are elderly adults whose memory for everyday events is attenuated by age-related decline in cognitive functions such as constructed autobiographical memories.

REFERENCES

Baddeley, A. D., & Wilson, B. A. (1986). Amnesia, autobiographical memory and confabulation. In D.C. Rubin (Ed.), *Autobiographical memory* (pp. 225–252). Cambridge, UK: Cambridge University Press.

Berry, E., Kapur, N., Williams, L., Hodges, S., Watson, P., Smyth, G., et al. (2007). The use of a wearable camera, SenseCam, as a pictorial diary to improve autobiographical memory in a patient with limbic encephalitis: A preliminary report. *Neuropsychological Rehabilitation*, *17*(4/5), 582–601.

Browne, G., Berry, E., Kapur, N., Hodges, S., Smyth, G., Watson, P., & Wood, K. (2011). SenseCam improves memory for recent events and quality of life in a patient with memory retrieval difficulties. *Memory*, *19*, 713–722.

Cabeza, R., & St. Jacques, P. (2007). Functional neuroimaging of autobiographical memory. *Trends in Cognitive Science*, *11*(5), 219–227.

Cermak, L. S., & O'Connor, M. (1983). The anterograde and retrograde retrieval ability of a patient with amnesia due to encephalitis. *Neuropsychologia*, *21*, 213–234.

Conway, M. A. (2005). Memory and the self. *Journal of Memory and Language*, *53*(4), 594–628.

Conway, M. A. (2009). Episodic memories. *Neuropsychologia*, *47*, 2305–2313.

Conway, M. A., & Pleydell-Pearce, C. W. (2000). The construction of autobiographical memories in the self-memory system. *Psychological Review*, *107*, 261–268.

Kopelman, M. D., Wilson, B. A., & Baddeley, A. D. (1989). The autobiographical memory interview – a new assessment of autobiographical and personal semantic memory in amnesic patients. *Journal of Clinical and Experimental Neuropsychology*, *11*(5), 724–744.

Loveday, C., & Conway, M. A. (2010). *Memory for a day: On the forgetting of everyday events*. Manuscript in preparation.

Nyberg, L., Cabeza, R., & Tulving, E. (1996). PET studies of encoding and retrieval: The HERA model. *Psychonomic Bulletin & Review*, *3*(2), 135–148.

Tulving, E., Kapur, S., Craik, F. I., Moscovitch, M., & Houle, S. (1994). Hemispheric encoding/retrieval asymmetry in episodic memory: Positron emission tomography findings. *Proceedings of the National Academy of Sciences of the United States of America*, *91*(6), 2016–2020.

Velanova, K., Jacoby, L. L., Wheeler, M. E., McAvoy, M. P., Petersen, S. E., & Buckner, R. L. (2003). Functional-anatomic correlates of sustained and transient processing components engaged during controlled retrieval. *The Journal of Neuroscience*, *23*(24), 8460–8470.

Williams, H. L., Conway, M. A., & Baddeley, A. D. (2008). The boundaries of episodic memories. In T. F. Shipley & J. M. Zacks (Eds.), *Understanding events: From perception to action*. New York, NY: Oxford University Press.

Williams, J. M. G., Barnhofer, T., Crane, C., Hermans, D., Raes, F., Watkins, E., et al. (2007). Autobiographical memory specificity and emotional disorder. *Psychological Bulletin*, *133*(1), 122–148.

Williams, J. M. G., & Broadbent, K. (1986). Autobiographical memory in suicide attempters. *Journal of Abnormal Psychology*, *95*, 144–149.

MEMORY, 2011, 19 (7), 705–712
Psychology Press
Taylor & Francis Group

SenseCam as a rehabilitation tool in a child with anterograde amnesia

Katalin Pauly-Takacs[1], Chris J. A. Moulin[1], and Edward J. Estlin[2]

[1]Institute of Psychological Sciences, University of Leeds, UK
[2]Royal Manchester Children's Hospital, Manchester, UK

We present the case of a 13-year-old boy, CJ, with profound episodic memory difficulties following the diagnosis of a metastatic intracranial germ cell tumour and subsequent treatment with radiotherapy and chemotherapy. At the core of this study is the first application of SenseCam to a child with severe memory impairment. CJ was taken for a walk while he was wearing SenseCam. This included visiting four different locations. We manipulated the number of locations he could review on SenseCam "films" and then tested recognition memory (forced choice) for both reviewed and non-reviewed locations. We also collected his justifications for the choices he made. Our results indicate that repeated viewings of SenseCam images support the formation of personal semantic memories. Overall our results suggest that the use of SenseCam in memory rehabilitation extends beyond supporting episodic memory and recollection, and supports the feasibility of its use with children who have marked memory difficulties.

Keywords: Episodic memory; Brain tumours; Metastatic intracranial germinoma; Semantic memory; Autobiographical memory.

Deficits in memory function, attention and processing speed often occur in children who sustain brain tumours (Palmer, Reddick, & Gajjar, 2007). These impairments are partly attributed to standard treatment procedures (i.e., chemotherapy and cranial or craniospinal irradiation), but tumour infiltration of memory-related brain structures and other pre-treatment factors, such as hydrocephalus, are also considered to contribute to these deficits (Carpentieri et al., 2003). The adverse neurocognitive effects of whole brain radiotherapy in particular have been well documented in the literature, particularly in relation to children with medulloblastoma. The majority of the studies report a significant decline in general intellectual functioning after whole brain radiotherapy treatment (for review see Mulhern, Hancock, Fairclough, & Kun, 1992; Mulhern, Merchant, Gajjar, Reddick, & Kun, 2004).

Neuroimaging studies have identified a number of post-treatment changes in the brain that contribute to the better understanding of the underlying neuropathology of cognitive decline in this population. For example, a decrease in white matter in the brain and a decline in corpus callosum volume are thought to explain impairments in overall intellectual functioning (Reddick et al., 1998, 2005; Shan et al., 2006). In addition, Nagel et al. (2004) evaluated hippocampal volume development among children treated for

Address correspondence to: Katalin Pauly-Takacs, Institute of Psychological Sciences, University of Leeds, Leeds LS2 9JT, UK. E-mail: ps07kpt@leeds.ac.uk

We thank CJ and his parents for their unfailing cooperation and continuous support in this study. We wish to thank Richard Wilkie for advice regarding the visual layout of our testing material. We are also grateful to Martin Conway for his support and to Emma Berry for providing CJ with a SenseCam, which made this study possible.

© 2011 Psychology Press, an imprint of the Taylor & Francis Group, an Informa business
http://www.psypress.com/memory http://dx.doi.org/10.1080/09658211.2010.494046

medulloblastoma and found abnormally slow hippocampal growth, which gives insight as to why these children experience memory difficulties.

Memory enables us to accumulate knowledge about the world and ourselves. Two distinct memory systems support this process: Episodic memory is the capacity to encode and later recollect personally experienced events from the past that occurred in a particular spatial and temporal context, whereas semantic memory refers to factual knowledge about past experiences (Tulving, 1972; Wheeler, Stuss, & Tulving, 1997). The literature suggests that episodic memory is a more vulnerable system than semantic memory. Studies in healthy cognitive ageing, for instance, repeatedly find that older adults experience difficulty in retrieving episodic details of personally experienced events, whereas semantic access to memories remains intact in this population (e.g., Clarys, Bugaiska, Tapia, & Baudouin, 2009; Levine, Svoboda, Hay, Winocur, & Moskovitch, 2002; Piolino, Desgranges, Benali, & Eustache, 2002). Similarly, several case-studies in neuropsychology document at least some degree of preserved semantic memory function in various amnesic states, allowing the patient to acquire new semantic information despite profound episodic memory impairment (e.g., Hirst, Phelps, Johnson, & Volpe, 1988; Kitchener, Hodges, & McCarthy, 1998; McKenna & Gerhand, 2002; O'Kane, Kensinger, & Locascio, 2004; Skotko et al., 2004; Verfaellie, Koseff, & Alexander, 2000). This dissociation between episodic and semantic memory has been found to be most pronounced if amnesia was acquired in early childhood (Vargha-Khadem, Gadian, & Mishkin, 2001; Vargha-Khadem et al., 1997).

However, studies assessing cognitive function after treatment for a childhood brain tumour merely report full scale IQ ratings and relevant subtests (e.g., working memory) in characterising memory deficits. Reference to contemporary theories of memory and measurement of different aspects of memory function (i.e., episodic and semantic memory) that might be affected by childhood brain tumours is less well understood. How deficits in one or both of the above subsystems affect the way children process new autobiographical information is also unknown. Consequently, the rehabilitation of these aspects of memory function is not incorporated in existing intervention programs (Butler & Mulhern, 2005), nor are they considered in contemporary rehabilitation models for children with brain injury (Wright & Limond, 2004). The particular focus on abnormal hippocampal growth suggests that it is episodic memory that is specifically impaired in this group.

At the core of this study is the first application of SenseCam as a rehabilitation tool in a child with severe episodic memory impairment due to brain tumours and subsequent treatment. Existing technological memory aids assist patients in completing daily tasks by way of supporting prospective memory (Kapur, Glisky, & Wilson, 2004). SenseCam, however, is a unique device with the potential to support memory for past experiences. In addition, SenseCam offers an opportunity to assess and rehabilitate autobiographical memory. A pioneering study revealed that successive reviews of SenseCam "films" contributed to increased levels of recall as well as long-term consolidation of previously experienced events in an adult patient with hippocampal damage (Berry et al., 2007). However, the use of technological memory aids in children is not well documented in the literature. As is the case in adult rehabilitation, the tools reported in this literature (e.g., PDA) are developed to enhance the organisational skills of children, which will enable them to manage their daily activities independently (Gillette & DePompei, 2008).

In our study we aimed to explore the benefits of SenseCam in a single case. We were interested in how SenseCam supported two facets of autobiographical memory: personal semantic and personal episodic (Kopelman, Wilson, & Baddeley, 1989). We hypothesised that if repeated viewings of SenseCam "films" contribute to the consolidation of personally experienced events, then CJ's memory for places where his camera was "on" should be better than for those not recorded by the device.

CASE REPORT

CJ is a 13-year-old boy who was diagnosed at the age of 11 with a suprasellar germinoma and multiple periventricular and leptomeningeal metastases (Figure 1) in August 2006. Following the diagnosis he underwent chemotherapy with cisplatin, etoposide, and ifosfamide followed by radiotherapy (40 Gy to the whole brain and spine). The treatment was completed by the end of November 2006. During the time of CJ's presentation and treatment it was clear to the clinician that his memory function, to be formally tested later, was markedly impaired.

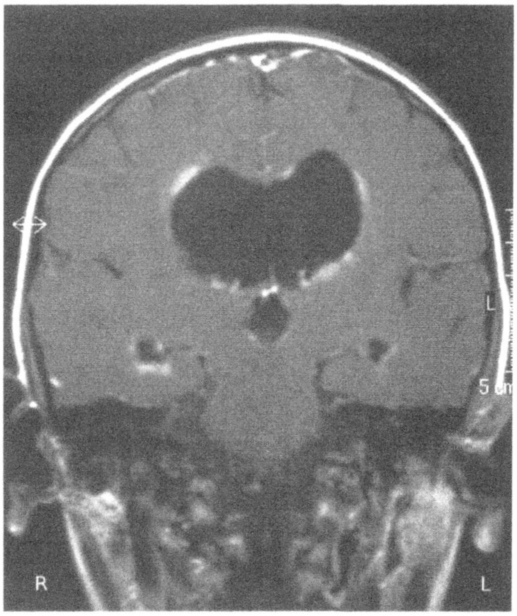

Figure 1. MRI image revealing the suprasellar primary germ cell tumour, extensive periventricular and leptomeningeal metastases (contrasted in white), and ventricular dilatation (coronal T1 weighted sequence with gadolinium).

MRI scans were taken regularly after the treatment was completed, and these confirmed that CJ remains in complete remission from his cancer. However, a marked and generalised cerebral atrophy and associated extensive white matter loss remains (Figure 2). This includes bilateral volume loss in the hippocampus.

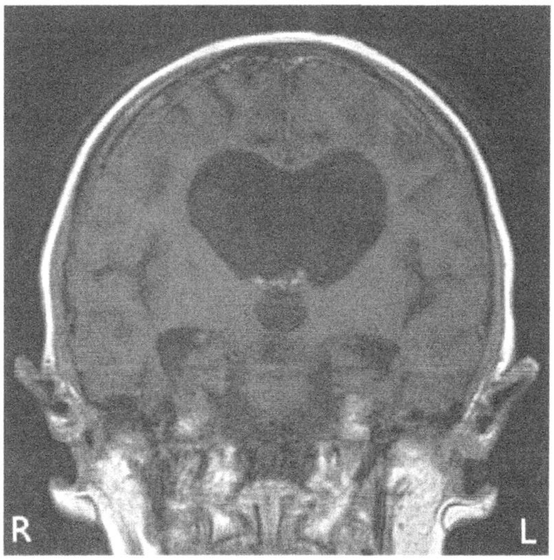

Figure 2. CJ's brain following treatment with chemotherapy and radiotherapy. There is a complete response to therapy; marked and generalised cerebral atrophy and loss of hippocampal volume remain. (coronal T1 weighted sequence with gadolinium).

CJ was unable to maintain a record of ongoing activities (e.g., he could not remember why he went upstairs) or recount recently experienced events (e.g., could not give a coherent account of what happened yesterday on the way back home). His behaviour became somewhat disinhibited in social situations and he tended to repeat stereotyped phrases. Additionally, due to deterioration of the optic nerve, CJ's sight in his right eye as well as his peripheral vision was poor. As a consequence, he experienced difficulties in carrying out movements that required hand–eye coordination. For example, he was reluctant to write. There was no indication of language impairment; his spontaneous speech was fluent and syntactically correct. Overall, CJ gave the impression of a friendly and ingenious young man who had very little awareness of his difficulties. Following treatment he attended school for about 3 hours per day, and required full 1:1 supervision for basic classroom tasks. Prior to his illness CJ was a very able child with exemplary scholastic achievement who had won a scholarship to an independent school for boys.

Anterograde amnesia was most conspicuous in CJ's everyday life. His parents made every effort to alleviate their son's memory loss: before being introduced to SenseCam they used videos and still images taken by a mobile phone to support CJ's memory. His parents reported significant improvements in CJ's general cognitive state and mood as a result. We saw CJ and his parents initially in February 2008, when they expressed their interest in SenseCam and agreed to participate in a study. They also gave written consent for disseminating the results of this study in scientific reports.

NEUROPSYCHOLOGICAL ASSESSMENT

A summary of CJ's test results can be found in Table 1. Results on the Wechsler Intelligence Scale for Children (Wechsler, 2003) indicate that CJ's verbal abilities and premorbid semantic knowledge base are well preserved. However, his perceptual reasoning, working memory, and processing speed scores are all in the extremely low range. This is unsurprising considering that these aspects of cognition are often found to be impaired in children who sustain brain tumours (Palmer et al., 2007). CJ's scores on the Children's Memory Scale (Cohen, 1997) reflect severe impairment across all

TABLE 1
Neuropsychological assessment (July 2008)

Test	*Composite score*	*Percentile rank*
WISC-IV		
Verbal comprehension	96	39
Perceptual reasoning	57	0.2
Working memory	54	0.1
Processing speed	50	0.1
CMS		
Visual immediate memory	50	<0.1
Visual delayed memory	50	<0.1
Verbal immediate memory	54	0.1
Verbal delayed memory	54	0.1
Attention and concentration	82	12
Learning	50	<0.1
Delayed recognition	66	1

CJ's performance indices on the WISC-IV and CMS tests. WISC-IV = Wechsler Intelligence Scale for Children – Fourth Edition; CMS = Children's Memory Scale.

aspects of memory function. His memory deficit in particular is best illustrated by a simple figure we asked him to copy and to then recall immediately, as with the Rey figure (Figure 3). This shows his difficulty in retaining the relational structure of an image. His reliance on knowledge rather than remembering is also demonstrated by his adding an element that is semantically related but was not part of the original figure: CJ completed the figure with a pot of gold next to the rainbow (labelled as A in figure).

METHOD

A memory walk with SenseCam

The walk. SenseCam is a small, wearable camera that was invented by Microsoft Research Cambridge (Hodges et al., 2006). CJ was taken for a walk in a novel environment while he was wearing the device. We deliberately chose locations with more salient features (such as a glass floor, tall columns, and a long corridor). The walk comprised four key locations, all at the University of Leeds campus; a visit to an art gallery, a coffee-break, a visit to a church, and a visit to a long corridor. We spent between 15 and 20 minutes in each location. During the walk we conversed with CJ about the surroundings in order to generate contextual information on which he could later be tested. For example, we told him facts such as, "This is the longest corridor in Europe". Crucial to this study, in two locations CJ's SenseCam was turned on; in the other two it was off. In order to be able to later test his memory for all visited places, a second SenseCam was worn by the experimenter. CJ's parents were informed that their son's memory for the walk would be tested on later occasions using the recorded SenseCam images. They were instructed to review the SenseCam recordings with CJ every second day in the 2 weeks following the walk. They were instructed to encourage their son to recall as much of the walk as he could while watching the SenseCam "movie" and to prompt him with questions when necessary but without giving him the correct answer. They were asked not to discuss the event (i.e., the walk) outside the review sessions. The parents reported that CJ had reviewed the SenseCam "movie" seven times.

CJ's memory for the walk was tested on three occasions employing a two-alternative forced choice recognition memory paradigm with SenseCam image pairs. In each set the target images depicted a scene of the *memory walk* while the foil images were taken from the experimenter's SenseCam at different times and places. Distractors were carefully selected to match the images on similarity. Outdoor–outdoor and indoor–indoor images were paired at all times. Similarly, care was taken to match the reviewed and non-reviewed images as much as it was possible based on the available recordings. This task was designed to be easy in keeping with CJ's severe impairment—two independent raters completed the test and could correctly segment the images into CJ's or experimenter's image on 90% of the pairs.

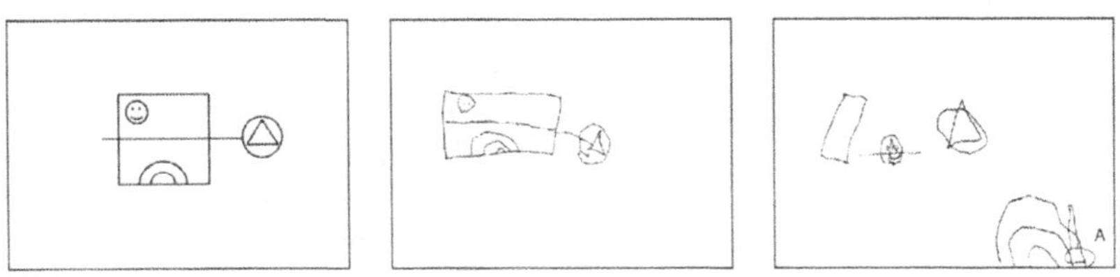

Figure 3. CJ's copy and immediate recall of a simple figure.

Test of shorter-term retention. The first test took place 2 weeks after the *memory walk.* A total of 30 image pairs were shown to CJ, which represented two experimental conditions and one control condition:

1. Reviewed condition (10 images from two locations): CJ's SenseCam was on at the time of the experience, therefore he had the opportunity to review these images.
2. Non-reviewed condition (10 images from two locations): CJ's SenseCam was off at the time of the experience, therefore he did not have the opportunity to review these images. In half of the target images people present in the event were visible, while the other half of these pictures depicted only the environment. At test CJ was asked which one of the two images depicted his day. Once he made a choice we also asked him to justify it (i.e., What makes you think ...?).
3. Because we used a second SenseCam it was possible to provide 10 control pairs where the target image included CJ himself. This was to confirm that CJ could see the images well and had understood the task. Performance on these images was 100% and is not discussed again.

Test of longer-term retention. CJ was retested on the same set of image-pairs 10 weeks after the walk. He did not review the recordings between the first and second test.

Follow-up. A final test took place 15 weeks after the walk with different materials. The testing material comprised 20 image pairs, 10 from each experimental condition. However, in this set the target images depicted only the environment without anyone being visible in them. We made this change in the testing material because we wanted to be sure that CJ's memory for the walk was not biased by simply recognising his parents in the images.

RESULTS

The proportion of pictures where CJ correctly selected his own images is shown in Figure 4.

Test of shorter-term retention. CJ's performance was significantly above chance in both reviewed and non-reviewed conditions, $p = .009$ (binomial probability). This suggests that SenseCam images

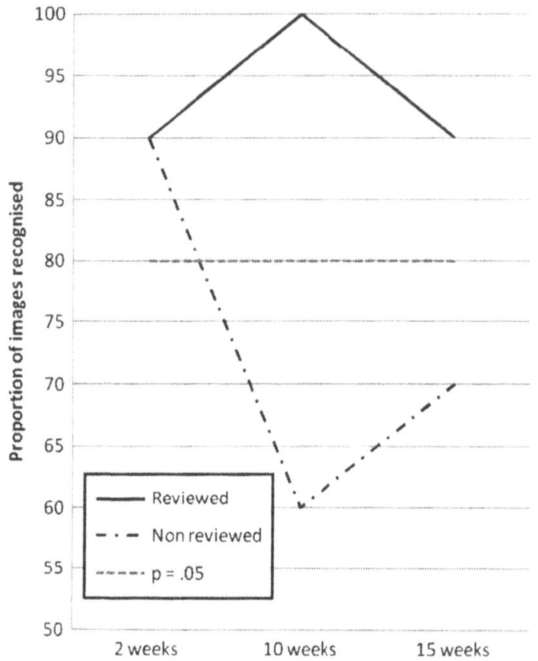

Figure 4. CJ's recognition memory for reviewed and non-reviewed locations of the *memory walk.*

of reviewed and non-reviewed events cued CJ's memory equally well 2 weeks after the experience. Incorrect answers were given to images without a person, whereas responses to images with a person visible in them were always correct, and he justified his choices with the recognition of that person: "*That's mum. That's my day.*" Some of the comments he made about his choices indicate that his recognition memory relies on familiarity rather than recollection; his justifications do not usually exceed the assertion of "*I have been there*" or "*I have seen that.*" However, other responses and justifications suggest successful encoding and retention of contextual details. These justifications refer to knowledge and information relevant to the experience but are not evident in the pictures themselves: e.g., "*Longest corridor in Europe. I have been there.*" In some cases he justified his answer with the recognition of a certain object in the image: "*Greek pillars. I have been there*" or "*I have seen those Greek pillars.*" However, on testing him it was revealed that the *Greek pillar* was not only a powerful aid for his recognition memory but also produced erroneous familiarity judgements and overgeneralisations. The most prominent example of this was when CJ erroneously chose a foil image featuring pillars using the *Greek pillars* justification over the target image.

Test of longer-term retention. A total of 10 weeks after the experience, CJ's responses differed with regard to whether or not he had reviewed the images. In the review condition he performed at ceiling, $p = .0009$ (binomial probability), but in the non-reviewed condition his performance was not significantly above chance, $p = .205$ (binomial probability). His justifications given in the first test persisted over this time period. When present in an image, the *Greek pillars* continued to guide his decisions. As in the previous test, this made him erroneously choose the foil. Strikingly, this is an image in which his parents were visible.

Follow-up. A total of 15 weeks after the walk, CJ's recognition memory performance continued to be significantly above chance for the images of the reviewed locations, $p = .009$ (binomial probability), but was not significantly above chance in the non-reviewed condition, $p = .117$ (binomial probability). These results suggest that CJ does hold more permanent representations in his memory of those places that he repeatedly viewed as SenseCam images.

DISCUSSION

We reported the case of a 13-year-old boy, CJ, with severe episodic memory difficulties following multiple brain tumours and subsequent chemotherapy and radiotherapy treatment.

Formal neuropsychological assessment indicated severe impairment across all aspects of memory function affecting both recall and recognition. However, his verbal abilities and premorbid knowledge base are well preserved.

At the core of this study was the evaluation of the effectiveness of SenseCam as a rehabilitation tool. Because recall data would not have been possible to collect due to the nature of CJ's impairment, our approach to the question was to measure his recognition memory for SenseCam-recorded events in a forced choice recognition memory paradigm. Although standardised tests indicated severe impairment in his recognition memory as well, our procedure had a crucial element that made it different from standard tests of recognition: CJ had the opportunity to rehearse the target items before testing. Therefore we were interested to see whether repeated viewings of SenseCam "films" would increase CJ's recognition memory for the experienced events.

Our results confirm a previous finding: repeated viewings of SenseCam images play an important role in the long-term retention of personally experienced events (Berry et al., 2007). Crucially, CJ's recognition memory for the walk was equally good for reviewed and non-reviewed locations in a shorter-term delay (2 weeks), but differences in his performance were observed in the longer term (10 and 15 weeks) where reviewed locations were consistently better recognised. In the case of reviewed locations, a large number of his justifications given for correct responses reflected conceptual knowledge about the place in the absence of recollecting any specific details of the experience, for example: "*Longest corridor in Europe. I have been there*" or "*Leeds Art Gallery. I have been there.*" This suggests that, at least in this case, repeated viewings of SenseCam images supported the formation of personal semantic memories, but did not appear to support the formation of episodic memories.The pattern of the results confirm that CJ's memory performance is affected by his use of the device: although non-reviewed locations were recognised after a 2-week delay, the justifications given for these choices reflected *familiarity* rather than conceptual knowledge, for example: "*I have seen that before*". Furthermore, as opposed to reviewed ones, non-reviewed locations were no longer recognised at an above-chance level after longer delays.

It has been suggested previously that SenseCam images provide potent cues to mentally re-experiencing past events and thus support episodic memory (Conway, St. Jacques, & Cabeza, 2008). However, we suggest that if reviewing of SenseCam images is not sufficient to support recollective experience due to brain damage, then given sufficient amount of rehearsal they will still support the formation of personal semantic memories. These semantic facts will later be accessible but not accompanied by autonoetic consciousness (Wheeler et al., 1997). This is something future SenseCam research should consider in all participant groups.

Our results are consistent with those found in a study carried out with healthy individuals, where *known* events supported by SenseCam showed greater stability over time than supported *remembered* and unsupported *known* events (Sellen et al., 2007).

Repeated viewing of SenseCam images was a crucial element of our procedure and we suggested that this type of practice contributed to better recognition memory, which then supported the formation of personal semantic memories. One negative effect of rehearsing the experience via SenseCam was that at times it also produced overgeneralisations and thus erroneous familiarity judgements (see the "Greek pillars" example in the results section). This is not unlike the DRM-type error produced on word lists where, in cases of memory impairment, gist recall is uncorrected due to a lack of ability to retrieve the specifics of the situation (Hudon et al., 2006). This effect is also one that future studies should take into account where better memory performance is expected as a function of repeated SenseCam viewings.

The finding that rehearsal of personally experienced events via SenseCam supports the formation of personal semantic memories after injury has important implications for rehabilitation. Few studies investigated the ability to acquire postmorbid personal semantic memories in amnesia. Studies carried out with adult cases are inconclusive as to whether the formation of new personal semantic memories dissociates from the formation of more general semantic knowledge. For example a patient, AC, reported by Van der Linden, Brédart, Depoorter, and Coyette (1996) retained the ability to acquire semantic memories in both the personal and public domain despite severe episodic memory impairment. However another patient, RS, reported by Kitchener et al. (1998) scored in the definitely abnormal range for all three periods on the personal semantic component of the Autobiographical Memory Interview despite having been able to acquire information about famous people and public events since the onset of his illness. In the light of our findings it is likely that SenseCam would be useful in such cases as RS.

The question of how children with hippocampal damage are able to process autobiographical information after injury is absent from the literature. By our view, SenseCam is an ideal clinical tool to assess this aspect of memory function. Furthermore, as our results suggest it is also a unique rehabilitation device for children with hippocampal damage whose self-development is set back due to their profound episodic memory impairment. The life-long use of SenseCam could increase their self-knowledge even in the absence of re-experiencing the self at a specific moment in the past.

In conclusion, SenseCam has been proven to be a useful rehabilitation tool for CJ's memory. Our most prominent finding was that SenseCam is powerful in the formation of personal semantic memories, which suggests that its use in rehabilitation extends beyond supporting episodic memory, and supports the feasibility of its use with children who have marked memory difficulties.

REFERENCES

Berry, E., Kapur, N., Williams, L., Hodges, S., Watson, P., Smyth, G., et al. (2007). The use of a wearable camera, SenseCam, as a pictorial diary to improve autobiographical memory in a patient with limbic encephalitis: A preliminary report. *Neuropsychological Rehabilitation, 17*, 582–601.

Butler, R. W., & Mulhern, R. K. (2005). Neurocognitive interventions for children and adolescents surviving cancer. *Journal of Pediatric Psychology, 30*, 65–78.

Carpentieri, S. C., Waber, D. P., Pomeroy, S. L., Scott, R. M., Goumnerova, L. C., Kieran, M. W., et al. (2003). Neuropsychological functioning after surgery in children treated for brain tumor. *Neurosurgery, 52*, 1348–1354.

Clarys, D., Bugaiska, A., Tapia, G., & Baudouin, A. (2009). Ageing, remembering and executive function. *Memory, 17*, 158–168.

Cohen, M. (1997). *Children's Memory Scale*. New York, NY: The Psychological Corporation.

Conway, M. A., St. Jacques, P., & Cabeza, R. (2008). *Reliving autobiographical memories for everyday events: An fMRI study using SenseCam*. Second Annual SenseCam Collaborator's Meeting, Cambridge, UK.

Gillette, Y., & DePompei, R. (2008). Do PDAs enhance the organization and memory skills of students with cognitive disabilities? *Psychology in the School, 7*, 665–677.

Hirst, W., Phelps, E. A., Johnson, M. K., & Volpe, B. T. (1988). Amnesia and second language learning. *Brain and Cognition, 8*, 105–116.

Hodges, S., Williams, L., Berry, E., Shahram, I., Srinivasan, J., Butler A., et al. (2006). SenseCam: A retrospective memory aid. In P. Dourish & A. Friday (Eds.), *Proceedings of the Eight International Conference on Ubiquitous Computing, Ubicomp 2006, LNCS 4206* (pp. 177–193). Berlin, Germany: Springer.

Hudon, C., Belleville, S., Souchay, C., Gely-Nargeot, M. C., Chertkow, H., & Gauthier, S. (2006). Memory for gist and detail information in Alzheimer's disease and mild cognitive impairment. *Neuropsychology, 20*, 566–577.

Kapur, N., Glisky, E., & Wilson, B. A. (2004). Technological memory aids for people with memory deficits. *Neuropsychological Rehabilitation, 14*, 41–60.

Kitchener, E. G., Hodges, J. R., & McCarthy, R. (1998). Acquisition of post-morbid vocabulary and semantic facts in the absence of episodic memory. *Brain, 121*, 1313–1327.

Kopelman, M. D., Wilson, B. A., & Baddeley, A. D. (1989). The Autobiographical Memory Interview – A new assessment of autobiographical and personal semantic memory in amnesic patients. *Journal of Clinical and Experimental Neuropsychology, 11*, 724–244.

Levine, B., Svoboda, E., Hay, J. F., Winocur, G., & Moscovitch, M. (2002). Aging and autobiographical memory: Dissociating episodic from semantic retrieval. *Psychology and Aging, 17*, 677–689.

McKenna, P., & Gerhand, S. (2002). Preserved semantic learning in an amnesic patient. *Cortex, 38*, 37–58.

Mulhern, R. K., Hancock, J., Fairclough, D., & Kun, L. (1992). Neuropsychological status of children treated for brain tumors: A critical review and integrative analysis. *Medical and Pediatric Oncology, 20*, 181–191.

Mulhern, R. K., Merchant, T. E., Gajjar, A., Reddick, W. E., & Kun, L. (2004). Late neurocognitive sequelae in survivors of brain tumors in childhood. *Lancet Oncology, 5*, 399–408.

Nagel, B. J., Palmer, S. L., Reddick, W. E., Glass, J. O., Helton, K. J., Wu, S., et al. (2004). Abnormal hippocampal development in children with medulloblastoma treated with risk-adapted irradiation. *American Journal of Neuroradiology, 25*, 1575–1582.

O'Kane, G., Kensinger, E. A., & Corkin, S. (2004). Evidence for semantic learning in profound amnesia: An investigation with patient HM. *Hippocampus, 14*, 417–425.

Palmer, S. L., Reddick, W. E., & Gajjar, A. (2007). Understanding the cognitive impact on children who are treated for medulloblastoma. *Journal of Pediatric Psychology, 32*, 1040–1049.

Piolino, P., Desgranges, B., Benali, K., & Eustache, F. (2002). Episodic and semantic remote autobiographical memory in ageing. *Memory, 10*, 239–257.

Reddick, W. E., Glass, J. O., Palmer, S. L., Wu, S., Gajjar, A., Langston, J. W., et al. (2005). Atypical white matter volume development in children following craniospinal irradiation. *Neuro-Oncology, 7*, 12–19.

Reddick, W. E., Mulhern, R. K., Elkin, T. D., Glass, J. O., Merchant, T. E., & Langston, J. W. (1998). A hybrid neural network analysis of subtle brain volume differences in children surviving brain tumors. *Magnetic Resonance Imaging, 16*, 413–421.

Sellen, A., Fogg, A., Aitken, M., Hodges, S., Rother, C., & Wood, K. (2007). *Do life-logging technologies support memory for the past? An experimental study using SenseCam*. In Proceedings of the Conference on Human Factors in Computing Systems, CHI'07, Irvine, CA.

Shan, Z. Y., Liu, J. Z., Glass, J. O., Gajjar, A., Li, C. I., & Reddick, W. E. (2006). Quantitative morphologic evaluation of white matter in survivors of childhood medulloblastoma. *Magnetic Resonance Imaging, 24*, 1015–1022.

Skotko, B. G., Kensinger, E. A., Locascio, J. J., Einstein, G., Rubin, D. C., Tupler, L. A., et al. (2004). Puzzling thoughts for HM: Can new semantic information be anchored to old semantic memories? *Neuropsychology, 18*, 756–769.

Tulving, E. (1972). Episodic and semantic memory. In E. Tulving & W. Donaldson, (Eds.), *Organization of memory* (pp. 31–43). New York, NY: Academic Press.

Van der Linden, M., Brédart, S., Depoorter, N., & Coyette, F. (1996). Semantic memory and amnesia: A case study. *Cognitive Neuropsychology, 13*, 391–413.

Vargha-Khadem, F., Gadian, D. G., & Mishkin, M. (2001). Dissociations in cognitive memory: The syndrome of developmental amnesia. *Philosophical Transactions of the Royal Society of London, 356*, 1435–1440.

Vargha-Khadem, F., Gadian, D. G., Watkins, K. E., Connelly, A., Van Paesschen, W., & Mishkin, M. (1997). Differential effects of early hippocampal pathology on episodic and semantic memory. *Science, 277*, 376–380.

Verfaellie, M., Koseff, P., & Alexander, M. P. (2000). Acquisition of novel semantic information in amnesia: Effects of lesion location. *Neuropsychologia, 38*, 484–492.

Wechsler, D. (2003). *Wechsler Intelligence Scale for Children – Fourth Edition*. San Antonio, TX: Harcourt Assessment, Inc.

Wheeler, M., Stuss, D. T., & Tulving, E. (1997). Toward a theory of episodic memory: The frontal lobes and autonoetic consciousness. *Psychological Bulletin, 121*, 331–354.

Wright, I., & Limond, J. (2004). A developmental framework for memory rehabilitation in children. *Pediatric Rehabilitation, 7*, 85–96.

MEMORY, 2011, 19 (7), 713–722

Psychology Press
Taylor & Francis Group

SenseCam improves memory for recent events and quality of life in a patient with memory retrieval difficulties

Georgina Browne[1], Emma Berry[1,2], Narinder Kapur[3], Steve Hodges[4], Gavin Smyth[4], Peter Watson[5], and Ken Wood[4]

[1]Neuropsychology Department, R3 Neurosciences, Addenbrooke's Hospital, Cambridge, UK
[2]Doctorate in Clinical Psychology, University of Hertfordshire, UK
[3]Research Department of Clinical, Experimental and Health Psychology, University College London, UK
[4]Microsoft Research Ltd, Cambridge, UK
[5]MRC Cognition and Brain Sciences Unit, Cambridge, UK

A wearable camera that takes pictures automatically, SenseCam, was used to generate images for rehearsal, promoting consolidation and retrieval of memories for significant events in a patient with memory retrieval deficits. SenseCam images of recent events were systematically reviewed over a 2-week period. Memory for these events was assessed throughout and longer-term recall was tested up to 6 months later. A written diary control condition followed the same procedure. The SenseCam review procedure resulted in significantly more details of an event being recalled, with twice as many details recalled at 6 months follow up compared to the written diary method. Self-report measures suggested autobiographical recollection was triggered by the SenseCam condition but not by reviewing the written diary. Emotional and social wellbeing questionnaires indicated improved confidence and decreased anxiety as a result of memory rehearsal using SenseCam images. We propose that SenseCam images provide a powerful boost to autobiographical recall, with secondary benefits for quality of life.

Keywords: SenseCam; Autobiographical memory; Rehabilitation.

The cognitive profile of Alzheimer's disease (AD) is well documented and emphasises marked deficits in episodic memory related to rapid forgetting of new information (Morris & Becker, 2004). A related diagnosis, mild cognitive impairment (MCI), is reached when patients display similar memory decline (i.e., greater than would be expected for their age), but do not display either reduced functioning in other cognitive domains or impaired activities of daily living, both of which are required for a diagnosis of AD (Grundman et al., 2004; Petersen et al., 1999).

A common presenting problem in both these populations is loss of autobiographical memory

Address correspondence to: Georgina Browne, R3 Neurosciences, Box 83 Addenbrooke's Hospital, Cambridge CB2 0QQ, UK. E-mail: georgina.browne@nhs.net

The authors would like to thank Mr and Mrs W for kindly agreeing to participate in the study. They also greatly appreciate the advice of Professor Martin Conway in preparing the manuscript.

Georgina Browne and Emma Berry have received consultancy fees from Microsoft Research, Cambridge. Narinder Kapur has received grant support and consultancy fees from Microsoft Research, Cambridge. Funding: Microsoft Research Ltd, Roger Needham Building, JJ Thomson Avenue, Cambridge CB3 0FB, UK.

© 2011 Psychology Press, an imprint of the Taylor & Francis Group, an Informa business
http://www.psypress.com/memory http://dx.doi.org/10.1080/09658211.2011.614622

(Dorrego et al., 1999; Hodges, 2006; Leyhe, Muller, Milian, Eschweiler, & Saur, 2009; Murphy, Troyer, Levine, & Moscovitch, 2008; Rubin, 1999), perhaps one of the most devastating effects of episodic memory decline. Autobiographical memory is regarded as a specific component of episodic memory and "refers to a person's recollection of past incidents and events, which occurred at a specific time and place" (Kopelman, 2002, p. 192). The term has received increasing attention over the last two decades, and accordingly there have been increasing attempts to define it. Tulving (2002) elaborated on his notion of re-experiencing to state that autobiographical remembering, or autonoetic awareness, is special in that one effectively undertakes mental time travel to recollect the original event as it occurred in the past. Notably, Brewer (e.g., 1988, 1996) has undertaken many extensive and thorough reviews of the literature and similarly concluded that autobiographical memory is a kind of "reliving of the individual's phenomenal experience during that earlier moment" (Brewer, 1996, p. 60). He contends that this particular kind of personal recollection is largely experienced as a visual mental image, representing salient information about the original event: the place, actions, people, objects, which may also engender associated thoughts and emotions.

It is unsurprising, then, that autobiographical memory is thought to play an intrinsic role in the development and maintenance of a stable sense of self. Conway (2005) has described the reciprocal nature of the relationship between memory and the self, suggesting that the coherence of the working self is maintained by the encoding and consolidation of episodic memories, and subsequent access to and construction (and reconstruction) of these memories. In turn, a coherent and stable self promotes higher self-esteem, a positive sense of wellbeing and associated physical health benefits. Indeed, there is evidence to suggest that reduced sense of self-identity in AD is related to poor autobiographical memory functioning (Addis & Tippett, 2004).

Moreover, memories are intrinsically pleasurable. They are not only cherished by the individual but they also have a social function—when memories are shared they facilitate intimacy and bonding within relationships and shared experiences lead to socially constructed memories (Nelson, 2000; Singer, 2006). There is evidence to suggest that when people are feeling depressed they draw on positive memories to lift their mood (Josephson, Singer, & Salovey, 1996). It is not surprising, then, that memory impairment can lead to a disruption of close relationships (Robinson & Swanson, 1990, cited in Baddeley, Eysenck, & Anderson, 2009), and reduction in self-confidence, social withdrawal, anxiety, and depression (Ballard, Boyle, Bowler, & Lindesey, 1996). Clare (2003) suggests that loss to social and psychological function is commonplace following cognitive deterioration.

There are therefore an increasing number of interventions focussing on cognitive rehabilitation. While the effectiveness of pharmacological interventions has yet to be conclusively demonstrated in AD and MCI populations (Raschetti, Albanese, Vanacore, & Maggini, 2007), there are an increasing number of non-medical interventions that may provide a suitable alternative.

Cognitive interventions, for example, are typically aimed at helping people to re-learn skills and information, or teaching compensatory strategies according to aims and goals set by the individual (Wilson, 2002). Following a recent meeting in Canada, a set of evidence-based guidelines were drawn up in response to the systematic review of 314 studies looking at the diagnosis and treatment of MCI (Chertkow et al., 2008). The team found four studies indicating improved cognition (working memory and verbal episodic memory) following cognitive training in the MCI population. However, these studies were either not randomised controlled trials (RCTs), the gold standard for measuring treatment success, or had small sample sizes, and thus the guidelines drawn up by Chertkow et al. (2008) concluded that while cognitive stimulation should be promoted in this population as part of a healthy lifestyle, there was as yet insufficient evidence to advocate the implementation of cognitive therapy as a treatment for MCI. One large-scale study undertaken with healthy older adults in America found that cognitive training delayed both cognitive and functional decline over a 5-year period (Willis et al., 2006). This study is supported by a number of RCTs similarly reporting positive effects of cognitive training in healthy older adults (Belleville, 2008). In conjunction with the association between intellectually stimulating activity and reduced risk of developing Alzheimer's disease (cf. Chertkow et al., 2008), such results may well generalise to the memory impaired populations. One methodological issue with studies investigating cognitive outcome is that they predominantly measure success in terms of performance on standardised cognitive assessments, which may have poor ecological validity and therefore tell us little about the impact on the individual's everyday activities and quality of life.

Cognitive and psychosocial rehabilitation has recently been the focus of an RCT investigating the use of a new evidence-based program in the memory-impaired population (Stuss et al., 2007). Stuss and his colleagues targeted memory, goal management, and psychosocial functioning as areas for improvement within the intervention. Their long-term follow-up results indicated maintenance of improved cognitive (Winocur, Craik, et al., 2007) and psychosocial functioning (Winocur, Palmer, et al., 2007), and highlighted the important and reciprocal relationship between these domains.

As yet, however, none of the treatments available focuses on improving autobiographical memory specifically. Current advances in assistive technologies have led to new interventions in the clinical setting; however it remains the case that most memory aids focus on systems for improving prospective memory (cf. Wilson, 2002), such as remembering appointments and shopping lists. Given the link between intact autobiographical memory and psychological and social wellbeing, rehabilitating recent autobiographical memory may lead to improvements in quality of life for people with memory loss and their carers. Berry et al. (2007) report the use of a wearable camera, SenseCam, which led to improved autobiographical memory for recent events in a patient with amnesia. We sought to replicate these findings and gain an index of impact on quality of life. The current study thus describes the use of SenseCam in a patient with memory retrieval difficulties, who was initially diagnosed with MCI and has not progressed to AD.

METHOD

Participant

Demographic details. Mrs W, a retired social worker, was diagnosed with mild cognitive impairment at the age of 55 and commenced taking a cholinesterase inhibitor (Aricept). She began participation in this study 10 months after her initial diagnosis and completed the study a further 10 months later. She lives at home with her husband, Mr W, and continues to lead a very active and full life.

Clinical details. Table 1 shows Mrs W's cognitive test profile at her initial diagnostic memory clinic assessment, and highlights memory impairment greater than expected for her age, with acceptable performance across other cognitive domains. At the time of diagnosis she was managing activities of daily living without difficulty.

At the time of writing—that is, 12 months post-study—Mrs W's condition had not progressed. Her scores on cognitive assessment had in fact improved following the SenseCam intervention such that her subsequent memory test performance was considered normal for her age: she scored 85/100 on Addenbrooke's Cognitive Exam Revised (ACE-R) and 27/30 on the Mini Mental State Exam (MMSE). Magnetic resonance imaging (MRI) and Pittsburgh Compound-B (PIB) scanning were inconsistent with Alzheimer's disease as a probable diagnosis, and she continues to be reviewed in our memory clinic.

Procedure

This single-case study followed a within-participant longitudinal design, comparing the effects of using SenseCam versus a written diary to aid retrospective recall of significant personal events.

There were two conditions: SenseCam facilitated recall and written diary facilitated recall. Each of the two conditions comprised two phases: in phase 1 recall of an event was tested over a 2-week period and in phase 2 longer-term recall of the event was tested a number of months later.

For the collection of SenseCam stimuli, Mrs W wore a small (6 cm × 8 cm × 2 cm) wide-angled lens camera, SenseCam, around her neck to collect images of significant personal events. Image capture was triggered automatically by the camera in response to changes in light, temperature, and motion, and by default every 30 seconds. Mrs W was not required to actively participate in the collection of the images: she did not need to remember to take the pictures herself and her full engagement in the activity was not disrupted by taking the pictures. Following an event Mr W uploaded the images onto a standard PC, ready for review the following day.

During phase 1 Mrs W wore the camera when she and her husband were doing something that

TABLE 1
Cognitive assessment details for Mrs W at point of diagnosis

Test	*Raw score*	*Statistic score*
General batteries		
ACE*	72/100*	> 5 SDs below mean*
MMSE*	25/30*	> 3 SDs below mean*
Verbal memory		
WMS-III Logical Memory		
Immediate Recall*	4*	%ile < 1st*
Delayed Recall*	4*	%ile < 1st*
Non-verbal memory		
Rey Figure Delayed Recall	3/36*	%ile < 10th*
PAL		
3 Pattern Tries	3	> 1 SD below mean
3 Pattern Errors*	3*	> 3 SDs below mean*
6 Pattern Errors*	42*	> 5 SDs below mean*
Verbal skills		
Graded Naming Test	23/30	%ile = 75th
Category Fluency		
Animals	14	%ile = 16th–19th
Fruit	19	%ile = 79th–82nd
Dogs	10	%ile = 31st–38th
TEA Elevator Counting with Distraction	7	%ile = 12th–21st
Executive functioning		
Trails B		
Time	92	Within normal limits
Errors	0	Within normal limits
Stroop errors	23*	Impaired*

SD = standard deviation; %ile = percentile, *indicates impairment relative to age-matched control group.

she particularly wanted to remember, such as a meal out with their granddaughter, or a trip to the seaside. Mr W made notes of the main event details, against which Mrs W's recall was subsequently tested. Mr W was asked to record facts, such as "we took the train to London" as well as any significant thoughts or emotions associated with the event. The day following the event Mr W asked his wife one cueing question, for example, "What do you remember of our trip to x?". He allowed his wife to free recall as much of the event as possible and scored her responses against his notes. If, for example, she recalled 9 of 12 items that he had written down, she scored 75%. Recall was tested in this same way every 2 days for 2 weeks.

Immediately following each recall test Mr and Mrs W reviewed the images together, which were played on a standard PC as a rapid slide show, talking through the event as they went along. Note, then, that the first recall test on day 1 occurred before any review of the event had taken place, and all subsequent memory tests reflect recall of the event in relation to her score on day 1. A total of six events were recorded in this way and results were averaged across trials.

After intervals of 1 month, 3 months, and 6 months without reviewing the images, Mrs W's longer-term recall of the events was reassessed (phase 2). A written diary control condition followed the same protocol, substituting Mr W's notes for the SenseCam images as the means by which to review the events. Mrs W reviewed just two events using this method, since she found it impacted negatively on her emotional wellbeing and did not want to continue with this part of the study.

Phase 1 baseline data were also collected for Mrs W's normal rate of forgetting over a 2-week period using no memory aids or other means of rehearsal. Mr and Mrs W experienced a significant event together, for which Mr W made notes as described above. No stimuli prompting recall or rehearsal of the event were looked at or discussed over the next 2 weeks. At the end of the 2-week period, Mr W tested Mrs W's memory for the event. Two events were recorded in this way.

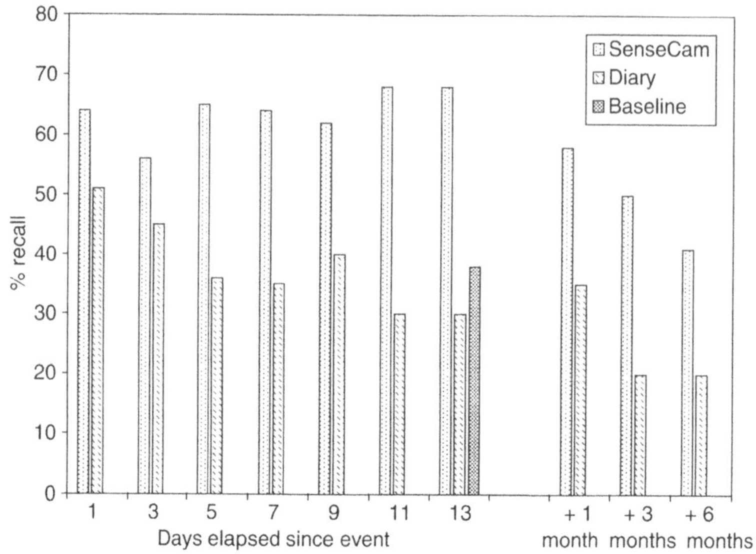

Figure 1. Average recall for SenseCam-reviewed versus diary-reviewed events.

Treatment order (and thus data collection) ran from baseline to SenseCam to written diary conditions. That is, baseline data were actually collected at the start of the study. This was followed by all data collection for phase 1 of the SenseCam condition, which was followed by all phase 1 data collection for the written diary condition. Phase 2 data collection followed accordingly. This order of data collection was intended to control for the possibility of cognitive recovery (spontaneous or otherwise) to Mrs W's cognition as a variable in explaining any superior SenseCam results, should we find them.

Measures

Three standardised measures were used to record Mrs W's psychological and social functioning: the Self-Image Profile for Adults (Butler & Gasson, 2004), the State-Trait Anxiety Inventory for adults (Spielberger, Gorsuch, Lushene, Vagg, & Jacobs, 1983), and Beck's Depression Inventory – Second Edition (Beck, Steer, & Brown, 1996). These measures were undertaken at the beginning of the study and at the end of phases 1 (2 week retention) and 2 (longer-term retention) of the SenseCam condition. Two in-house qualitative measures were developed to assess Mrs W's experience of using SenseCam and the written diary as memory aids and were administered at the end of phase 1 in both conditions. The first in-house measure comprised a semi-structured interview using open-ended questions to generate qualitative feedback about the experience of using SenseCam and the written diary. For example, Mrs W was asked, "How do you feel about using SenseCam/a written diary to help your memory?" The second measure was a quality of life assessment that used Likert scales to rate the impact of using the aids in terms of subjective levels of stress, confidence, ability to cope at home, and memory function. For example, Mrs W was asked, "As a result of using SenseCam/a written diary, do you think there is any difference in how 'stressed out' you are?" and asked to grade her response on a scale where -5 indicated worse and $+5$ indicated better.

Statistical analysis

For each condition, chi-squared analyses were used to compare the mean recall scores across the two conditions. For remaining measures of psychosocial functioning, these scores were plotted and reviewed non-statistically.

RESULTS

Overall, the proportion of events recalled was significantly greater for the SenseCam condition than the diary condition, $\chi^2(1) = 29.25$, $p < .001$. Figure 1 details Mrs W's average recall of an event over time for the two conditions. Using SenseCam, her recall over the 2-week reviewing period ranged from 64% on day 1 to 68% on

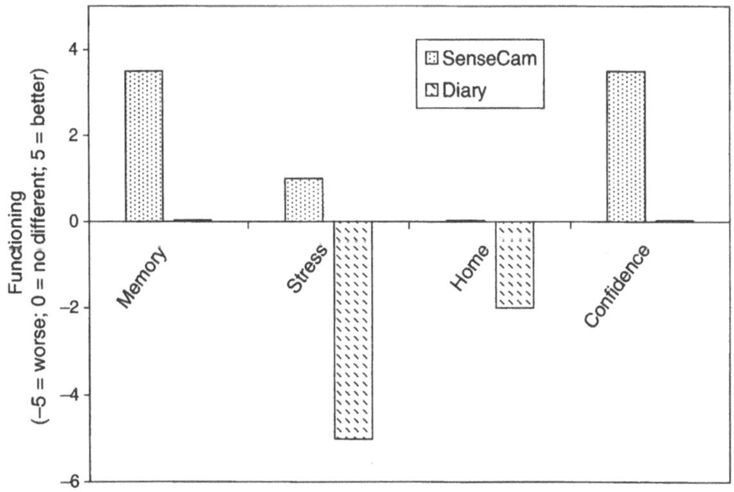

Figure 2. Impact of using SenseCam and a written diary as memory aids on Mrs W's day-to-day wellbeing.

day 13, which compared to a drop from 51% to 30% using the diary review method. Her baseline rate of forgetting over the 2-week period indicated an average of 38% recall on day 13, suggesting that the written diary made no difference to her normal rate of forgetting.

Longer-term follow-up data also indicated superior performance for SenseCam over written diary-facilitated recollection. Over the course of 6 months without reviewing images or diary, while there was decline in Mrs W's memory for all events, at 6 months' follow-up she recalled twice as many details for SenseCam-reviewed events (41%) than diary-reviewed events (20%).

Figure 2 shows Mrs W's subjective response to using SenseCam and the written diary as memory aids. She thought using SenseCam made no difference to her ability to cope at home, but led to improvements in her memory, level of stress, and self-confidence. Using the written diary made no difference to her memory or level of self-confidence, but had a negative impact on her level of stress and ability to cope at home.

Qualitatively, Mrs W reported much enjoyment from using SenseCam, and stated that it had had a positive impact on her memory: "it was like having another pair of eyes or another person with you helping you remember" since the SenseCam images were "actually what my eyes were seeing" or "re-experiencing". She said that looking back over the images "jogged my memory of things that I didn't remember that were in the back of my mind ... things that normally I would just forget ... [it was] as if I was back on the trip again". Mrs W reported that these memories were "all there" and "just came rolling out" and on occasion she was able to recall information not recorded in the SenseCam images, such as conversations that had taken place and her feelings about particular events.

Mr and Mrs W both thought using SenseCam had been beneficial for their relationship as they spent more time together talking about recent events: Mrs W stated "we can sit and talk together about where we've been". Mrs W further noted that "if you have memory problems, you have low confidence" but since using SenseCam improved her memory, she had "more confidence talking about things" and thus noted an improvement in her day-to-day self-assurance.

This contrasted with Mrs W's experience of using the diary, which her husband reported did not stimulate "actual recall" of the event. Mrs W said, "If I just talk about [an event], I drift off and don't remember it". She even felt unsure that the events depicted by the diary were ones that had actually happened: "[Mr W] tells me [about the trip] but I don't know whether I really did it ... I had to take [Mr W"s] word for it", and this led to bickering and tension between Mrs W and her husband. She stated that she "hated" the written diary condition, which was therefore discontinued after collecting data for two events. There was no change to scores on the standardised measures of anxiety, depression, or self-image, which were all within the normal range both pre and post SenseCam intervention.

DISCUSSION

Regular review of SenseCam images resulted in superior recall of recent events compared to reviewing a written diary, and this effect was maintained in the long term. These results are consistent with a number of other recent studies showing improved memory following SenseCam use (e.g., Berry, Browne, Kapur, Watson, & Hodges, 2011; Berry et al., 2007; Lee & Dey, 2008; St. Jacques, Lowder, Conway, & Cabeza, 2011).

A preliminary study investigating the neural activation associated with SenseCam facilitated recollection in healthy adults found that stimulation of hippocampal networks resulted in moderate improvement on tests of general cognitive functioning, and concluded that it may have been the use of SenseCam that ultimately facilitated this effect (St. Jacques et al., 2011). Thus it could also be argued, albeit very speculatively at this stage, that SenseCam use could, in part, account for the improvement seen in clinic from moderate memory impairment at the time of initial MCI diagnosis to normal memory functioning (on standardised tests) nearly 3 years later.

An alternative account for the cognitive recovery could be that Mrs W's memory difficulties had no neurological basis in the first instance, and subsequently resolved spontaneously. Indeed, a fifth of people initially diagnosed with MCI may spontaneously recover normal cognitive functioning (Solfrizzi et al., 2004). If Mrs W belongs to this group, one would expect to see increasingly better results as data collection for the study progresses. Indeed this may in part account for the superior performance of the SenseCam data over the baseline data. However, by this argument, the written diary should outperform both baseline and SenseCam, since the timeline for data collection ran from baseline to SenseCam to written diary conditions. It does not: SenseCam results are superior despite the possible improvement over time to general cognition, and baseline and written diary results are equivalent in effect. This would seem to lend weight to concluding that SenseCam is a better tool for facilitating autobiographical recollection than a written diary. That is, Mrs W's cognition may have recovered spontaneously over the course of the study, irrespective of SenseCam use, which nevertheless outperforms the written diary as a memory aid.

A third possibility that may account for Mrs W's improved cognition is that she is one of the 10–20% who respond to cholinesterase inhibitors (cf. Lemstra, Richard, & van Gool, 2007), with which she was treated following her initial diagnosis. However, it would be extremely rare to see such a striking effect in terms of improved cognitive function (cf. Hogan et al., 2008). Furthermore, this argument is subject to the same criticism of treatment order effect noted previously, and thus the conclusion that SenseCam outperforms the written diary as a tool for facilitating autobiographical recollection still holds.

This study also highlights the positive impact SenseCam had on quality of life, secondary to improved autobiographical memory. Our findings are consistent with a recent study that also reports improved psychosocial functioning following the use of SenseCam (Crete-Nishihata et al., 2011). Mrs W noted improved memory and thus self-esteem and confidence as a result of using SenseCam. She and her husband both commented on the increased time they spent discussing activities they had done together and that this had had a positive influence on their relationship. This contrasted with their experience of using a written diary as a memory aid, which Mrs W indicated impacted negatively on her stress levels and on her ability to cope at home. She disliked using the diary as she found it did not promote memory of events. Undertaking the recall tests in this condition led to squabbling with her husband, as she could not recall the events when they reviewed the notes together and they argued about what had really happened.

It is possible that this reported benefit to quality of life following the use of SenseCam may have been facilitated simply by taking part in the research: receiving innovative technology and regular input from a member of the research team may have positively biased Mr and Mrs W's perceived impact of using SenseCam. Nevertheless, Mrs W appeared to genuinely enjoy reviewing activities using the SenseCam images, as observed by one of the authors (GB). On one occasion she was asked to look through a set of images taken 8 months previously and that she had never seen before. She did not recall the event until about half way through the set when one particular image "jumped out" at her. The image was of her dog jumping up at a visitor. At this point Mrs W clapped her hands, laughed and remarked, "now I remember", and recalled the entire event.

Mrs W described such recollections as if she were "re-experiencing" the event, which may provide insight into the mechanisms facilitating recall when using SenseCam. Firstly, there may be individual or single images that act as "trigger" images cueing recall for the entire event (see also our observations in Berry et al., 2011), perhaps akin to what Croucher, Calder, and Barnard (2006) call "impact images". Secondly, Mrs W's description mirrors that used by Tulving (2002) when he referred to autobiographical recollection as a "conscious re-experiencing of past experiences". Indeed, the properties of SenseCam imagery correspond well with the properties of autobiographical memory: they are largely visual (Brewer, 1988), and represent a time-compressed, summary record from the first person perspective (Conway, 2005). As such, they may provide a powerful cue to the recollection of personal events, enabling effective retrieval and consolidation of the memory in long-term storage.

Our findings have important implications for cognitive therapy in both the MCI population and, more broadly, the ageing population. It is clear that memory decline can lead to poor psychosocial functioning (Ballard et al., 1996; Clare, 2003). This study complements this evidence: Mrs W's poor recall for events led to reduced psychosocial functioning. Moreover, as her memory for events improved, so too did her psychological wellbeing and her relationship with her husband. While there remains a need for large-scale RCTs investigating the effects of cognitive rehabilitation in both dementia and normal ageing, there are nevertheless increasing numbers of small-scale research and single-case studies that suggest benefits to both cognitive function and psychosocial wellbeing in MCI and AD (e.g., Berry et al., 2011; Brooker & Duce, 2000; Clare et al., 2009; Kurz, Pohl, Ramsenthaler, & Sorg, 2009; Massimi et al., 2008. For reviews see also Chertkow et al., 2008; Clare & Woods, 2004; Hogan et al., 2008; Woods & Roth, 2005) and a small number of promising large-scale studies and RCTs in the normal ageing population (e.g., Ball et al., 2002; Stuss et al., 2007; Willis et al., 2006. For reviews see Belleville, 2008; Chertkow et al., 2008).

It remains the case, however, that cognitive rehabilitation programmes typically focus on activities such as memory training, problem solving, reality orientation, and reminiscence therapy, and not on activities for improving autobiographical memory. There currently exists a small but compelling literature that SenseCam is effective at improving memory for recent significant events (e.g., Berry et al., 2007, 2009; Berry et al., 2011; Lee & Dey, 2008; St. Jacques et al., 2011). In conjunction with both the evidence for improved psychosocial functioning following cognitive rehabilitation, and the literature linking intact autobiographical memory with self-identity and thus self-esteem, there is good evidence to suggest that memory rehabilitation programmes should aim to include methods for improving recent autobiographical memory, and more specifically, that devices such as SenseCam may be effective tools for this purpose.

REFERENCES

Addis, D. R., & Tippett, L. J. (2004). Memory of myself: Autobiographical memory and identity in Alzheimer's disease. *Memory, 12*, 56–74.

Baddeley, A., Eysenck, W., & Anderson, M. C. (2009). *Memory.* Hove, UK: Psychology Press.

Ball, K., Berch, D. B., Helmers, K. F., Jobe, J. B., Leveck, M. D., Mariske, M., et al. (2002). Effects of cognitive training interventions with older adults: A randomized controlled trial. *Journal of the American Medical Association, 288*, 2271–2281.

Ballard, C. G., Boyle, A., Bowler, C., & Lindesay, J. (1996). Anxiety disorders in dementia sufferers. *International Journal of Geriatric Psychiatry, 11*, 987–990.

Beck, A. T., Steer, R. A., & Brown, G. K. (1996). *Beck depression inventory – second edition.* London: The Psychological Corporation: Harcourt Brace & Company.

Belleville, S. (2008). Cognitive training for persons with mild cognitive impairment. *International Psychogeriatrics, 20*, 57–66.

Berry, E., Browne, G., Kapur, N., Watson, P., & Hodges, S. (2011). *The use of SenseCam improves memory for recent significant events in patients with mild to moderate Alzheimer's disease: a series of single case studies.* Manuscript in preparation.

Berry, E., Hampshire, A., Rowe, J., Hodges, S., Kapur, N., Watson, P., et al. (2009). The neural basis of effective memory therapy in a patient with limbic encephalitis. *Journal of Neurology, Neurosurgery, and Psychiatry with Practical Neurology, 80*, 1202–1205.

Berry, E., Kapur, N., Williams, L., Hodges, S., Watson, P., Smyth, G., et al. (2007). The use of a wearable camera, SenseCam, as a pictorial diary to improve autobiographical memory in a patient with limbic encephalitis. *Neuropsychological Rehabilitation, 17*, 582–681.

Brewer, W. F. (1988). Qualitative analysis of the recalls of randomly sampled autobiographical events. In M. M. Gruneberg, P. E. Morris, & R. N. Sykes (Eds.), *Practical aspects of memory: current research and issues.* Chichester, UK: Wiley.

Brewer, W. F. (1996). What is recollective memory? In D. C. Rubin (Ed.), *Remembering our past: Studies in autobiographical memory* (pp. 19–66). Cambridge, UK: Cambridge University Press.

Brooker, D., & Duce, L. (2000). Wellbeing and activity in dementia: A comparison of group reminiscence therapy, structured goal-directed group activity and unstructured time. *Aging & Mental Health, 4*, 354–358.

Butler, R. J., & Gasson, S. L. (2004). *The self image profile for adults.* London: Harcourt Assessment.

Chertkow, H., Massoud, F., Nasreddine, Z., Belleville, S., Joanette, Y., Bocti, C., et al. (2008). Diagnosis and treatment of dementia: 3. Mild cognitive impairment and cognitive impairment without dementia. *Canadian Medical Association Journal, 178*, 1273–1285.

Clare, L. (2003). Neuropsychological rehabilitation for people with dementia. In B. A. Wilson (Ed.), *Neuropsychological rehabilitation: Theory and practice* (pp. 197–215). Lisse, The Netherlands: Swets & Zeitlinger.

Clare, L., van Paasschen, J., Evans, S. J., Parkinson, C., Woods, R. T., & Linden, D. E. (2009). Goal-oriented cognitive rehabilitation for an individual with mild cognitive impairment: Behavioural and neuroimaging outcomes. *Neurocase, 16*, 1–14.

Clare, L., & Woods, R. T. (2004). Cognitive training and cognitive rehabilitation for people with early-stage Alzheimer's disease: A review. *Neuropsychological Rehabilitation, 14*(4), 385–401.

Conway, M. (2005). Memory and the self. *Journal of Memory and Language, 53*, 594–628.

Crete-Nishihata, M., Baecker, R. M., Massimi, M., Ptak, D., Campigotto, R., Kaufman, L. D., et al. (2011). *Reconstructing the past: Personal memory technologies are not just personal and not just for memory.* Manuscript in preparation.

Croucher, C. J., Calder, A. J., & Barnard, P. J. (2006). *Impact, arousal and the recollection of emotional pictures.* Paper presented at the Joint Meeting of the Experimental Psychology Society with Nederlandse Vereninging voor Psychonomie, Birmingham.

Dorrego, M. R., Sabe, L., Cuerva, A. G., Kuzis, G., Tiberti, C., Boller, R., et al. (1999). Remote memory in Alzheimer's disease. *The Journal of Neuropsychiatry and Clinical Neurosciences, 11*, 490–497.

Grundman, M., Peterson, R. C., Ferris, S. H., Thomas, R. G., Aisen, P. S., Bennett, D. A., et al. (2004). Mild cognitive impairment can be distinguished from Alzheimer disease and normal aging for clinical trials. *Archives of Neurology, 61*, 59–66.

Hodges, J. R. (2006). Alzheimer's centennial legacy: Origins, landmarks and the current status of knowledge concerning cognitive aspects. *Brain, 129*, 2811–2822.

Hogan, B. D., Bailey, P., Black, S., Carswell, A., Chertkow, H., Clarke, B., et al. (2008). Diagnosis and treatment of dementia: 5. Nonpharmacologic and phpharmacologic therapy for mild to moderate dementia. *Canadian Medical Association Journal, 179*, 1019–1026.

Josephson, B., Singer, J. A., & Salovey, P. (1996). Mood regulation and memory: Repairing sad moods with happy memories. *Cognition and Emotion, 10*, 437–444.

Kopelman, M. D. (2002). Retrograde amnesia. In A. D. Baddeley, M. D. Kopelman, & B. A. Wilson (Eds.), *The handbook of memory disorders: second edition* (pp. 189–208). Chichester, UK: John Wiley & Sons Ltd.

Kurz, A., Pohl, C., Ramsenthaler, M., & Sorg, C. (2009). Cognitive rehabilitation in patients with mild cognitive impairment. *International Journal of Geriatric Psychiatry, 24*, 163–168.

Lee, M. L., & Dey, A. K. (2008). Lifelogging memory applicance for people with episodic memory impairment. Proceedings of the 10th International Conference on Ubiquitous Computing. *Ubicomp '08, 344*, 44–53.

Lemstra, A. W., Richard, E., & van Gool, W. A. (2007). Commentary: Cholinesterase inhibitors in dementia: Yes, no, or maybe? *Age and Ageing, 36*, 625–627.

Leyhe, T., Muller, S., Milian, M., Eschweiler, G. W., & Saur, R. (2009). Impairment of episodic and semantic autobiographical memory in patients with mild cognitive impairment and early Alzheimer's disease. *Neuropsychologia, 47*, 2464–2469.

Massimi, M., Berry, E., Browne, G., Smyth, G., Watson, P., & Baecker, R. M. (2008). An exploratory case study of the impact of ambient biographical displays on identity in a patient with Alzheimer's disease. *Neuropsychological Rehabilitation, 18*, 742–765.

Morris, J. C., Storandt, M., Miller, J. P., McKeel, D. W., Price, J. L., Rubin, E. H., et al. (2001). Mild cognitive impairment represents early-stage Alzheimer disease. *Archives of Neurology, 58*, 397–405.

Morris, R., & Becker, J. (2004). *Cognitive neuropsychology of Alzheimer's disease* (2nd ed.). Oxford, UK: Oxford University Press.

Murphy, K. J., Troyer, A. K., Levine, B., & Moscovitch, M. (2008). Episodic, but not semantic, autobiographical memory is reduced in amnestic mild cognitive impairment. *Neuropsychologia, 46*, 3116–3123.

Nelson, K. (2000). The origins of autobiographical memory. In U. Neisser & I. E. Hyman (Eds.), *Memory observed: Remembering in natural contexts.* New York: Worth Publishers.

Petersen, R. C., Smith, G. E., Waring, S. C., Ivnik, R. J., Tangalos, E. G., & Kokmen, E. (1999). Mild cognitive impairment: Clinical characterization and outcome. *Archives of Neurology, 56*, 303–308.

Raschetti, R., Albanese, E., Vanacore, N., & Maggini, M. (2007). Cholinesterase inhibitors in mild cognitive impairment: A systematic review of randomised trials. *Public Library of Science: Medicine, 4*, e338.

Rubin, D. C. (1999). *Remembering our past: Studies in autobiographical memory.* Cambridge, UK: Cambridge University Press.

Singer, J. A. (2006). Memory, emotion and psychotherapy: Maximising the positive functions of self-defining memories. In B. Uttl, N. Ohta, & A. L. Sigenthaler (Eds.), *Memory and emotion: Interdisciplinary perspectives* (pp. 211–232). Oxford, UK: Blackwell Publishing.

Solfrizzi, V., Panza, F., Colacicco, A. M., D'Introno, A., Capurso, C., Torres, S., et al. (2004). Vascular risk factors, incidence of MCI, and rates of progression to dementia. *Neurology, 63*, 1882–1891.

Spielberger, C. D., Gorsuch, R. L., Lushene, R., Vagg, P. R., & Jacobs, G. A. (1983). *State-trait anxiety inventory for adults*. Redwood City, CA: Mind Garden Inc.

St. Jacques, P. L., Conway, M. A., Lowder, M., & Cabeza, R. (2011). *Two ways of accessing the past: Hippocampal connectivity during autobiographical memory elicited by verbal versus visual cues*. Manuscript submitted for publication.

Stuss, D. T., Robertson, I. H., Craik, F. I. M., Levine, B., Alexander, M. P., Black, S., et al. (2007). Cognitive rehabilitation in the elderly: A randomized trial to evaluate a new protocol. *Journal of the International Neuropsychological Society*, *13*, 120–131.

Tulving, E. (2002). Episodic memory: From mind to brain. *Annual Review of Psychology*, *53*, 1–25.

Willis, S. L., Tennstedt, S. L., Marsiske, M., Ball, K., Elias, J., Koepke, K. M., et al. (2006). Long-term effects of cognitive training on everyday functional outcomes in older adults. *Journal of the American Medical Association*, *296*, 2805–2814.

Wilson, B. (2002). Management and remediation of memory problems in brain-injured adults. In A. D. Baddeley, M. D. Kopelman, & B. A. Wilson (Eds.), *The handbook of memory disorders: Second edition* (pp. 655–682). Chichester, UK: John Wiley & Sons Ltd.

Winocur, G., Craik, F. I., Levine, B., Robertson, I. H., Binns, M. A., Alexander, M., et al. (2007). Cognitive rehabilitation in the elderly: Overview and future directions. *Journal of the International Neuropsychological Society*, *13*, 166–171.

Winocur, G., Palmer, H., Dawson, D., Binns, M. A., Bridges, K., & Stuss, D. T. (2007). Cognitive rehabilitation in the elderly: An evaluation of psychosocial factors. *Journal of the International Neuropsychological Society*, *13*, 153–165.

Woods, R., & Roth, A. (2005). Effectiveness of psychological interventions with older people. In A. Roth & P. Fanagy (Eds.), *What works for whom? A critical review of psychotherapy research* (pp. 425–446). New York, NY: The Guilford Press.

MEMORY, 2011, 19 (7), 723–732

Psychology Press
Taylor & Francis Group

Gender differences in autobiographical memory for everyday events: Retrieval elicited by SenseCam images versus verbal cues

Peggy L. St. Jacques[1], Martin A. Conway[2], and Roberto Cabeza[1]

[1]Duke University, Durham, NC, USA
[2]University of Leeds, UK

Gender differences are frequently observed in *autobiographical memory* (AM). However, few studies have investigated the neural basis of potential gender differences in AM. In the present functional MRI (fMRI) study we investigated gender differences in AMs elicited using dynamic visual images vs verbal cues. We used a novel technology called a SenseCam, a wearable device that automatically takes thousands of photographs. SenseCam differs considerably from other prospective methods of generating retrieval cues because it does not disrupt the ongoing experience. This allowed us to control for potential gender differences in emotional processing and elaborative rehearsal, while manipulating how the AMs were elicited. We predicted that males would retrieve more richly experienced AMs elicited by the SenseCam images vs the verbal cues, whereas females would show equal sensitivity to both cues. The behavioural results indicated that there were no gender differences in subjective ratings of reliving, importance, vividness, emotion, and uniqueness, suggesting that gender differences in brain activity were not due to differences in these measures of phenomenological experience. Consistent with our predictions, the fMRI results revealed that males showed a greater difference in functional activity associated with the rich experience of SenseCam vs verbal cues, than did females.

Keywords: Episodic memory; Autobiographical memory; Gender; fMRI; Functional neuroimaging.

Gender differences have frequently been observed in autobiographical memory (AM), which refers to memory for events from our personal past. Several studies have documented superior AMs in females compared to males (for a review see Andreano & Cahill, 2009). For example, compared to males, females recall longer and more detailed AMs (e.g., Friedman & Pines, 1991; Pillemer, Wink, DiDonato, & Sanborn, 2003; Pohl, Bender, & Lachmann, 2005; Ross & Holmberg, 1992; Seidlitz & Diener, 1998), are more accurate at dating their AMs (e.g., Skowronski & Thompson, 1990), and are faster to recall AMs (e.g., Davis, 1999). In contrast, other studies have failed to find gender differences in AM (e.g., Rubin, Schulkind, & Rahhal, 1999). The lack of gender differences in behaviour does not necessarily imply that there are no gender differences in AM retrieval (e.g., Piefke, Weiss, Markowitsch, & Fink, 2005). However, the bases of potential gender differences during AM retrieval are not well understood. In the present study we employed functional MRI (fMRI) to

Address correspondence to: Peggy L. St. Jacques, Department of Psychology, Harvard, 33 Kirkland Street, William James Hall, Cambridge, MA, 02138, USA. E-mail: peggyls@wjh.harvard.edu.

The authors would like to thank Matthew W. Lowder for help with participant testing. This research was supported by a grant from Microsoft Research Cambridge and the National Institute of Health RO1 AG23770, both awarded to RC.

© 2011 Psychology Press, an imprint of the Taylor & Francis Group, an Informa business
http://www.psypress.com/memory http://dx.doi.org/10.1080/09658211.2010.516266

examine brain activity underlying potential gender differences in AM retrieval.

Reported gender differences in AM have been linked to differences in emotional processing and elaborative rehearsal (for reviews see Andreano & Cahill, 2009; Piefke & Fink, 2005). According to the affective intensity hypothesis females' superior AM is due to increased emotional processing that subsequently enhances memory recall. For example, females recall more emotional AMs (e.g., Friedman & Pines, 1991; Fujita, Diener, & Sandvik, 1991), more emotional information (e.g., Bauer, Stennes, & Haight, 2003; Bloise & Johnson, 2007), and rate their memories as being more emotional (e.g., Seidlitz & Diener, 1998). Moreover, sex differences have been observed in brain activity during emotional tasks (e.g., Cahill et al., 2001; Canli, Desmond, Zhao, & Gabrieli, 2002). In contrast, the elaborative rehearsal hypothesis suggests that females are better at remembering their life's experiences because of more frequent and elaborative rehearsal (e.g., Seidlitz & Diener, 1998). Support for this hypothesis is provided by evidence that females discuss events at more detailed length (Friedman & Pines, 1991; Seidlitz & Diener, 1998) and that parents discuss AMs in a more elaborative way with daughters compared to sons (for a review see Fivush & Nelson, 2004).

Alternatively, gender differences in AM might be due to more general cognitive differences in verbal and spatial processing (cf. Andreano & Cahill, 2009; Piefke & Fink, 2005). A substantial body of literature shows that females outperform males on verbal tasks such as phonological fluency, whereas males outperform females on spatial tasks such as mental rotation and navigation (for a review see Andreano & Cahill, 2009). However, previous studies examining gender differences in AM have relied on verbal cues to elicit AMs and verbal processing strategies to determine the quality of retrieval, in which males might have more disadvantage. Moreover, individual differences in phonological fluency accounts for potential differences in the level of detail in verbal recall of AMs (Addis, Sacchetti, Ally, Budson, & Schacter, 2009). In contrast, functional neuroimaging studies of AM have suggested that there is substantial overlap in the brain regions recruited during navigation (for a meta-analysis see Spreng, Mar, & Kim, 2009) and particular spatial abilities (for reviews see Hassabis & Maguire, 2007; Moscovitch et al., 2005), suggesting that these processes are very important in AM retrieval. Furthermore, episodic memory tests that have controlled for verbal processing have observed less-robust gender differences (for a review see Andreano & Cahill, 2009). Thus it is possible that the reported gender differences in behavioural studies of AM might be the result of potential biases favouring verbal processing in the method of elicitation and evaluation of the retrieved events.

One solution to examine AM retrieval in a more unbiased way is to use functional neuroimaging to examine covert retrieval of AMs. Gender differences should be observed in the AM retrieval network if females rely more on verbal processing, whereas males rely more on spatial processing during AM recall. Piefke et al. (2005) is the only functional neuroimaging study to our knowledge, which has investigated gender differences in AM retrieval. In this functional MRI (fMRI) study, participants were asked to recall AMs elicited via verbal sentences describing particular autobiographical events generated in a pre-scan interview. Females recruited the prefrontal cortex (PFC), a region that is associated with increased control over the recovery of information (for a review see Miller & Cohen, 2001). Piefke et al. (2005) interpreted the greater recruitment of the PFC as reflecting a greater reliance on temporal context when females retrieve AMs. In contrast, males recruited the parahippocampal gyrus, a region associated with bottom-up visuospatial processing (for a review see Burgess, Maguire, & O'Keefe, 2002). Thus the findings of Piefke et al. (2005) are consistent with the idea that gender differences in AM might be due to differences in retrieval strategy. However, it is not clear whether the use of more spatial cues might attenuate some of these potential gender differences in cognitive strategy during AM retrieval.

To address these issues, we investigated potential gender differences in AMs elicited using verbal cues versus dynamic visual images. We employed a novel technology called a SenseCam (Microsoft Research Cambridge; http://research.microsoft.com/sensecam/) to prospectively collect dynamic, visuospatial cues to elicit AMs during fMRI scanning. SenseCam is a small wearable digital camera that has electronic sensors (e.g., light, heat, etc.) that can automatically trigger thousands of photographs in a single day (see Figure 1A). This differs considerably from the normal way in which we can use a camera to generate retrieval cues (Cabeza et al., 2004; St. Jacques, Rubin, Labar, & Cabeza, 2008), because it does not disrupt the ongoing experience of events through the act of taking a photograph (for a review see Cabeza & St. Jacques, 2007). Moreover, the SenseCam images can provide effective retrieval cues to elicit everyday AMs, which are less likely to be emotionally intense and elaboratively rehearsed compared to memories that participants retrieve themselves (e.g., Seidlitz & Diener, 1998). Participants wore the SenseCam for a week while it automatically recorded photographs, and they also kept a schedule of their daily activities. Following a delay of a week, participants came in for their fMRI session in which they were asked to covertly recall the events depicted in short SenseCam (SC) clips versus verbal cues (VC) garnered from the daily schedule, then to rate their subjective feeling of re-experience using a reliving rating. We examined the interaction between gender (males, females) and type of cue (SC, VC) on brain activity sensitive to reliving during AM retrieval. Based on reported gender differences in the reliance on spatial vs verbal processing, we predicted that males would retrieve more richly experienced AMs when cued via the SenseCam images (SC) versus the verbal cues (VC), whereas females would show an equal benefit for both types of cues.

METHOD

Participants

There were 23 participants (12 females, and 11 males; age range: 18–35 years) who were healthy, right-handed, and without history of neurological or psychiatric episodes (for demographic characteristics see Table 1). Participants gave written informed consent for a protocol approved by the Duke University Institutional Review Board. Participants were tested on subsets of executive function (Intra-Extra Dimensional Set Shifting, Spatial Span, Spatial Working Memory, Rapid Visual Information Processing), visual memory ability (Paired-Associated Learning, Pattern Recognition Memory), and speed of processing (Movement Time and Reaction Time) included in the Cambridge Neuropsychological Test Automated Battery (CANTABeclipse, version 2.0; Cambridge Cognition Ltd.), as well as vocabulary ability using the Shipley Vocabulary Test. Using Bonferroni correction to control for multiple *t*-tests we found no significant gender differences across these cognitive tasks or in the demographic characteristics of the participants (see Table 1).

Procedure

Prospective collection. Retrieval cues were prospectively collected across a period of 6 days, in which participants wore the SenseCam and kept a schedule of each day's activities to be used to parse the SenseCam images into events. The daily schedule was recorded at the end of each day along with a unique identifier to distinguish that particular day from others (e.g., "Today was the day I had lunch with Ben"). Participants were instructed to write about 10–15 brief sentences, one for each major event during the day (e.g., "Had breakfast", "went to the grocery store . . ."). Participants were not informed that their written schedules would be later used to test their memory for the events, and debriefing after scanning confirmed that no

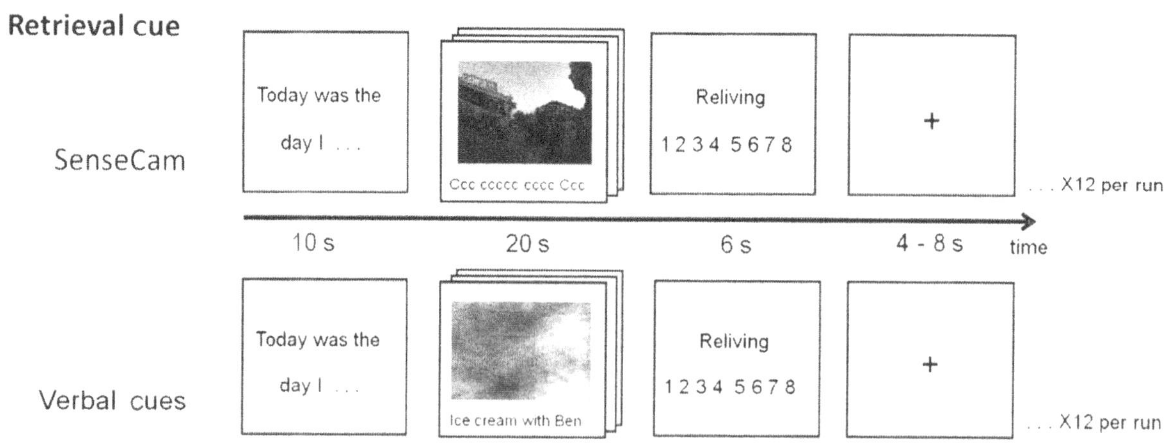

Figure 1. The experimental design depicting the study conditions. To view this figure in colour, please see the online issue of the journal.

TABLE 1
Demographic information by gender

	Females	*Males*	*t (21)*
n	12	11	
Age	23.08 (2.23)	24.45 (4.72)	0.90
Years of education	16.17 (1.75)	15.91 (2.17)	− 0.32
Shipley vocabulary	33.75 (2.99)	34.73 (3.44)	0.73
Executive tasks			
Spatial working memory			
Between errors	6.75 (9.38)	10.18 (12.78)	0.74
Strategy	24.58 (5.45)	28.55 (7.54)	1.45
Spatial span	7.58 (1.16)	8.18 (0.75)	1.45
Rapid visual information processing	0.95 (0.03)	0.98 (0.02)	2.60
Intra-extra dimensional set shifting			
Stages completed	9.00 (0.00)	9.00 (0.00)	n/a
Total errors	9.25 (2.34)	10.45 (2.50)	1.19
Memory tasks			
Paired associate learning	2.17 (2.17)	5.36 (5.26)	1.94
Pattern recognition	96.53 (3.91)	96.59 (3.64)	0.04
Memory			
Speed Tasks			
Movement time (ms)	363.89 (75.81)	351.16 (58.65)	− 0.45
Reaction time (ms)	309.73 (44.75)	318.56 (57.51)	0.41

Mean (Standard Deviation); *p <. 001.

participant suspected a memory test. Then 3 days were randomly assigned to the SC condition and 3 days to the VC condition. For each day, 12 events were selected to be tested in the scanner. Participants also viewed SenseCam images from other people's cameras in separate runs, which were included for additional analyses that were not the focus on the present investigation (St. Jacques, Conway, Lowder, & Cabeza, 2011).

fMRI scanning. The scanning session took place 1 week following the last day the SenseCam was worn (mean length of delay = 8 days, $SD = 1.2$). Participants did not view the photographs prior to fMRI scanning. There were six fMRI runs blocked by condition and presented in an alternating order (i.e., ABABAB), counterbalanced across participants based on a Latin square design. The structure of the runs was similar in each condition (see Figure 1). Each run began with a 10-second title screen (i.e., "Today was the day I ...") and consisted of 12 cues presented in chronological order from that day, for a total of 36 events per condition across three runs. The cues were presented for 20 seconds, and participants were instructed to recall the events depicted. The cues in the SC condition consisted of 40 SenseCam pictures depicting a single event and presented at a rate of two pictures per second; the cues in the VC condition consisted of a short description of a single event. To control for differences in the visual input, a static string of letters was presented in the SC condition, whereas participant-specific, Fourier-transformed SenseCam images were presented at a rate of two pictures per second in the VC condition. Thus the visual input between the conditions was identical.

Following the cue presentation participants indicated the subjective experience associated with each cue. Participants rated the subjective experience of recollection, *reliving*, which refers to how much they were able to re-experience the event depicted as if it were happening right now or as if they were mentally travelling back to the time when the event occurred. It is important to note that reliving is similar to other subjective measures of recollection, such as the remember/know paradigm (Yonelinas, 2002). For example, in the remember/know paradigm, participants are asked to use introspection to classify items as recollected (vivid re-experiencing of the original event and its context) or merely familiar. Although introspection has its limitations, the results of hundreds of remember/know studies are highly consistent with findings of hundreds of studies using objective measures of recollection, such as source memory (Yonelinas, 2002). However, there are some critical differences between the reliving scale and remember/know paradigm, which make the reliving scale a better measure for AM. First, the reliving scale could be considered a better subjective measure of recollection in AM than remember/know because it does not require the assumption of a dual-process model (Wixted, 2007; Yonelinas, 2002). Second, reliving is a better predictor of recollection in AMs compared to the remember/know scale, which is a better predictor of confidence in AMs (Rubin, Schrauf, & Greenberg, 2003). Ratings were conducted on an 8-point scale from low to high, and were self-paced (up to 6 seconds). Following a response, a fixation cross was presented for a jittered interval between 4 and 8 seconds plus any remaining time from the response period.

Post-scanning. Immediately following the scanning session, participants viewed the identical SC and VC runs and answered additional questions on a small set of subjective ratings to ensure that the events selected for inclusion in the SC vs VC conditions were unbiased. More ratings were not included due to time constraints. Participants were asked to rate the events on the following properties: Importance ($1 = \text{low}$ to $8 = \text{high}$), Vividness ($1 = \text{low}$ to $8 = \text{high}$), Emotion ($-4 =$ intense negative to $4 =$ intense positive), and Uniqueness ($1 = \text{low}$ to $8 = \text{high}$) associated with the event. For more details on the instructions provided to participants, please see the Appendix.

fMRI methods

Image acquisition. Scanning was conducted using a 4T GE magnet. Anatomical scanning included a T1-weighted sagittal localiser series and 3D fast spoiled gradient echo recalled (SPGR) structural images were acquired in the coronal plane (256^2 matrix, $TR = 12.3$ ms, $TE = 5.4$ ms, flip angle $= 20°$, $FOV = 240$, 68 slices, 1.9 mm slice thickness). Coplanar functional images were acquired using an inverse spiral sequence (64^2 image matrix, $TR = 2000$ ms, $TE = 6$ ms, $FOV = 240$, flip angle $= 60°$, 34 slices, 3.8 mm slice thickness).

fMRI analyses. Image processing and analyses were performed using Statistical Parametric Mapping software in Matlab (SPM5; Wellcome Department of Imaging Neuroscience). Functional images were corrected for slice acquisition order, realigned to correct for motion artefacts, spatially normalised to a standard stereotactic space, and spatially smoothed using an 8-mm isotropic Gaussian kernel. Evoked haemodynamic responses for the cue were modelled with a boxcar function corresponding to the 20-second phase of presentation, convolved with a canonical haemodynamic response function within the context of the General Linear Model (GLM). Evoked haemodynamic responses for the ratings were modelled with a delta (stick) function, convolved with a canonical haemodynamic response function.

SenseCam retrieval vs verbal cue retrieval. To examine brain activity in the SC condition we employed the GLM to examine the neural correlates modulated by reliving using a random-effects parametric approach via the first-order parametric modulation option integrated in SPM5. The parametric approach ensures that potential gender differences reflect memory (i.e., fluctuations in activity tracking reliving) rather than other perceptual differences (e.g., exploration of the visual stimulus). Data analysis was confined to the first 5 seconds of the retrieval blocks (i.e., presentation of the stimulus) to reduce potential differences in the number of retrieval cues provided by the two conditions. Subsequently, we conducted two-sample t-tests to examine the interaction between gender and memory cue ($p = .005$, > 10 voxel extent threshold) and the main effect of gender across both cueing manipulations, and then inclusively masked this statistical image with the corresponding statistical map for the effect of interest at $p = .005$ (i.e., SenseCam > Verbal Cues in Males, etc.). Thus the resulting pattern of group differences in activity had to clear two hurdles: (1) the difference should be significant within one group, and (2) the difference should be significantly larger within one group compared to the other group. Given the a priori role of the medial temporal lobe (MTL) in AM (Cabeza & St. Jacques, 2007; Maguire, 2001; McDermott, Szpunar, & Christ, 2009; Spreng et al., 2009; Svoboda, McKinnon, & Levine, 2006) we conducted an additional a priori region of interest (ROI) here at $p = .05$ using the Talairach Daemon Atlas Labels (Lancaster, Summerin, Rainey, Freitas, & Fox, 1997; Lancaster et al., 2000), implemented within the PickAtlas software (Maldjian, Laurienti, Kraft, & Burdette, 2003), also using an extent threshold of > 10 voxels.

RESULTS

Behavioural

The behavioural results indicated that there were no gender differences in the phenomenological experience of memory retrieval measured by reliving, importance, vividness, emotion, and uniqueness, or in reaction times to make these subjective ratings (for means and standard deviations see Table 2). We conducted multiple repeated-measures ANOVAs (Gender × Cue) using Bonferroni correction separately on each of the subjective ratings and reaction time measures ($p < .005$). Both females and males gave higher reliving ratings, $F(1, 21) = 32.60$, $p < .001$, and vividness ratings, $F(1, 21) = 78.79$, $p < .001$, for AMs elicited in the SC versus VC conditions. Furthermore, both genders made faster reliving ratings, $F(1, 21) = 17.80$, $p < .005$, for the SC versus VC conditions. There were no other gender or cueing differences. These results suggest that any gender differences in functional activity cannot be explained by potential gender differences in the phenomenological experience of recall—at least as measured by reliving, emotion, importance, vividness—of the AMs and the uniqueness of the events.

TABLE 2
Mean behavioral responses by gender

	Females	*Males*
SenseCam		
Subjective ratings		
Reliving	5.10 (0.48)	4.97 (0.65)
Vividness	4.75 (0.42)	4.59 (0.86)
Emotional intensity	1.91 (0.24)	1.96 (0.41)
Importance	3.15 (0.70)	3.53 (0.85)
Uniqueness	4.29 (0.57)	4.22 (0.77)
Reaction time (s)		
Reliving	1.12 (0.38)	1.75 (0.77)
Vividness	1.75 (0.52)	2.09 (0.71)
Emotional intensity	1.81 (0.46)	1.88 (0.46)
Importance	2.09 (0.79)	3.04 (1.33)
Uniqueness	2.09 (0.55)	2.30 (0.79)
Verbal cue		
Subjective ratings		
Reliving	4.06 (0.60)	4.25 (0.62)
Vividness	3.67 (0.68)	3.55 (0.47)
Emotional intensity	1.93 (0.32)	1.79 (0.36)
Importance	3.11 (0.70)	3.37 (0.78)
Uniqueness	4.13 (0.62)	3.71 (0.67)
Reaction time (s)		
Reliving	0.95 (0.36)	1.44 (0.52)
Vividness	1.71 (0.56)	2.03 (0.65)
Emotional intensity	1.70 (0.50)	2.08 (0.78)
Importance	2.06 (0.89)	3.29 (1.28)
Uniqueness	1.94 (0.47)	2.37 (1.14)

Mean (Standard Deviation).

fMRI

As predicted, we found that males showed greater increase in activity sensitive to reliving AMs elicited in the SC versus VC condition, whereas females showed equivalent sensitivity to reliving in both cueing types (see Table 3 and Figure 2). There was greater activity in MTL (left hippocampus), retrosplenial cortex, left inferior frontal gyrus (IFG), and right occipital cortex that was positively correlated with reliving ratings to a greater extent for males vs females in the SC vs VC conditions. Further, when we separately examined the influence of gender within each condition we found that males recruited less activity sensitive to reliving for AMs elicited in the VC condition when compared to females. Specifically, males recruited less hippocampus ($x = -26$, $y = -33$, $z = 2$; $t = 2.44$, 11 voxels) and IFG (BA 45; $x = -45$, $y = 19$, $z = 20$; $t = 4.11$, 34 voxels), which overlapped with those showing the gender × cue interaction effects. There were no significant effects of gender that were common to both the SC and VC conditions, suggesting that cue independent effects of reliving were not influenced by gender. In sum, these results suggest that females were equally sensitive to reliving AMs in both conditions, but that males benefited more from the rich visuospatial cues provided by the SenseCam images than the verbal cues.

DISCUSSION

The present study investigated the interaction between gender and the type of cue to elicit AMs during functional scanning. We used a novel technology called a SenseCam to prospectively collect dynamic, visuospatial cues to elicit everyday AMs in the scanning environment. This allowed us to control for potential differences in the emotional intensity and rehearsal of retrieved events. The behavioural results revealed that there were no gender differences in the reliving, emotion, importance, vividness, of the AMs and the uniqueness of the events. Consistent with our predictions, however, the fMRI results revealed that males showed a greater difference in functional activity associated with the rich experience

TABLE 3
Gender x Cue effect

Region	*BA*	*H*	*x*	*y*	*z*	*t*	*Voxels*
SenseCam vs Verbal cue							
Males > Females							
Inferior frontal gyrus	45	L	−48	19	17	3.34	19
*Hippocampus	–	L	−22	−33	2	2.49	14
Retrosplenial cortex	29	C	0	−39	16	3.89	15
Occipital cortex	18	R	30	−94	12	3.85	15
Females > Males	No significant voxels						
Verbal cue vs SenseCam	No significant voxels						

Talaraich Coordinates Reported. BA, Brodmann's Area; H, Hemisphere. *Region of Interest.

of visuospatial versus verbal cues, than did females.

Males and females might rely on different cognitive strategies during memory retrieval. Previous evidence has indicated an advantage for males on spatial tasks, whereas females show greater advantage on verbal tasks (cf. Andreano & Cahill, 2009; Piefke & Fink, 2005). Consistent with this finding, one previous fMRI study examining gender effects on AM found that males relied more on MTL regions associated with visuospatial processing, whereas females relied more on PFC regions linked to controlled processes, such as temporal context (Piefke et al., 2005). Substantial evidence has suggested that females have superior AMs compared to males (for reviews see Andreano & Cahill, 2009; Piefke & Fink, 2005). However, the female advantage might be less robust once potential gender differences in these cognitive strategies are controlled (for review see Andreano & Cahill, 2009). Consistent with this idea, we found that males,

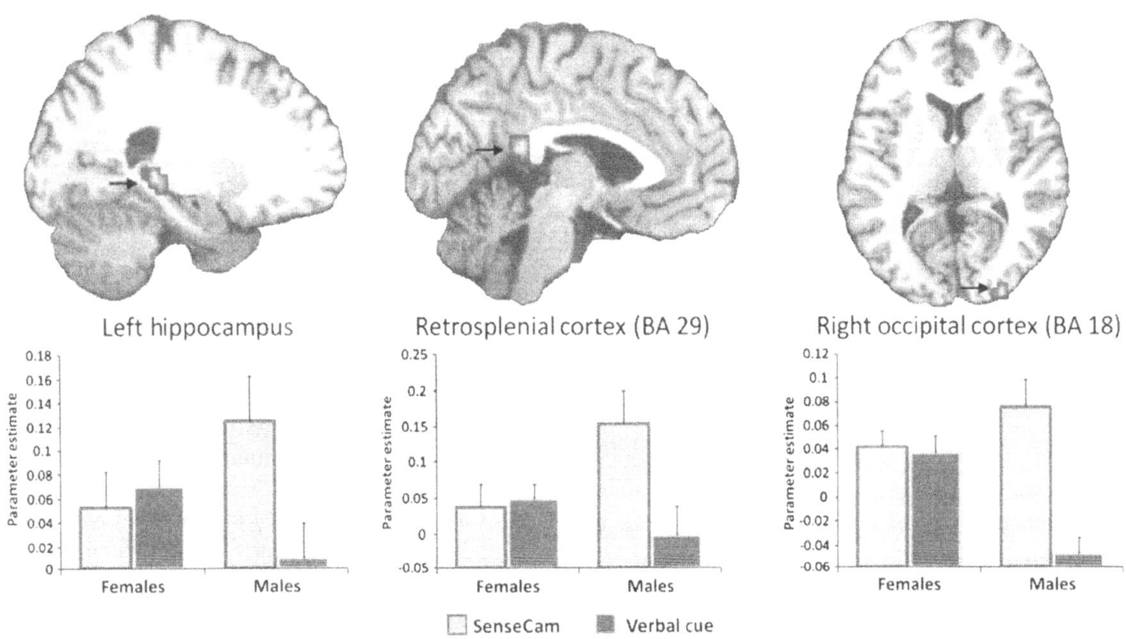

Figure 2. The results of the two-sample *t*-test showing the effects of gender on cue type for functional activity sensitive to the experience of reliving. Males recruited more richly experienced autobiographical memories cued by the SenseCam than the verbal cues, whereas females showed an equivalent sensitivity to reliving in functional activations for both cueing types. Error bars indicate standard error of the mean. To view this figure in colour, please see the online issue of the journal.

compared to females, showed greater recruitment of brain regions sensitive to reliving of AMs elicited by visuospatial cues than verbal cues.

The present findings are less amenable to alternative accounts of potential gender differences in AM, which have linked better memory in females to differences in the amount of rehearsal or emotional intensity (for reviews see Andreano & Cahill, 2009; Piefke & Fink, 2005), since we queried for very recent, everyday AMs. Participants did keep a daily schedule of events, which may have involved some minimal rehearsal and perhaps lessened the influence of the SenseCam cues, when compared to the verbal cues. However, potential gender differences in the influence of rehearsal provided by the daily schedule could not easily explain the greater sensitivity to reliving elicited by the SenseCam images in males.

In the present study we showed that gender differences were directly linked to memory experience by examining brain activity that was parametrically modulated by participant ratings of reliving. Males showed greater sensitivity to the experience of reliving when cued by the visuospatial cues in a number of brain regions. First, there was greater sensitivity to reliving in the hippocampus, a region associated with spatial memory (for a review see Burgess et al., 2002), and to recollection processes (for a review see Diana, Yonelinas, & Ranganath, 2007). Furthermore, functional neuroimaging studies of AM have shown that the amount of details associated with retrieval modulates activity in the left hippocampus (e.g., Addis, McIntosh, Moscovitch, Crawley, & McAndrews, 2004), and patient evidence links this region to recollection of AMs (e.g., Steinvorth, Corkin, & Halgren, 2006). Second, males showed greater sensitivity to reliving when cued by the visuospatial cues in the retrosplenial cortex. Previous functional neuroimaging studies have found the retrosplenial cortex to be sensitive to the amount of reliving associated with AM retrieval (Daselaar et al., 2008), and damage here can result in amnesia (e.g., Valenstein et al., 1987). Third, there was greater sensitivity to reliving in males in the occipital cortex. The occipital cortex is associated with the visual imagery that is critical to AM retrieval (Greenberg & Rubin, 2003), and has been linked to the rich elaboration of AMs (Conway, Pleydell-Pearce, & Whitecross, 2001; Daselaar et al., 2008). In sum, males and females showed a differential effect of reliving AMs cued by visuospatial versus verbal cues, with males showing a greater effect of visuospatial compared to verbal cues and females showing equal sensitivity to both cues.

Conclusion

The present findings demonstrate the potential of using SenseCam to prospectively generate everyday AMs, which was particularly advantageous to the current investigation of gender differences in functional neuroimaging of AMs. We found that males had a differential effect on brain activity recruited when retrieving richly re-experienced AMs elicited by the SenseCam images, whereas females showed an equal effect to both SenseCam and verbal cues. The findings emphasise the importance of using unbiased measures to elicit and evaluate AMs when examining gender differences.

REFERENCES

Addis, D. R., McIntosh, A. R., Moscovitch, M., Crawley, A. P., & McAndrews, M. P. (2004). Characterizing spatial and temporal features of autobiographical memory retrieval networks: A partial least squares approach. *NeuroImage*, *23*(4), 1460–1471.

Addis, D. R., Sacchetti, D. C., Ally, B. A., Budson, A. E., & Schacter, D. L. (2009). Episodic simulation of future events is impaired in mild Alzheimer's disease. *Neuropsychologia*, *47*, 2660–2671.

Andreano, J. M., & Cahill, L. (2009). Sex influences on the neurobiology of learning and memory. *Learning & Memory*, *16*(4), 248–266.

Bauer, P. J., Stennes, L., & Haight, J. C. (2003). Representation of the inner self in autobiography: Women's and men's use of internal states language in personal narratives. *Memory*, *11*(1), 27–42.

Bloise, S. M., & Johnson, M. K. (2007). Memory for emotional and neutral information: Gender and individual differences in emotional sensitivity. *Memory*, *15*(2), 192–204.

Burgess, N., Maguire, E. A., & O'Keefe, J. (2002). The human hippocampus and spatial and episodic memory. *Neuron*, *35*(4), 625–641.

Cabeza, R., Prince, S. E., Daselaar, S. M., Greenberg, D. L., Budde, M., Dolcos, F., et al. (2004). Brain activity during episodic retrieval of autobiographical and laboratory events: An fMRI study using a novel photo paradigm. *Journal of Cognitive Neuroscience*, *16*(9), 1583–1594.

Cabeza, R., & St. Jacques, P. L. (2007). Functional neuroimaging of autobiographical memory. *Trends in Cognitive Science*, *11*(5), 219–227.

Cahill, L., Haier, R. J., White, N. S., Fallon, J., Kilpatrick, L., Lawrence, C., et al. (2001).

Sex-related difference in amygdala activity during emotionally influenced memory storage. *Neurobiology of Learning & Memory, 75*(1), 1–9.

Canli, T., Desmond, J. E., Zhao, Z., & Gabrieli, J. D. (2002). Sex differences in the neural basis of emotional memories. *Proceedings of the National Academy of Sciences USA, 99*(16), 10789–10794.

Conway, M. A., Pleydell-Pearce, C. W., & Whitecross, S. E. (2001). The neuroanatomy of autobiographical memory: A slow wave cortical potential study of autobiographical memory. *Journal of Memory & Language, 45*, 493–524.

Daselaar, S. M., Rice, H. J., Greenberg, D. L., Cabeza, R., LaBar, K. S., & Rubin, D. C. (2008). The spatiotemporal dynamics of autobiographical memory: Neural correlates of recall, emotional intensity, and reliving. *Cerebral Cortex, 18*(1), 217–229.

Davis, PJ. (1999). Gender differences in autobiographical memory for childhood emotional experiences. *Journal of Personality and Social Psychology, 76*, 498–510.

Diana, R. A., Yonelinas, A. P., & Ranganath, C. (2007). Imaging recollection and familiarity in the medial temporal lobe: a three-component model. *Trends in Cognitive Science, 11*(9), 379–386.

Fivush, R., & Nelson, K. (2004). Culture and language in the emergence of autobiographical memory. *Psychological Science, 15*(9), 573–577.

Friedman, A., & Pines, A. (1991). Sex differences in gender-related childhood memories. *Sex Roles, 25*, 25–32.

Fujita, F., Diener, E., & Sandvik, E. (1991). Gender differences in negative affect and well-being: The case for emotional intensity. *Journal of Personality and Social Psychology, 61*(3), 427–434.

Greenberg, D. L., & Rubin, D. C. (2003). The neuropsychology of autobiographical memory. *Cortex, 39*(4-5), 687–728.

Hassabis, D., & Maguire, E. A. (2007). Deconstructing episodic memory with construction. *Trends in Cognitive Science, 11*(7), 299–306.

Lancaster, J. L., Summerin, J. L., Rainey, L., Freitas, C. S., & Fox, P. T. (1997). The Talairach Daemon, a database server for Talairach Atlas Labels. *Neuroimage*, 5(4:S633).

Lancaster, J. L., Woldorff, M. G., Parsons, L. M., Liotti, M., Freitas, C. S., Rainey, L., et al. (2000). Automated Talaraich atlas labels for functional brain mapping. *Human Brain Mapping, 10*, 120–131.

Maguire, E. A. (2001). Neuroimaging studies of autobiographical event memory. *Philosophical Transactions of the Royal Society in London B: Biological Sciences, 356*(1413), 1441–1451.

Maldjian, J. A., Laurienti, P. J., Kraft, R. A., & Burdette, J. H. (2003). An automated method for neuroantomic and cytoarchitectonic atlas-based interrogation of fMRI data sets. *Neuroimage, 19*, 1233–1239 (WFU Pickatlas, version 1232.1233).

McDermott, K. B., Szpunar, K. K., & Christ, S. E. (2009). Laboratory-based and autobiographical retrieval tasks differ substantially in their neural substrates. *Neuropsychologia, 47*(11), 2290–2298.

Miller, E. K., & Cohen, J. D. (2001). An integrative theory of prefrontal cortex function. *Annual Review of Neuroscience, 24*, 167–202.

Moscovitch, M., Rosenbaum, R. S., Gilboa, A., Addis, D. R., Westmacott, R., Grady, C., et al. (2005). Functional neuroanatomy of remote episodic, semantic and spatial memory: A unified account based on multiple trace theory. *Journal of Anatomy, 207*(1), 35–66.

Piefke, M., & Fink, G. R. (2005). Recollections of one's own past: The effects of aging and gender on the neural mechanisms of episodic autobiographical memory. *Anatomy and Embryology, 210*(5–6), 497–512.

Piefke, M., Weiss, P. H., Markowitsch, H. J., & Fink, G. R. (2005). Gender differences in the functional neuroanatomy of emotional episodic autobiographical memory. *Human Brain Mapping, 24*(4), 313–324.

Pillemer, D. B., Wink, P., DiDonato, T. E., & Sanborn, R. L. (2003). Gender differences in autobiographical memory styles of older adults. *Memory, 11*(6), 525–532.

Pohl, R. F., Bender, M., & Lachmann, G. (2005). Autobiographical memory and social skills of men and women. *Applied Cognitive Psychology, 19*, 745–759.

Ross, M., & Holmberg, D. (1992). Are wives memories for events in relationships more vivid than their husband's memories? *Journal of Social and Personal Relationships, 9*, 585–604.

Rubin, D. C., Schrauf, R. W., & Greenberg, D. L. (2003). Belief and recollection of autobiographical memories. *Memory & Cognition, 31*(6), 887–901.

Rubin, D. C., Schulkind, M. D., & Rahhal, T. A. (1999). A study of gender differences in autobiographical memory: Broken down by age and sex. *Journal of Adult Development, 6*(1), 61–71.

Seidlitz, L., & Diener, E. (1998). Sex differences in the recall of affective experiences. *Journal of Personality and Social Psychology, 74*(1), 262–271.

Skowronski, J. J., & Thompson, C. P. (1990). Reconstructing the dates of events: Gender differences in accuracy. *Applied Cognitive Psychology, 4*, 371–381.

Spreng, R. N., Mar, R. A., & Kim, A. S. (2009). The common neural basis of autobiographical memory, prospection, navigation, theory of mind, and the default mode: A quantitative meta-analysis. *Journal of Cognitive Neuroscience, 21*(3), 489–510.

St. Jacques, P. L., Conway, M. A., Lowder, M. W., & Cabeza, R. (2011). Watching my mind unfold vs yours: An fMRI study using a novel camera technology to examine neural differences in self-projection of self vs other perspectives. *Journal of Cognitive Neuroscience, 23*(6), 1275–1284.

St. Jacques, P. L., Rubin, D. C., Labar, K. S., & Cabeza, R. (2008). The short and long of it: Neural correlates of temporal-order memory for autobiographical events. *Journal of Cognitive Neuroscience, 20*(7), 1341–1367.

Steinvorth, S., Corkin, S., & Halgren, E. (2006). Ecphory of autobiographical memories: An fMRI study of recent and remote memory retrieval. *Neuroimage, 30*, 285–298.

Svoboda, E., McKinnon, M. C., & Levine, B. (2006). The functional neuroanatomy of autobiographical memory: A meta-analysis. *Neuropsychologia, 44*(12), 2189–2208.

Valenstein, E., Bowers, D., Verfaellie, M., Heilman, K. M., Day, A., & Watson, R. T. (1987). Retrosplenial amnesia. *Brain, 110*(6), 1631–1646.

Wixted, J. T. (2007). Dual-process theory and signal-detection theory of recognition memory. *Psychological Review, 114*(1), 152–176.

Yonelinas, A. P. (2002). The nature of recollection and familiarity: A review of 30 years of research. *Journal of Memory and Language, 46*, 441–517.

APPENDIX

After viewing each event you will be making four different ratings:

1. Importance. You will be rating how important, or significant, this event is to your life. Some events are more personally meaningful than others because they impart an important message or represent an anchor, critical juncture, or turning point. Other events are relatively insignificant and do not carry any sort of personal meaning to you. Rate each event on a scale of 1 (not at all important) to 8 (very important).
2. Vividness. You will be rating how vivid each memory is. You may find that some memories are fuzzier than others, with bits and pieces missing, and it takes a great deal of effort to consciously reconstruct the event. On the other hand, some memories are full and detailed, with virtually no missing information. Rate each memory on a scale of 1 (vague; unclear; not at all vivid) to 8 (completely clear; very vivid).
3. Emotion. You will be rating the emotional content associated with recalling the event. This scale is a little different from the others in that we are trying to capture two types of information. First you will decide whether retrieving this memory represents negative emotions or positive emotions for you. If the memory is negative you will be using the keys on the left; if it is positive you will be using the keys on the right. Then we are also interested in the intensity of that emotion. Some of your memories may be extremely sad, while others may be just somewhat sad. Similarly, some of your memories may be extremely happy and exciting, whereas others may just be pleasing or calming. Rate each memory on a scale from –4 (intense negative) to 4 (intense positive). Memories that carry virtually no emotional content should be rated –1 or 1. We are interested the emotion associated with retrieving the event now in the present, rather than the emotion that might have been attached to the event during the time it occurred.
4. Uniqueness. You will be rating how unique each event is to your life. There are certain events we all do regularly, as part of a daily routine, that may seem mundane or commonplace. Alternatively, there are other events we rarely experience that we may regard as different or special. Rate the uniqueness of each event on a scale from 1 (something you do every day) to 8 (something completely unique that you rarely do).

Psychology Press
Taylor & Francis Group

An fMRI study of long-term everyday memory using SenseCam

F. Milton[1], N. Muhlert[2], C. R. Butler[3], A. Smith[2], A. Benattayallah[4], and A. Z. Zeman[2]

[1]Department of Psychology, University of Exeter, Exeter, UK
[2]Department of Neurology, Peninsula Medical School, University of Exeter, Exeter, UK
[3]Department of Clinical Neurology, University of Oxford, Oxford, UK
[4]Peninsula MR Research Centre, Peninsula Medical School, Exeter, UK

We used a novel automatic camera, SenseCam, to investigate recognition memory for real-life events at a 5-month retention interval. Using fMRI we assessed recollection and familiarity memory using the remember/know procedure. Recollection evoked no medial temporal lobe (MTL) activation compared to familiarity and new responses. Instead, recollection activated diverse regions in neocortex including medial prefrontal cortex. We observed decreased activation in anterior hippocampus/ anterior parahippocampal gyrus (aPHG) at 5 months compared to a 36-hour retention interval. Familiarity was associated with greater activation in aPHG and posterior parahippocampal gyrus (pPHG) than recollection and new responses. Familiarity activation decreased over time in anterior hippocampus/ aPHG and posterior hippocampus/pPHG. The engagement of neocortical regions such as medial prefrontal cortex at a 5-month delay, together with the reduced MTL activation at 5 months relative to at 36 hours is in line with the assumptions of Consolidation theory. SenseCam provides a valuable technique for assessing the processes that underlie remote everyday recognition memory.

Keywords: fMRI; Recognition memory; SenseCam; Recollection; Familiarity; Consolidation.

Recognition memory is often believed to be the result of two distinct processes: *recollection*, which supports the ability to recognise an item based on contextual information; and *familiarity*, the ability to recognise an item based on memory strength in the absence of contextual details (Mandler, 1980). An alternative view proposes that, rather than reflecting distinct underlying processes, familiarity and recollection differ in the strength of a common memory signal (Dunn, 2004; Kirwan, Wixted, & Squire, 2008).

There has recently been intense interest in the neural correlates of recognition memory. These studies have typically used laboratory stimuli such as words (Eldridge, Knowlton, Furmanski, Bookheimer, & Engel, 2000), objects (Vilberg & Rugg, 2007), and visual scenes (Montaldi, Spencer, Roberts, & Mayes, 2006). Several approaches have been taken to distinguish the neural correlates of recollection and familiarity including confidence ratings, associative recognition, source memory, and the remember-know paradigm (for a review, see Yonelinas, 2002).

Recollection memory has been associated with increased hippocampal and posterior parahippocampal gyrus (pPHG) activity compared to familiarity (e.g., Eldridge et al., 2000; Wheeler & Buckner, 2004). Meanwhile, familiarity is typically linked to perirhinal and anterior parahippocampal regions (aPHG; e.g., Henson, Cansino,

Address correspondence to: F. Milton, Washington Singer Laboratories, Perry Road, Exeter, EX4 4QG UK. E-mail: f.n.milton@exeter.ac.uk
This research was supported by grants from the Great Western Research Initiative and Microsoft Research.

© 2011 Psychology Press, an imprint of the Taylor & Francis Group, an Informa business
http://www.psypress.com/memory http://dx.doi.org/10.1080/09658211.2011.552185

Herron, Robb, & Rugg, 2003). These regional activations broadly support *dual-process* accounts of recognition memory (e.g., Aggleton & Brown, 1999; Diana, Yonelinas, & Ranganath, 2007), which propose that recollection is supported by the hippocampus, whereas familiarity is supported by aPHG, including perirhinal cortex.

Most recognition studies have used short retrieval delays (i.e., less than 1 day). However, in our everyday environment we are often required to recognise items that have not been seen for a considerable time. It is therefore important to understand the neural substrates of recognition memory for items encountered in the remote past. The extent to which the hippocampus and other medial temporal lobe (MTL) structures are involved in declarative memory processes such as recognition memory has been the subject of considerable debate. One theory, known as the standard consolidation model (Squire, Stark, & Clark, 2004) posits that the hippocampus has a time dependent role in declarative memory. Initially, memory retrieval is believed to be dependent on the hippocampus, but over time memory traces are reorganised to become less dependent on the hippocampus, allowing retrieval from distributed neocortical structures alone. In contrast, according to multiple trace theory (MTT; Nadel & Moscovitch, 1997), the hippocampus is involved in retrieval of episodic memories throughout the lifetime. With time, activation in the hippocampus should remain as great or even increase due to the laying down of separate (multiple) traces each time a memory is retrieved.

Several recent fMRI studies have used a prospective recognition memory paradigm to investigate long-term recognition memory processes. For instance, Viskontas, Carr, Engel, and Knowlton (2009) used high-resolution scanning of the MTL to reveal that 1 week after initial encoding the subiculum was involved in recollection memory. Similarly, Bosshardt et al. (2005) found greater activation in bilateral hippocampus when viewing stimuli learned 1 month before scanning compared to stimuli learned 1 day before. Relatedly, Suchan, Gayk, Schmid, Koster, and Daum (2008) used the remember/know procedure to measure recognition memory over a period of 6 weeks. For remember responses they found consistent hippocampal activity over time. Familiarity responses resulted in decreased perirhinal cortex activation over time. Nevertheless, Suchan et al. (2008) argued that familiarity activation remained relatively stable over time, suggesting it lasts at least up to 6 weeks after encoding. Both Bosshardt et al. (2005) and Suchan et al. (2008) argued that their findings provide support for MTT, although it is possible that their time delays were insufficient for consolidation effects in MTL to be observable.

Dolcos, LaBar, and Cabeza (2005) used a longer retrieval delay, testing recognition memory after a 1-year interval. While their interest was primarily on the effect emotion has on long-term recognition memory, some of their findings are relevant to the current issue. In particular, they found that, after a 1-year delay, there was greater activation in the head of right hippocampus and bilaterally in the hippocampus tail for remember compared to know responses.

While the majority of prospective recognition memory studies have observed hippocampal activity at long retrieval delays, Takashima et al. (2006) found somewhat discrepant results. They tested recognition memory at four time periods ranging from hours to 3 months after encoding. They found that hippocampal activation decreased over time and linked this to memory consolidation.

Evidence from retrospective neuroimaging studies of remote autobiographical memory is related to the current issue (for a review see Svoboda, McKinnon, & Levine, 2006) and also shows discrepancies between studies. A number of these studies have found no effect of the age of memories on hippocampus activity (Ryan et al., 2001; Steinvorth, Corkin, & Halgren, 2006), while others have found increased hippocampal activity for remote compared to recent memories (e.g., Rekkas & Constable, 2005). However, several studies have observed a decrease in hippocampus activity over time suggesting disengagement of this region from long-term memory processes (Niki & Luo, 2002; Piefke et al., 2003).

Outside the MTL several regions have been linked with long-term recognition memory. In particular, the ventrolateral (Bosshardt et al., 2005) and medial prefrontal cortices (mPFC; Dolcos et al., 2005; Takashima et al., 2006) consistently activate at long time intervals. One suggestion is that mPFC, rather than the hippocampus, may integrate information from multiple neocortical regions during remote memory retrieval (Takashima et al., 2006). Additionally, long-term recognition memory often engages lateral temporal lobes (e.g., Bosshardt et al., 2005; Dolcos et al., 2005). Retrospective autobiographical memory studies also consistently activate prefrontal cortex (e.g., Addis, Moscovitch, & McAndrews, 2004; Maguire & Frith, 2003) and lateral temporal cortex (e.g., Gilboa, Winocur, Grady, Hevenor, & Moscovitch, 2004; Ryan et al., 2001).

The prospective recognition memory studies discussed, while varying in the time delay, all used laboratory-based stimuli. Indeed there has been a dearth of studies investigating everyday recognition processes (although see Cabeza et al., 2004). In this study we used a novel wearable camera, SenseCam, to acquire images of everyday events and gave participants a recognition test after a 5-month interval. SenseCam, which is activated by a range of environmental sensors taking an average of one image every 30 seconds without user involvement, appears to be an ideal technique to investigate recognition memory. First, the automatic capture of images is methodologically advantageous because it reduces the intentional encoding of the items that will be tested later. This paradigm therefore allows more direct insight into the neural substrates of everyday recognition memory than previous work. Second, the complexity of the stimuli and their personal nature make them ideally suited to investigate recognition over lengthy delays because they are likely to minimise the risk of accuracy floor effects. In addition, the level of contextual detail available is likely to vary between images, permitting exploration of remote recollection and familiarity memory.

In summary this is, as far as we are aware, the first study to examine the neural correlates of recollection and familiarity memory for remote everyday events. In particular, our study assessed MTL involvement in recollection and familiarity processes over time. Additionally, we examined whether neocortical regions such as prefrontal cortex and lateral temporal lobes are involved in remote everyday recognition memory.

METHOD

Participants

A total of 10 right-handed participants from the University of Exeter (6 male, 4 female), ranging in age from 18 to 25 years, took part in the study. Participants were paid £15 for their participation. Participants gave informed consent according to procedures approved by the Psychology Ethics Committee, University of Exeter.

fMRI data acquisition

Structural and functional imaging was performed with a 1.5-T Phillips Gyroscan magnet equipped with a Sense coil. A T2*-weighted echo planar sequence was used (TR = 3000ms, Te = 45ms, flip angle = 90°, 32 transverse slices, 3.5 × 2.5 × 2.5 mm ascending acquisition). A total of 280 volumes were acquired in each of the two runs per participant. An additional 5 "dummy" scans were performed before each run prior to the stimulus sequence. A T1-weighted structural MRI scan was also acquired (Tr = 25ms, Te = 4.1ms, flip angle = 30°, 160 axial slices, 1.6 × 0.9 × 0.9 mm).

Equipment

The SenseCam (sized 6.5cm wide × 7cm high × 1.5 cm long) is built around a PIC 18F8722 6 MIPS microcontroller with 128KB of flash memory (Hodges et al., 2006). SenseCam is worn round the neck, with pictures captured using a fish eye lens. This maximises the field of view and ensures that objects at head height are photographed. Images were captured automatically approximately every 30 seconds.

Procedure

Participants wore a SenseCam for two days while undertaking their everyday activities. Participants performed an initial recognition memory task inside the scanner approximately 36 hours and then again approximately 5 months after acquisition of the images. We chose an interval of 5 months in order to extend the results of previous studies of remote recognition memory, which have typically used shorter delays than this (e.g., Bosshardt et al., 2005; Suchan et al., 2008; Takashima et al., 2006; Viskontas et al., 2009; although see Dolcos et al., 2005) while keeping the events sufficiently recent for participants to be able to recognise them with a good degree of accuracy. The procedure for the two recognition memory sessions was identical and the images used were the same for both retrieval sessions. This paper focuses on the long delay condition (5 months) but uses the short delay condition (36 hours) to investigate how the neural basis of everyday memory changes over time. Results from the short delay condition will be presented in a forthcoming paper. Participants were not informed of the long delay session until 4 months after the first session.

Before each scanning session participants were trained to distinguish between different types of recognition memory. Participants saw a series of images, some of which were theirs (old), and the rest were images acquired by other participants (new), which had the same general characteristics (e.g., similar types of event, brightness). Participants were asked to report whether images were "remembered" or "known" (Tulving, 1985). The instructions outlining this distinction were modelled on those of Rotello, Macmillan, and Reeder (2004; see also Rajaram, 1993). Specifically, "remembering" was defined as the ability to be consciously aware of some aspect or aspects of what happened or what was experienced at the time the photo was taken (e.g., what one was thinking or doing at the time). "Knowing" was described as the feeling that the event was familiar while being unable to recollect anything about its occurrence or what was experienced at the time of its occurrence. Participants were all able to verbalise this distinction. Participants completed a training session to further familiarise them with these judgements. A total of 15 trials (10 "old", 5 "new" images) were randomly presented.

Inside the scanner, images were presented on a back-projection screen positioned at the foot end of the scanner and viewed via a mirror mounted on a head coil. Recognition judgements were measured using two fibreoptic button boxes held in the participants' right and left hands. E-Prime (Psychology Software Tools, Inc., Pittsburgh.) was used for the presentation and timing of stimuli and collection of response data.

There were 120 trials in the scanning session; 80 "old" and 40 "new"[1] images. The events recorded by participants were all characteristic of everyday experiences and were evenly distributed throughout the acquisition period. Images were selected so that unique events were presented. In other words, images were excluded if they displayed the same activity as one of the previously selected images (e.g., looking at the same shelf in a shop, looking out of a window, or waiting in a queue). There were six blocks of 20 images and the presentation order of the stimuli was randomised. The session was divided into two runs, each lasting 14 minutes, with three blocks presented in each run. At the end of each of the six blocks a message appeared for 12 seconds saying, "That is the end of the block. Please take a short break." This was followed by a message lasting 1500 ms instructing participants to "Get ready to start the next block." Participants were also given the opportunity to rest for as long as they required between the two scanning runs.

Trials began with a blank screen lasting 250–3750 ms, followed by a fixation cross for 150 ms. An image was then presented for 4000 ms during which time participants were asked not to respond. This was followed by instructions, which remained on the screen for 3000 ms, asking participants to classify the image as "Remember", "Know", or "New". If no response was made during this interval, a message appeared saying, "Time out!!" "Remember" and "Know" responses were made using the response box in one hand, "New" responses using the response box in the other hand. The hand corresponding to these judgements was counterbalanced.

A further message then appeared which varied according to the judgement participants made. For "Remember" responses, participants had to distinguish between high and low level of detail. "Know" images were to be divided into high and low familiarity. These sub-categories were collapsed at analysis to improve statistical power. For "New" images, participants had to press any button. Participants had 3000 ms to respond; if no response was made in this time, the "Time out!!" message appeared.

Immediately after the recognition task a post-scan interview was administered in which participants were presented with four "remember" and four "know" images. Participants described their memory for these events, which was scored by the experimenter on a scale from 0 (no details) to 3 (many details). Participants also rated events for memory strength on a scale of 1 (very vague) to 6 (very clear).

Analysis of fMRI data

Image preprocessing and analyses were performed using SPM5 (www.fil.ion.ucl.ac.uk/spm). Functional

[1]The "new" images are not in the strictest sense new but were also encountered (for 4000 ms) in the 36-hour retrieval session. We used the same stimuli in both sessions to ensure that differences between old and new stimuli were unlikely to be the result of exposure in the initial session rather than the personal experiencing of the event itself. The crucial difference between old and new stimuli is therefore the personal experience with the old stimuli but not with the new stimuli. We used the term "new" to make instructions to participants consistent across sessions; however, we accept that "lure" may be a more adequate description for the foils.

images were corrected for acquisition order, and realigned to correct for motion artefacts. A mean image created from the realigned images was coregistered with the structural T1 volume and the structural volumes spatially normalised. The spatial transformation was applied to the realigned T2* volumes which were spatially smoothed using a Gaussian kernel of 8-mm full-width half maximum. A high pass filter of 128 s was applied. The BOLD response was modelled by a canonical haemodynamic response function together with its temporal and dispersion derivatives. The six head movement parameters were included as confounds. Onset of the image was considered the beginning of the trial. First-level linear contrasts of parameter estimates for each voxel were generated and a random effects analysis performed.

Pairwise contrasts for memory types comprising at least eight events were conducted using repeated-measures *t*-tests with a significance threshold of $p < .001$ (uncorrected) and a cluster threshold of five contiguous voxels. Region of interest (ROI) analyses were conducted in bilateral MTL based on a priori hypothesis that this region is active during recognition memory. The ROI mask was applied using the WFU Pickatlas (Maldjian, Laurienti, Burdette, & Kraft, 2003). Coordinates were transformed from normalised MNI space to Talairach space (http://imaging.mrc-cbu.cam.ac.uk/imaging/MniTalairach).

RESULTS

Behavioural analyses

Table 1 displays the mean proportions for remember, know, misses, correct rejections (i.e., new stimuli that were correctly classified as new), and false alarms (i.e., new stimuli that were incorrectly classified as old) responses. A total of 2% of trials were excluded from analyses because participants failed to respond in time. All participants made sufficient responses of each type (at least eight events) to be included in all the contrasts. The relatively low number of incorrectly rejected old items (18%) and incorrectly accepted new items (11%) precluded further analyses of these classification types.

TABLE 1
Proportion of recognition responses for old and new items

	Old items			*New items*	
	Remember	*Know*	*Miss*	*CR*	*FA*
Mean	.27	.52	.18	.89	.11
SD	.13	.14	.17	.09	.09

SD = Standard Deviation; CR = Correct rejection; FA = False alarm.

The post-scan ratings revealed that participants recalled more details for images classified as Remember ($M = 1.86$, $SD = .47$) than those classified as Know ($M = .78$, $SD = .47$), $t(8) = 6.5$, $p < .001$. This occurred even though the post-scan test was self-paced, providing participants more opportunity to retrieve specific details for familiarity responses than in the scanner. Perceived memory strength was greater for Remember ($M = 3.52$, $SD = 1.08$) than Know responses ($M = 1.72$, $SD = .61$), $t(8) = 5.5$, $p = .001$. These findings suggest that participants could distinguish between recollection and familiarity processes.

Imaging analyses

MTL region of interest (ROI) analyses at 5 months. The following analyses used a significance threshold of $p < .01$ (uncorrected) and a cluster threshold of five contiguous voxels. There was no significant activation for Remember relative to New responses (i.e., correct rejections), while Know compared to New stimuli elicited greater activation in regions of right aPHG and bilateral pPHG (Figure 1a). A contrast comparing Remember to Know responses revealed no regions of significant activation, while comparing Know with Remember yielded activation in two clusters in right pPHG and one cluster in left pPHG (Figure 1b; Table 2). New responses produced greater activation than Remember responses in right aPHG and bilateral pPHG (Figure 1c). The New – Know contrast (Figure 1d) produced activation in two clusters in right aPHG and right pPHG.

Extra-MTL analyses at 5 months. These analyses used a significance threshold of $p < .001$ and a cluster threshold of five contiguous voxels. There was extensive extra-MTL activation in the Remember–Know contrast (Table 2) comprising activation in left superior frontal gyrus, left dorsolateral prefrontal cortex (DLPFC), right mPFC, right thalamus, right precuneus, and left inferior temporal cortex. The Know–Remember contrast (Table 2) revealed activity in right insula, right posterior cingulate, and right cerebellum.

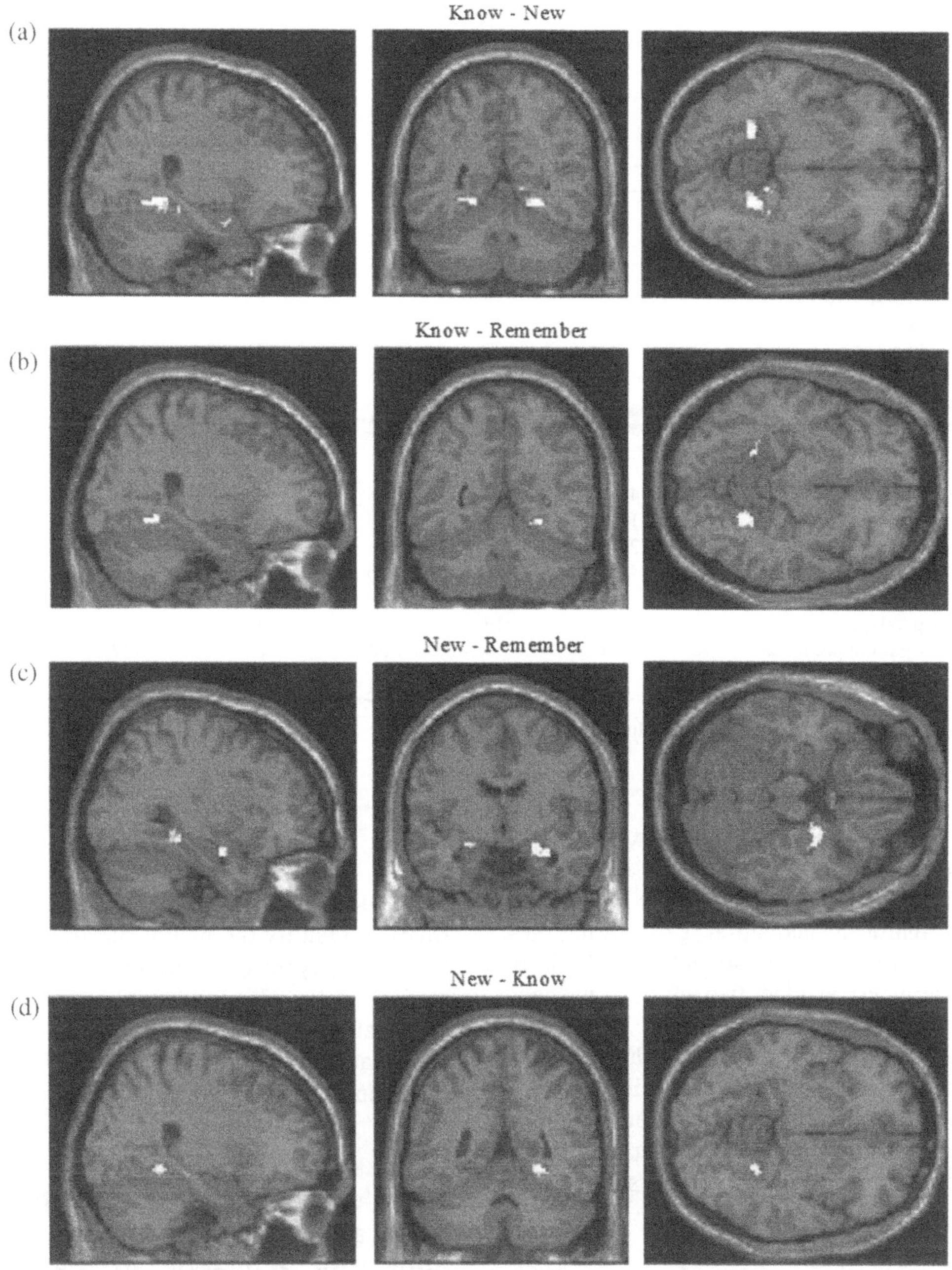

Figure 1. Regions in MTL where activation was greater for (a) Know than New responses; (b) Know compared to Remember responses; (c) New than Remember responses; (d) New than Know responses. To view this figure in colour, please see the online issue of the journal.

Remember compared to New (Figure 2a) induced greater activation in myriad regions including left ventrolateral frontal cortex (VLFC), anterior cingulate, cingulate gyrus, left inferior parietal lobe, left superior temporal gyrus, and right cerebellum. The Know–New contrast (Figure 2b) evoked activation in bilateral mPFC, right VLFC, bilateral insula, left inferior and left superior temporal lobe together with middle occipital gyrus. The New–Remember contrast (Figure 2c) included activation in mPFC, right middle frontal gyrus, bilateral insula, left cingulate gyrus and right precuneus. New compared to Know (Figure 2d) elicited activation in left VLFC, left anterior cingulate, right superior temporal gyrus, right thalamus, right precuneus, and right cuneus.

Short versus long delay for MTL ROI analyses. These analyses used thresholds of $p < .01$

TABLE 2
Regions showing significant activation for Remember compared with Know responses and for Know compared with Remember responses

Region	Cluster size	BA	Talairach coordinates			z-score
			x	*y*	*z*	
Remember – Know						
Right anterior cingulate	44	25	4	19	−4	4.19*
Right thalamus	26	–	12	−3	9	4.05*
Left superior frontal cortex	9	6	−18	28	54	3.91*
Right precuneus	42	31	2	−47	34	3.75*
Left cingulate gyrus		31	−8	−41	32	3.62*
Left dorsalateral frontal cortex	5	46	−48	28	24	3.68*
Right occipital lobe	7	19	48	−72	−3	3.56*
Right medial prefrontal cortex	6	10	2	52	1	3.19*
Know – Remember						
Right posterior cingulate	46	29	18	−46	12	4.26*
Right insula	14	13	30	8	12	3.92*
Right cerebellum	26	–	16	−48	−18	3.68*
Right posterior parahippocampal gyrus	46**	19	26	−53	−6	3.17*
Left posterior parahippocampal gyrus	47**	19	−22	−47	−6	2.99
Right posterior parahippocampal gyrus	31**	–	32	−26	−12	2.98

BA = Brodmann's area; * = $p < .001$; ** = cluster size at $p < .01$.

(uncorrected) and five contiguous voxels. A contrast comparing Remember activity at the long delay (5 months) to the short delay (36 hours) found no significant activation. Contrasting Remember activity for the short delay to the long delay (Figure 3a) yielded two clusters in right hippocampus/aPHG.

For familiarity, no regions produced more activation over a long than a short delay. There was greater activation in right anterior hippocampus/aPHG and right posterior hippocampus/pPHG for Know responses at the short delay relative to at the long delay (Figure 3b).

Short versus long delay for extra-MTL analyses. These analyses used thresholds of $p < .001$ and five contiguous voxels. No significant recollection activation was observed at the long relative to the short delay. Recollection at the short delay compared to the long delay induced activation in right cingulate gyrus and left thalamus (Table 3).

There was no significant familiarity-based activation at the long compared to the short delay. Meanwhile, there was greater familiarity activation at the short relative to the long delay in bilateral mPFC, the lateral globus pallidus and left caudate body (Table 3).

DISCUSSION

This study combined the use of SenseCam with fMRI to identify the neural substrates associated with everyday recognition memory over a 5-month retrieval delay. This condition was compared to an identical recognition memory test conducted approximately 36 hours after the event. We discuss the main findings of our experiment in turn.

Recollection elicits no activation in the MTL at a 5-month delay; there is familiarity activation in the MTL but this is reduced over time

No MTL regions evoked greater activation for Remember compared to either Know or New responses. The lack of MTL activation for long-term recollection responses is also illustrated by contrasting the 5-month to the 36-hours retrieval condition. No regions were more active at 5 months than at 36 hours but two regions in right anterior hippocampus/aPHG activated more at 36 hours than at 5 months.

There was greater MTL activation for Know compared to Remember responses in bilateral

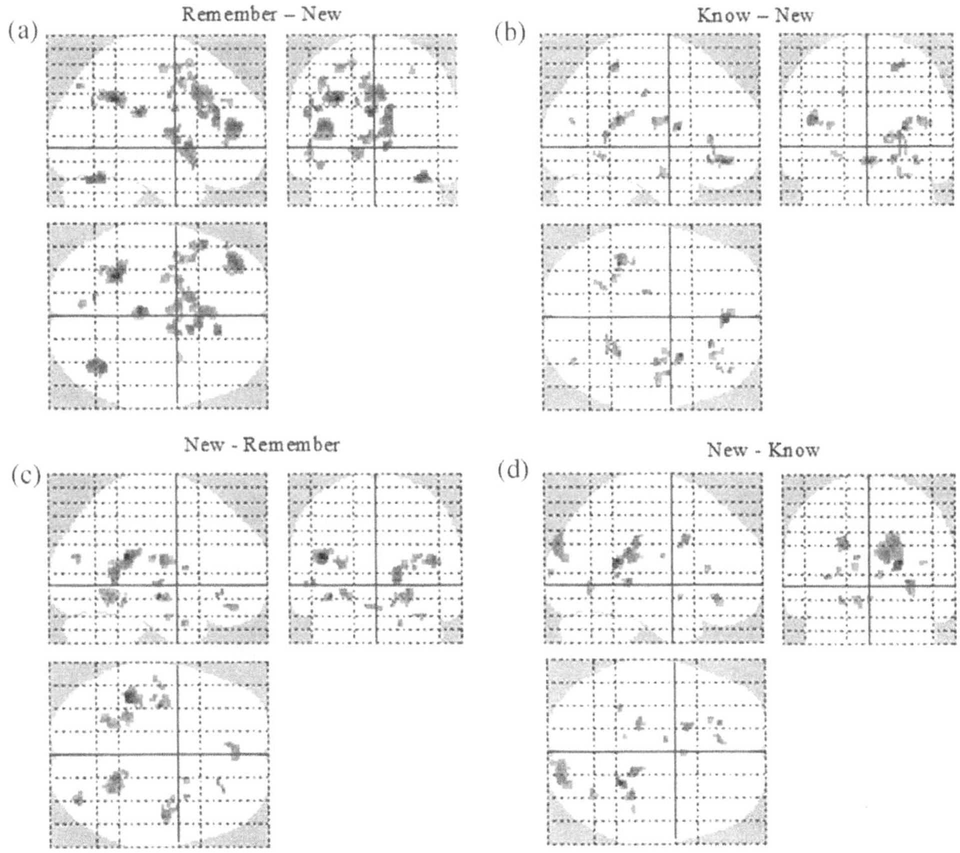

Figure 2. Whole brain analyses showing significant activation for (a) Remember compared to New responses; (b) Know compared to New responses; (c) New compared to Remember; (d) New compared to Know responses.

pPHG. Additionally, familiarity recruited clusters in aPHG and pPHG relative to New stimuli. No region of MTL was more active at the long than the short delay for familiarity memory, while a region in anterior hippocampus/aPHG and two clusters in posterior hippocampus/pPHG activated more at the short than the long delay.

These results suggest that recognition processes become disengaged from the MTL over time and are consistent with Takashima et al. (2006) who also showed a decrement of MTL activation across time. Nevertheless, the greater MTL activation for familiarity than recollection at a 5-month retrieval delay is noteworthy and broadly supportive of Suchan et al. (2008) who argued that the neural signal of familiarity-based activation is relatively durable. Furthermore, an explanation for this finding does not directly emerge from single-process memory strength accounts (e.g., Dunn, 2004).

Familiarity involved both aPHG and pPHG. Greater aPHG activation has frequently been observed for familiarity compared to recollection responses (e.g., Daselaar, Fleck, & Cabeza, 2006; Henson, Rugg, Shallice, Josephs, & Dolan, 1999). The greater aPHG activation for familiarity than New stimuli may reflect retrieval processes. However, the pPHG activation is more surprising. While this region has been implicated in familiarity processes (Daselaar et al., 2006), it is inconsistent with many previous studies (e.g., Davachi, Mitchell, & Wagner, 2003; Ranganath, Yonelinas, Cohen, Dy, Tom, & D'Esposito, 2003) and dual-process models (e.g., Aggleton & Brown, 1999) that link this region to recollection. One potential explanation for the pPHG activation for familiarity responses compared to New stimuli is that memory processes are seldom "process-pure" (Diana et al., 2007; Wais, Mickes, & Wixted, 2008) and recollection processes may be partially contributing to this effect. This, however, fails to explain why pPHG activation was also greater for familiarity compared to recollection, because a process contamination explanation would also predict greater recollection activity in this region. Our findings therefore appear more consistent

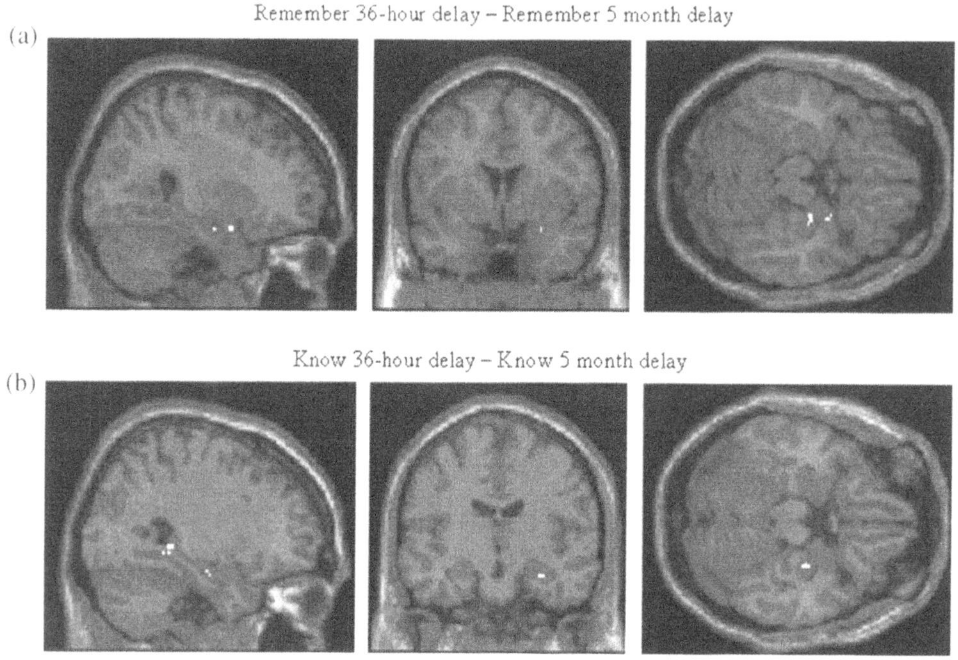

Figure 3. Regions in MTL where activation was greater for (a) Remember at short delay (36 hours) than Remember at long delay (5 months); (b) Know at short delay than Know at long delay. To view this figure in colour, please see the online issue of the journal.

with the idea that pPHG is involved in familiarity processes for everyday recognition. Familiarity has been linked with greater perceptual processing than recollection (Daselaar et al., 2006; Yonelinas, 2002) and the pPHG has strong connections with sensory areas (Daselaar et al., 2006). Increased pPHG activation for familiarity responses may therefore reflect the perceptual processes involved in such judgements. Nevertheless, regardless of the paradigm used, process impurity is a potential

TABLE 3
Regions showing significant activation for a short (36 hours) compared to a long (5 months) retrieval delay

			Talairach coordinates			
Region	*Cluster size*	*BA*	*x*	*y*	*z*	*z-score*
Remember (36 hours) – Remember (5 months)						
Left thalamus (pulvinar)	33	–	−8	−32	11	3.74*
Right cingulate gyrus	5	–	22	5	27	3.56*
Right anterior parahippocampal gyrus	5**	34	28	1	−15	2.83
Right anterior parahippocampal gyrus	9**	–	28	−10	−15	2.83
Right hippocampus		–	30	−12	−6	2.59
Know (36 hours) – Know (5 months)						
Lateral globus pallidus	16	–	24	−20	−1	4.83*
Right prefrontal cortex	19	10	16	31	−5	3.71*
Left caudate body	12	–	−20	5	24	3.63*
Left prefrontal cortex	12	10	−38	42	15	3.42*
Right Hippocampus	5**		30	−12	−6	2.73
Right Hippocampus	13**	–	30	−39	0	2.69
Right posterior parahippocampal gyrus	7**	–	32	−39	−3	2.67

BA = Brodmann's area; * = $p < .001$; ** = cluster size at $p < .01$.

issue for all studies attempting to distinguish between separate memory processes. Future work using SenseCam should therefore use alternative measurements such as confidence ratings to further assess whether pPHG involvement is a robust characteristic of everyday familiarity memory.

There is greater activation in regions of the MTL for New compared to old stimuli

Regions of aPHG and pPHG also yielded greater activation for New stimuli than Remember and Know responses. Novel stimuli have been linked with greater aPHG activation than old stimuli (e.g., Montaldi et al., 2006), which may reflect a novelty signal (Daselaar et al., 2006) or less-efficient item representation (Diana et al., 2007). Meanwhile, several studies have found regions of pPHG that activate more for new than old stimuli, possibly reflecting incidental encoding processes (e.g., Johnson, Muftuler, & Rugg, 2008; Stark & Okado, 2003; Vilberg & Rugg, 2009).

Remote recollection recruits a number of extra-MTL regions

In contrast to the lack of recollection based activation in MTL, diverse extra-MTL regions were recruited by recollection memory. Regions activated by recollection compared to familiarity included left superior frontal gyrus, left DLPFC, right mPFC, and left anterior temporal cortex. Among the regions that recollection memory engaged to a greater extent than New stimuli were left VLFC, left inferior parietal lobe, and left superior temporal gyrus. Nevertheless, no regions induced greater activation at 5-months than at 36-hours retrieval delay. This may reflect general decay of the memory trace over time; however, given the limited increased activation at the short compared to the long delay (right cingulate gyrus and left thalamus), it appears that extra-MTL traces remain relatively stable, at least over a 5-month period.

For the regions linked to recollection, mPFC has been implicated in recollection processes (Yonelinas, Otten, Shaw, & Rugg, 2005), and may support self-referential mental activity (Gusnard, Akbudak, Schulman, & Raichle, 2001). mPFC has also been linked to long-term recognition processes (e.g., Dolcos et al., 2005; Takashima et al., 2006). Daselaar et al. (2006) and Henson et al. (1999) both observed greater left VLFC activation for recollection processes, possibly reflecting source retrieval (Nolde, Johnson, & Raye, 1998). The left superior frontal gyrus is involved with recollection (Vilberg & Rugg, 2007), while left DLPFC has been implicated in recollection based temporal-order judgements (St. Jacques, Rubin, LaBar, & Cabeza, 2008). The left inferior parietal lobe consistently activates more for old than new items (e.g., Henson et al., 1999; Wheeler & Buckner, 2004), while regions of left temporal cortex are engaged in long-term recognition memory (e.g., Bosshardt et al., 2005; Dolcos et al., 2005) and in autobiographical memory (e.g., Gilboa et al., 2004).

Diverse extra-MTL regions are recruited by remote familiarity memory

Familiarity also resulted in extra-MTL activations compared to recollection and New stimuli. Familiarity activity was elevated relative to recollection activation in right insula, right posterior cingulate, and right cerebellum. Relative to New stimuli, familiarity involved greater activity in bilateral mPFC, right VLFC, bilateral insula, and left temporal lobe. As for recollection, the bilateral medial frontal gyrus activation may reflect long-term memory retrieval, while right VLFC has been linked with active retrieval processes (e.g., Henson, Shallice, & Dolan, 1998), and with increasing activity as familiarity rises (Montaldi et al., 2006). The left insula has been shown to increase with familiarity (Yonelinas et al., 2005), while posterior cingulate (Daselaar et al., 2006) and left temporal lobe (Montaldi et al., 2006) are engaged in familiarity processes. There was no increased activity for familiarity over time in extra-MTL regions but there was reduced activation at the long compared to the short delay in two small regions of mPFC. Although this appears somewhat inconsistent with the idea that mPFC is involved in long-term memory, this may reflect reduced self-referential processing (Gusnard et al., 2001).

Methodological considerations

One methodological feature of our study is that we used the same images in both the short and long delay retrieval sessions (for a related technique see Viskontas et al., 2009). One reason for this was that participants did not generate a sufficient number of unique events to use different stimuli in each session. However, this approach had the advantage of equating perceptual qualities, event saliency, and personal significance across the sessions. Nevertheless, it is possible that this repetition of stimuli may have influenced the pattern of results to some degree. Specifically, participants may have recognised the image from the previous scanning session rather than through recognition of the event itself. We believe that this is unlikely due to the fact that the initial study provided only limited extra exposure to the stimuli (4000 ms) but future work could guard again this possibility by using different sets of target and novel images at each test interval. Our recent experience using SenseCam indicates that a "structured day"—for example a day spent at the zoo—provides a sufficiently rich source of photographs to allow the creation of several separate sets of material for subsequent memory testing (Muhlert, Milton, Butler, Kapur, & Zeman, 2010).

Conclusions

In summary, our results showed different patterns of activation in recollection and familiarity memory. In particular, after a 5-month retrieval delay we observed greater pPHG activation for familiarity than recollection memory. Furthermore, the reduced activation in the MTL at 5 months relative to at 36 hours for both recollection and familiarity memory is consistent with consolidation theory, which predicts disengagement of the MTL in recognition memory over time. The continued engagement of extra-MTL regions such as mPFC and lateral temporal cortex by both recollection and familiarity memory is also consistent with consolidation theory, which posits that remote memory continues to be supported by neocortical regions. Our findings demonstrate the value of SenseCam as a technique to investigate long-term everyday recognition memory.

REFERENCES

Addis, D. R., Moscovitch, M., & McAndrews, M. P. (2004). Consequences of hippocampal damage across the autobiographical network in left temporal lobe epilepsy. *Brain*, *130*, 2327–2342.

Aggleton, J. P., & Brown, M. (1999). Episodic memory, amnesia, and the hippocampal-anterior thalamic axis. *Behavioral & Brain Sciences*, *22*, 425–489.

Bosshardt, S., Degonda, N., Schmidt, C. F., Boesiger, P., Nitsch, R. M., Hock, C., et al. (2005). One month of human memory consolidation enhances retrieval-related hippocampal activity. *Hippocampus*, *15*, 1026–1040.

Cabeza, R., Prince, S. E., Daselaar, S. M., Greenberg, D. L., Budde, M., Dolcos, F., et al. (2004). Brain activity during episodic retrieval of autobiographical and laboratory events: An fMRI study using a novel photo paradigm. *Journal of Cognitive Neuroscience*, *16*, 1583–1594.

Daselaar, S. M., Fleck, M. S., & Cabeza, R. (2006). Triple dissociation in the medial temporal lobes: Recollection, familiarity, and novelty. *Journal of Neurophysiology*, *96*, 1902–1911.

Davachi, L., Mitchell, J. P., & Wagner, A. D. (2003). Multiple routes to memory: Distinct medial temporal lobe processes build item and source memories. *Proceedings of the National Academy of Sciences*, *100*, 2157–2162.

Diana, R. A., Yonelinas, A. P., & Ranganath, C. (2007). Imaging recollection and familiarity in the medial temporal lobe: A three-component model. *Trends in Cognitive Sciences*, *11*, 379–386.

Dolcos, F., LaBar, K. S., & Cabeza, R. (2005). Remembering one year later: Role of the amygdala and the media temporal lobe memory system in retrieving emotional memories. *Proceedings of the National Academy of Sciences*, *102*, 2626–2631.

Dunn, J. C. (2004). Remember-know: A matter of confidence. *Psychological Review*, *111*, 524–542.

Eldridge, L. L., Knowlton, B. J., Furmanski, C. S., Bookheimer, S. Y., & Engel, S. A. (2000). Remembering episodes: A selective role for the hippocampus during retrieval. *Nature Neuroscience*, *3*, 1149–1152.

Gilboa, A., Winocur, G., Grady, C. L., Hevenor, S. J., & Moscovitch, M. (2004). Remembering our past: Functional neuroanatomy of recollection of recent and very remote personal events. *Cerebral Cortex*, *14*, 1214–1225.

Gusnard, D. A., Akbudak, E., Schulman, G. L., & Raichle, M. E. (2001). Medial prefrontal cortex and self-referential mental activity: Relation to a default mode of brain function. *Proceedings of the National Academy of Sciences*, *98*, 4259–4264.

Henson, R. N. A., Cansino, S., Herron, J. E., Robb, W. G. D., & Rugg, M. D. (2003). A familiarity signal in human anterior cortex? *Hippocampus*, *13*, 259–262.

Henson, R. N. A., Rugg, M. D., Shallice, T., Josephs, O., & Dolan, R. J. (1999). Recollection and familiarity in recognition memory: An event related fMRI study. *The Journal of Neuroscience*, *19*, 3962–3972.

Henson, R. N. A., Shallice, T., & Dolan, R. J. (1998). Right prefrontal cortex and episodic memory retrieval: A functional MRI test of the monitoring hypothesis. *Brain*, *122*, 137–1381.

Hodges, S., Williams, L., Berry, E., Izadi, S., Srinivasan, J., Butler, A., et al. (2006). SenseCam: A retrospective memory aid. In P. Dourish & A. Friday (Eds.), *Ubicomp, LNCS 4206* (pp. 177–193). Berlin, Germany: Springer-Verlag.

Johnson, J. D., Muftuler, L. T., & Rugg, M. D. (2008). Multiple repetitions reveal functionally and anatomically distinct patterns of hippocampal activity during continuous recognition memory. *Hippocampus, 18*, 975–980.

Kirwan, C. B., Wixted, J. T., & Squire, L. R. (2008). Activity in the medial temporal lobe predicts memory strength, whereas activity in the prefrontal cortex predicts recollection. *The Journal of Neuroscience, 28*, 10541–10548.

Maguire, E. A., & Frith, C. D. (2003). Lateral asymmetry in the hippocampal response to the remoteness of autobiographical memories. *The Journal of Neuroscience, 23*, 5302–5307.

Maldjian, J. A., Laurienti, P. J., Burdette, J. B., & Kraft, R. A. (2003). An automated method for neuroanatomic and cytoarchitectonic atlas-based interrogation of fMRI data sets. *Neuroimage, 19*, 1233–1239.

Mandler, G. (1980). Recognising: The judgement of previous occurrence. *Psychological Review, 87*, 252–271.

Montaldi, D., Spencer, T. J., Roberts, N., & Mayes, A. (2006). The neural system that mediates familiarity memory. *Hippocampus, 16*, 504–520.

Muhlert, N., Milton, F., Butler, C. R., Kapur, N., & Zeman, A. Z. (2010). Accelerated forgetting of real-life events in transient epileptic amnesia. *Neuropsychologia, 48*, 3235–3244.

Nadel, L., & Moscovitch, M. (1997). Memory consolidation, retrograde amnesia and the hippocampal complex. *Current Opinion in Neurobiology, 7*, 217–227.

Niki, K., & Luo, J. (2002). An fMRI study on the time-limited role of the medial temporal lobe in long-term topographical autobiographic memory. *Journal of Cognitive Neuroscience, 14*, 500–507.

Nolde, S. F., Johnson, M. K., & Raye, C. L. (1998). The role of prefrontal cortex during tests of episodic memory. *Trends in Cognitive Sciences, 2*, 399–406.

Piefke, M., Weiss, P. H., Zilles, K., Markowitcsh, H. J., & Fink, G. R. (2003). Differential remoteness and emotional tone modulate the neural correlates of autobiographical memory. *Brain, 126*, 650–668.

Rajaram, S. (1993). Remembering and knowing: Two means of access to the personal past. *Memory & Cognition, 21*, 89–102.

Ranganath, C., Yonelinas, A. P., Cohen, M. X., Dy, C.J., Tom, S.M., & D'Esposito, M. (2003). Dissociable correlates of recollection and familiarity within the medial temporal lobes. *Neuropsychologia, 42*, 2–13.

Rekkas, P. V., & Constable, R. T. (2005). Evidence that autobiographic memory retrieval does not become independent of the hippocampus: An fMRI study contrasting very recent with remote events. *Journal of Cognitive Neuroscience, 17*, 1950–1961.

Rotello, C. M., Macmillan, N. A., & Reeder, J. A. (2004). Sum-difference theory of remembering and knowing: A two-dimensional signal-detection model. *Psychological Review, 111*, 588–616.

Ryan, L., Nadel, L., Keil, K., Putnam, K., Schnyer, D., Trouard, T., et al. (2001). Hippocampal complex and retrieval of recent and very remote autobiographical memories: Evidence from functional magnetic resonance imaging in neurologically intact people. *Hippocampus, 11*, 707–714.

Squire, L. R., Stark, C. E., & Clark, R. E. (2004). The medial temporal lobe. *Annual Review of Neuroscience, 27*, 279–306.

Stark, C. E. L., & Okado, Y. (2003). Making memories without trying: Medial temporal lobe activity associated with incidental memory formation during recognition. *The Journal of Neuroscience, 23*, 6748–6753.

St. Jacques, P., Rubin, D. C., LaBar, K. S., & Cabeza, R. (2008). The short and long of it: Neural correlates of temporal-order memory for autobiographical events. *Journal of Cognitive Neuroscience, 20*, 1327–1341.

Steinvorth, S., Corkin, S., & Halgren, E. (2006). Ecphory of autobiographical memories: An fMRI study of recent and remote memory retrieval. *Neuroimage, 30*, 285–298.

Suchan, B., Gayk, A. E., Schmid, G., Koster, O., & Daum, I. (2008). Hippocampal involvement in recollection but not familiarity across time: A prospective study. *Hippocampus, 18*, 92–98.

Svoboda, E., McKinnon, M. C., & Levine, B. (2006). The functional neuroanatomy of autobiographical memory: A meta-analysis. *Neuropsychologia, 44*, 2189–2208.

Takashima, A., Petersson, K. M., Rutters, F., Tendolkar, I., Jensen, O., Zwarts, M. J., et al. (2006). Declarative memory consolidation in humans: A prospective functional magnetic resonance imaging study. *Proceedings of the National Academy of Sciences, 103*, 756–761.

Tulving, E. (1985). Memory and consciousness. *Canadian Psychology, 26*, 1–12.

Vilberg, K. L., & Rugg, M. D. (2007). Dissociation of the neural correlates of recognition memory according to familiarity, recollection and amount of recollected information. *Neuropsychologia, 45*, 2216–2225.

Vilberg, K. L., & Rugg, M. D. (2009). An investigation of the effects of relative probability of old and new test items on the neural correlates of successful and unsuccessful source memory. *NeuroImage, 45*, 562–571.

Viskontas, I. V., Carr, V. A., Engel, S. A., & Knowlton, B. J. (2009). The neural correlates of recollection: Hippocampal activation declines as episodic memory fades. *Hippocampus, 19*, 265–272.

Wais, P. E., Mickes, L., & Wixted, J. T. (2008). Remember/know judgements probe degrees of recollection. *Journal of Cognitive Neuroscience, 20*, 400–405.

Wheeler, M. E., & Buckner, R. L. (2004). Functional-anatomic correlates of remembering and knowing. *NeuroImage, 21*, 1337–1349.

Yonelinas, A. P. (2002). The nature of recollection and familiarity: A review of 30 years of research. *Journal of Memory & Language, 46*, 441–517.

Yonelinas, A. P., Otten, L. J., Shaw, K. N., & Rugg, M. D. (2005). Separating the brain regions involved in recollection and familiarity in recognition memory. *The Journal of Neuroscience, 25*, 3002–3008.

MEMORY, 2011, 19 (7), 745–757

Psychology Press
Taylor & Francis Group

Exploration of use of SenseCam to support autobiographical memory retrieval within a cognitive-behavioural therapeutic intervention following acquired brain injury

Rob Brindley[1], **Andrew Bateman**[1,2], **and Fergus Gracey**[1,2]

[1]Oliver Zangwill Centre for Neuropsychological Rehabilitation, The Princess of Wales Hospital, Ely, Cambridgeshire, UK
[2]The Medical Research Council Cognition and Brain Sciences Unit, Cambridge, UK

Delivering effective psychotherapy to address the significant emotional consequences of acquired brain injury (ABI) is challenged by the presence of acquired cognitive impairments, especially retrieval of detailed autobiographical memories of emotional trigger events. Initial studies using a wearable camera (SenseCam) suggest long-term improvements in autobiographical retrieval of recorded events. In this study a single-case experimental design was implemented to explore the use of SenseCam as a memory aid for a man with a specific anxiety disorder and memory and executive difficulties following ABI. We predicted that SenseCam supported rehearsal of memories of events that trigger high levels of anxiety would yield improved retrieval of both factual detail and internal state information (thoughts and feelings) compared with a conventional psychotherapy aid (automatic thought record sheets, ATRs) and no strategy. The findings indicated SenseCam supported retrieval of anxiety trigger events was superior to ATRs or no strategy in terms of both detail and internal state information, with 94% of the information being recalled in the SenseCam condition, compared to 39% for the "no strategy" and 22% for the ATR conditions. It is concluded that SenseCam may be of use as a compensatory aid in psychotherapies relying on retrieval of emotionally salient trigger events.

Keywords: Acquired brain injury; Psychotherapy; Memory; Strategies; Anxiety.

Acquired brain injury (ABI) is associated with increased risk of developing emotional disorders. A recent meta-analytic review suggested both prevalence and lifetime incidence of depression following brain injury to be around 30%, and a four-fold increase in likelihood of suicide compared with rates in the general population has also been reported (Teasdale & Engberg,

Address correspondence to: Fergus Gracey, Oliver Zangwill Centre for Neuropsychological Rehabilitation, The Princess of Wales Hospital, Lynn Road, Ely, Cambridgeshire, CB6 1DN, UK. E-mail: fergus.gracey@ozc.nhs.uk

We would like to acknowledge the financial and practical support of Microsoft Research (Cambridge, UK). In particular we are indebted to Emma Berry, Georgina Browne, and Steve Hodges for their time and advice. We would also like to acknowledge Phil Barnard for his time and discussion with us on an early draft of the paper.

In addition, we would like to acknowledge the National Institute for Health Research "Collaborations for Leadership in Applied Health Research and Care" (CLAHRC) for Cambridgeshire and Peterborough for providing funding to support Fergus Gracey with the writing of this paper.

© 2011 Psychology Press, an imprint of the Taylor & Francis Group, an Informa business
http://www.psypress.com/memory http://dx.doi.org/10.1080/09658211.2010.493893

2001). Anxiety is frequently experienced, one meta-analysis reporting an overall prevalence of 29% for anxiety disorders following TBI (Epstein & Ursano, 1994), comorbid anxiety and depression also being common.

The development and evaluation of interventions for emotional disorders following brain injury is therefore critical. There is increasing support for the use of cognitive behavioural interventions with those experiencing emotional difficulties following ABI (Bradbury et al., 2008; Soo & Tate, 2007; Tiersky et al., 2005; Williams, Evans, & Fleminger, 2003a; Williams, Evans, & Wilson, 2003b). However, adaptations to address both the underlying causes of emotional disorder and the cognitive barriers to engagement in therapy are required. The experience of losing one's sense of self and identity can be one of the most devastating consequences following an acquired brain injury (ABI) (Bennett & Raymond, 1997). The emotional, cognitive, and physical impairments associated with ABI may result in significant changes to an individual's interpretation of themselves and the world around them (Gracey et al., 2008; Riley, Brennan, & Powell, 2004). These difficulties are often compounded by impairments in the retrieval and storage of autobiographical memory, whereby an individual may be unable to recall their pre-injury self and/or create a new concept of self (Coetzer, 2008; Kovarsky, Shaw, & Adingono-Smith, 2007; Nochi, 1998; Ownsworth, Turpin, Andrew, & Fleming, 2008). Ylvisaker and Feeney (2000) argue that the process of therapy for those with ABI should involve working with the individual towards developing a new or adjusted self-concept. The specific challenges of providing psychological therapy in the context of cognitive impairment have been discussed in the literature. The use of external memory aids, such as written diaries, audio recording, and audio-visual displays, have been suggested to support those with memory impairments within rehabilitation (Brown, Pinnington, & Ward, 2005; Evans, Wilson, Needham, & Brentall, 2003; Hibbard, Grober, Gordon, & Aletta, 1990; Judd & Wilson, 2005; Massimi et al., 2008; Whitehouse, 1994). A study of clinicians providing psychological therapy to people with ABI highlighted that acquired cognitive impairments (including problems with memory, executive functioning, self-awareness, and attention) impacting on therapy were a source of stress for clinicians (Judd & Wilson, 2005). In this study the use of behavioural experiments in CBT (in which change in cognitive content is addressed through testing predictions through activity-based experiments) was reported as especially useful by clinicians. McGrath and King (2004) describe the use of behavioural experiments in CBT to address common emotional issues following brain injury. Ylvisaker and Feeney (2000) present cases illustrating how cognitive strategies (such as metaphorical compaction and visual imagery) can be used in order to reduce working memory load to support the organisation of information and to facilitate the challenging process of identity change. However, despite the growing number of promising case studies and some outcome studies, systematic evaluation of potential supports for psychological therapy with this client group have not been carried out.

A particular challenge for the adaptation of CBT and other therapies post ABI is the lack of an integrated theoretical framework linking mood disorder, acquired cognitive impairment and change processes in therapy (but see Gracey, Evans, & Malley, 2009). Recent advances and developments in the theory and research behind cognitive-behavioural models of mood disorder propose information-processing accounts that may help make sense of how specific impairments may present a barrier to the kind of changes required to benefit from psychological therapy. The interacting cognitive subsystems model (ICS; Teasdale & Barnard, 1993) proposes that therapeutic change comes about as a result of changes at what is called the "implicational" level of meaning, rather than the alternative "propositional" level of meaning. The former deals with felt experience, linking representations of self and identity to multimodal representations of autobiographical experiences. The propositional system on the other hand represents logical relationships between concepts and is more akin to semantic rather than episodic storage. The model has been used to argue that the traditional CBT approach of identifying and challenging negative thoughts and maladaptive assumptions using logical argument is targeting change at the wrong level of meaning. The use of what have become known as "third generation" CBT techniques such as behavioural experiments, imagery, mindfulness-based techniques, and compassionate mind training has been advocated on the basis that such interventions address change at the more personally salient implicational level of meaning. Ylvisaker and Feeney (2000) have drawn on this model to support the techniques used in their "identity mapping" approach to addressing identity and self-regulation difficulties of people following brain injury.

Given the key role of engaging with rich personal experiences (either directly during in vivo intervention, or more usually through retrieval of autobiographical memories) in such CBT approaches, as well as the importance of accurate and detailed self-report of emotional trigger events, the need to support autobiographical retrieval in CBT following ABI is highlighted. Williams, Williams, and Ghadiali (1998) suggest that the use of automatic thought record (ATR) sheets, a standard CBT procedure, may be of help in supporting retrieval of events for people with brain injury. Given very promising initial results for supporting retrieval of specific events in those with significant memory problems (e.g., Berry et al., 2007), a possible additional therapeutic tool is an external memory aid known as SenseCam.

SenseCam is a wearable camera, which is able to take photos automatically in response to environmental changes without the involvement of the user. Images are taken using a fish-eye lens and, when the unit is worn around the neck, give an approximation of an individual's visual perspective. When these images are compiled and viewed consecutively, they create a "flip-book" effect. Berry et al. (2007) presents a case comparing SenseCam-supported rehearsal with diary-based rehearsal with a client experiencing severe memory difficulties resulting from limbic encephalitis. SenseCam-supported rehearsal was associated with longer-term improvement in autobiographical retrieval associated with the specific events recorded. Anecdotal accounts of clinicians and researchers using SenseCam suggest that users retrieve additional reflections on thoughts and feelings related to the event being reviewed. Berry et al. argue that these additional reflections, together with the inherent qualities of SenseCam images (e.g., sporadic capturing of images, image viewpoint, etc.), could be interpreted as the retrieval and consolidation of episodic memory specific to the recorded events, in line with the self-memory system (SMS; Conway, 2005) model.

These qualities of SenseCam "movies", together with the associated improvement in autobiographical memory, suggests that SenseCam could be a useful addition to cognitive behavioural therapy with those experiencing memory impairments. These qualities also suggest that SenseCam could be a useful addition to cognitive behavioural therapy in general, allowing greater access to an individual's experience and interpretation of lived events and thus may be particularly useful in working with experiences of events being used for behavioural experiments.

In this study preliminary work with an individual with acquired memory impairment and an anxiety disorder is explored, and the use of a traditional CBT approach of using automatic thought record sheets (ATRs) is compared with the use of SenseCam in supporting recall. The key questions identified with this study relate first of all to the relative efficacy of these strategies for supporting recall of anxiety-related trigger events, and second to the content of retrieved detail. Given findings from previous work with SenseCam, and in line with the predictions arising from the ICS model that SenseCam supports development of emotionally "hotter" implicational rather than emotionally "cold" propositional-level meanings, SenseCam-supported retrieval is expected to be superior to ATR-supported recall or no recall strategy in terms of amount recalled. In addition the content of SenseCam-supported retrieval is predicted to include a greater reference to internal states, such as thoughts and feelings. Finally, SenseCam-supported retrieval of an anxiety provoking trigger situation is predicted to be associated with a greater activation of anxious arousal (as measured by heart rate changes) than ATR supported or no strategy retrieval.

METHOD

Participant and clinical context

Neurological symptoms and background. Allan suffered injuries resulting from an assault when he was aged 21; a brain scan at the time indicated right frontal contusions, a small right subdural haemorrhage, a left temporo-occipital fracture, and a left temporal bone fracture. Allan also had a number of pre-existing neurological problems that were not identified until the time of the injury; hydrocephalus, arachnoid cyst malformation, migraines, and enlargement of the third and lateral ventricles. Prior to his injury, aside from migraines, Allan achieved normal milestones and at the time of his injury was a successful university student, active in a range of interests.

Previous neuropsychological assessment and rehabilitation. Allan was initially assessed at a holistic neuropsychological rehabilitation centre 5 months following the assault. A biopsychosocial approach to assessment was used in which the emotional consequences of Allan's acquired brain injury were formulated in conjunction with his other acquired difficulties and social participation restrictions (Williams & Evans, 2003; Wilson, Gracey, Evans & Bateman, 2009). The assessment identified a number of cognitive difficulties, including significant memory impairments, difficulties in sustaining attention, impaired verbal and figure recall, reduced verbal processing speed, and executive functioning deficits. Following this assessment, Allan participated in a 6-month rehabilitation programme at the centre. The programme aimed to support Allan in developing awareness and understanding of the consequences of his brain injury, adjusting emotionally, and developing strategies to manage his cognitive difficulties in the context of his main goal of returning to university to complete his degree. An outcome of rehabilitation was the development of a memory and planning system, including use of a "personal digital assistant" (PDA), which he continued to use routinely following the programme.

Psychological assessment and formulation. Allan was re-referred to the service 7 years post-injury to address anxiety symptoms impacting his ability to go out independently. Symptoms had become worse following a road traffic accident about a year prior to referral in which Allan was not physically hurt. Sudden onset of leg weakness, leading Allan to have to sit down, was reported to occur intermittently following the accident, with no neurological cause identified following thorough investigation. The initial assessment was aimed at formulating Allan's anxiety difficulties within the context of his brain injury and related difficulties with social participation. Assessment involved clinical interviews with Allan and his mother, in addition to client and informant versions of standardised questionnaires. A repeat neuropsychological assessment was not carried out at this point. However, Allan and his family reported ongoing difficulties especially with tasks requiring episodic memory, including autobiographical memory. At this time Allan self-reported physical sensations related to panic and anxiety within social situations, specifically leg weakness and increased frequency of migraines. Allan also reported ongoing problems in recalling autobiographical events where the detail of such events was lost after 7 days. As shown in Table 1, Allan's emotional symptoms placed him in the clinical range for anxiety (Beck Anxiety Inventory, BAI; Beck, Epstein, Brown, & Steer, 1988a; Beck, Steer, & Carbin, 1988b), panic (Mobility Inventory for Agoraphobia, MIA; Chambless, Caputo, Jasin, Gracely, & Williams, 1985), and depression (Beck Depression Inventory 2nd edition, BDI-II;

TABLE 1
Questionnaire measures taken at initial assessment

Measure	*Sub-scale*	*Score*	*Interpretation*
Beck Anxiety Inventory	–	16	Moderate anxiety
Beck Depression Inventory – II	–	23	Moderate depression
Robson Self Concept Questionnaire ($M = 137.8$, $SD = 19.1$)*	–	90	Low self-esteem
Mobility Inventory for Agoraphobia (rating 0-5: 0 = low or minimal, 5 = maximum)	Avoidance Alone	4.00	Within clinical range
	Avoidance Accompanied	2.37	Within clinical range
	Panic Frequency	3	Within clinical range
	Panic Intensity	3	Within clinical range
Mayo-Portland Adaptability Inventory (MPAI-4)	Total Score	50	Moderate Difficulties
	Ability	55	Moderate to Severe Difficulties
	Adjustment	50	Moderate Difficulties
	Participation	49	Mild to Moderate Difficulties

*See Robson (1989).

Beck, Steer, & Brown, 1996), and more than 2 standard deviations below the mean on a measure of self-esteem (Robson self-concept questionnaire, SCQ; Robson, 1989) indicating significantly low self-esteem. The Mayo-Portland Adaptability Inventory version 4 (MPAI-4; Malec, 2005) was completed by a significant other and provides an estimate of Allan's overall functioning post ABI in the moderate severity range.

These measures, together with Allan's self-reporting of anxiety-related symptoms arising in response to specific trigger situations and the alteration of his behaviours in relation to social situations, was sufficient to satisfy DSM-IV TR Axis I criteria for generalised social phobia (American Psychiatric Association, 2000). Also, due to the impact of cognitive and memory difficulties resulting from a non-progressive acquired brain injury upon the maintenance of these difficulties, social phobia was seen as an indirect consequence of a medical disorder on DSM-IV-TR Axis III (American Psychiatric Association, 2000).

Therapeutic intervention and rationale

The work described within this study was undertaken as a preliminary step in devising an adapted CBT approach, where the key concern related to compensation for memory impairment in such a way as to support cognitive emotional change at the implicational level of meaning. Work was carried out to systematically compare the relative efficacy of strategies for supporting recall in CBT prior to carrying out therapeutic intervention. A "memory testing stage" was conducted whereby the recall of events using either standard CBT thought record sheets or review of SenseCam footage would be compared. The experimental hypotheses are:

1. SenseCam-supported recall will lead to higher frequencies of recalled information units versus recall supported by ATRs or no strategy.
2. SenseCam-supported recall will elicit higher frequencies of specific emotional elements when compared with recall supported by ATRs or the no-recall strategy.
3. SenseCam-supported recall will elicit a higher mean heart rate when compared with recall supported by ATRs or the no-recall strategy.

Study design

The design employed was an adaptation of a single-case time-series design used by Berry et al. (2007) in their evaluation of SenseCam-supported recall versus diary and no strategy in an individual with memory difficulties post encephalitis. The first modification was the nature of the to-be-recalled event, which given the specific question regarding intervention in this case was the recall of events that routinely triggered an anxious reaction for Allan (we will call these "emotional trigger events"). A further modification related to the extent to which supported recall might also result in triggering of an anxiety-related physiological response (we will call this "affective arousal"). In order to address this a portable ECG device was worn by Allan across trigger events and free recall trials. Number of information units recalled, nature of recalled information and affective arousal (as inferred from heart rate) were compared across the recall strategies.

Measures

Autobiographical memory retrieval. Following Berry et al. (2007) this was calculated as proportion of information correctly recalled by Allan against the number of information units in a diary of the events as completed by a significant other.

Affective response. Heart rate information was collected during the three emotional trigger events and during all trials. Heart rate information was recorded using a wireless ECG monitor (ActiHeart; Brage, Brage, Franks, Ekelund, & Wareham, 2005) with chest electrodes. The sampling rate was 128 Hz (8mS) with an epoch of 15 seconds and inter-beat intervals were converted into heart rates (HR) of beats per minute (BPM). Mean HR was calculated over the duration of each event and the duration of each strategy trial, which is in line with current research procedures (Chida & Hamer, 2008; Lewis & Drewett, 2005; Story & Craske, 2008; Wilhelm & Roth, 2001). A comparison baseline HR was collected during a psychoeducation session with Allan previous to data collection, together with resting heart rate calculated from overnight sleep periods. The ActiHeart also has built in actimetry, which allows heart rate changes that occur without an accompanying significant change in activity levels to be identified. For the purposes of this study we operationally defined "anxious arousal" as increased heart rate in the absence of preceding and accompanying activity changes, and further confirmed the nature of the emotional arousal by checking that the images recorded by SenseCam corresponded to identified emotional trigger events for Allan.

Nature of recalled information. Content analysis was performed on the information recalled during strategy use. The amount of detail covered within a retrieved memory was calculated as described above on the basis of reference to specific details, thus providing a means of defining a retrieved memory in terms of amount of detail. Furthermore, units of recall considered specific and detailed were labelled as "specific elements", vague or general comments were labelled as "generic elements". Since the to-be-remembered events were specific events, within the method of the current study a memory described as general or lacking detail does not correspond to the "overgeneral" or "generic" types of autobiographical memory described respectively by Williams (1996) and Conway and Haque (1999). In order to capture the level of detail in reference to type of meaning (implicational versus propositional), relative frequencies of reference to internal state (thoughts, feelings, subjective experiences) were calculated for each condition. "Emotional elements" were defined as those containing reference to experienced thoughts and feelings, while "non-emotional elements" were defined as containing reference to factual information such as movements, actions, and information relating to the event. Therefore four categories of information elements were used to classify recalled information: general emotional, general non-emotional, specific emotional, and specific non-emotional. The proportion of the category elements to the overall number of elements retrieved was calculated across the seven trials.

Symptoms of anxiety and depression. In order to assess Allan's emotional disorder, and to create a baseline prior to the planned CBT intervention, anxiety (using the BAI), depression (BDI-II), and self esteem (Robson SCQ) were assessed on three occasions, twice prior to and once after this experiment.

Procedure

Allan and his family were asked to identify three events coming up in the family diary that he could participate in over the course of a week that would typically evoke a strong anxious reaction. Retrieval conditions were randomly allocated to each event: The events and corresponding conditions were:

- Event 1: accompanied trip to town for passport photographs – no strategy.
- Event 2: accompanied social event at hosts home – automatic through record sheets.
- Event 3: accompanied social event – meal out: SenseCam.

For each event, Allan was asked to maintain an automatic thought record, noting down the details of his experience that he felt would help him to recall the event at a later date. Allan also collected SenseCam images and heart rate information during all three events as described above. A member of Allan's family was asked to maintain a record of each event (relative diary), where they were asked to note down and identify the key steps or segments of each event (information units).

Allan's recall of these events was then obtained at 7 days post-event (in line with Allan's self-report of forgetting) and then twice a week over the course of 3 weeks, creating a total of seven trials. Each event was randomly allocated to a different strategy condition, prior to receiving any data from the client or their family. The automatic thought record and SenseCam experimental conditions were compared to a control "no strategy" condition. This control condition provided an estimate of Allan's forgetting of personally salient events, as detailed within the study design section.

At each trial, Allan reviewed the event using the specified strategy as much as he felt necessary, with the exception of the control condition. So for the SenseCam condition Allan watched the movie, and for the ATR condition he re-read the record entries for the event. Allan was given time to try to recall and think about the event for the "no strategy" condition. For the initial trial for each event Allan's recall was assessed before and after use of the strategy. Thereafter assessment of recall of the event occurred prior to strategy-supported rehearsal to counteract any possible effects from reviewing the material immediately before testing. For all trials, an audio recording of Allan's recall of the event was taken. Recall was examined using a "free recall with single prompt" approach, with the prompt being the title of the event as agreed with Allan and his family prior to data collection. Information recalled by Allan was compared with the information units identified within the relative diary and percentages of information units correct/identified were calculated for each event per testing session. Content analysis was carried out on the recalled information and spontaneous reflections made by Allan during the trial as described above (see Table 2).

RESULTS

Effectiveness of strategies in supporting recall of anxiety triggering events

Figure 1 shows Allan's average percentage recall of autobiographical events in regards to each strategy used. It illustrates that, over time, Allan's recall of autobiographical events was maintained and began to increase to approximately 94% during the testing period when using the SenseCam strategy. During the same period, the control and thought record conditions were associated with a steady decrease from 78% and 56% to 39% and 22% in recalled information respectively. This shows that SenseCam-supported retrieval was superior to both ATR-supported and no strategy conditions.

Emotional content and nature of supported recollections of anxiety triggering events

Content of recollections. Content analysis was performed on the verbal recall for the three events over each trial. Figure 2 shows the percentage of identified elements for each category of memory across the three conditions. SenseCam-supported recall was most closely associated with both emotional and non-emotional elements specific to that event. Conversely, both ATR-supported and no strategy retrieval provided a greater percentage of generic-level elements when compared with SenseCam-supported retrieval. However, for all three conditions specific non-emotional elements were the most prevalent category. This suggests that overall SenseCam-supported recall was superior to both ATR-supported and no strategy recall in the retrieval of specific emotional elements.

TABLE 2
Summary of data collection procedure

	Within event	*Initial testing (7 days post-event)*	*Trial 1 (7 days post-event)*	*Trials 2 to 7*
Event 1 – No strategy	Recording of all events using both strategies and HR recorded	Free recall of information units, no review, HR recorded	Free recall of information units and HR recorded	Free recall of information units and HR recorded at regular intervals over 3-week period
Event 2 – Review of event using thought record	Recording of all events using both strategies and HR recorded	Free recall of information units pre-review and HR recorded	Free recall of information units post-review and HR recorded	Free recall of information units pre-review and HR recorded at regular intervals over 3-week period
Event 3 – Review of event using SenseCam images	Recording of all events using both strategies and HR recorded	Free recall of information units pre-review and HR recorded	Free recall of information units post-review and HR recorded	Free recall of information units pre-review and HR recorded at regular intervals over 3-week period

HR = heart rate.

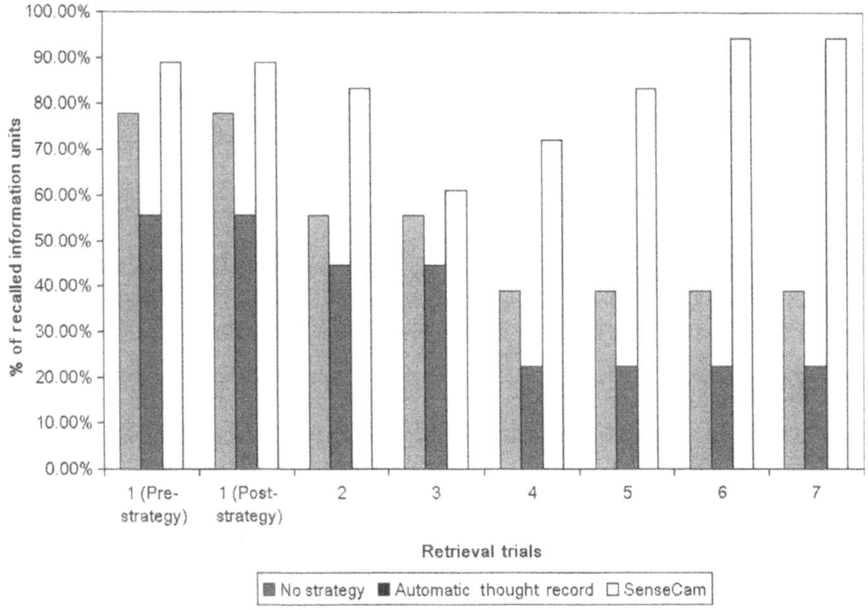

Figure 1. Mean percentage of information units recalled over a 4-week period.

Emotional arousal during recollection. Table 3 shows the mean heart rate in BPM over the course of the events, together with the mean BPM for each condition across all trials. The control condition shows a tendency for anxious arousal during recall to reduce over time following the event. Conversely, thought records and SenseCam conditions show BPM as elevated in the initial trial, decreasing again by trial 7.

In order to examine this dataset further, a non-parametric test of variance between the experimental and control conditions was adopted. The Kruskal-Wallis test was used, where the resulting chi-squared statistic was found to be not significant, $\chi^2(3) = 4.555$, $p = .207$. This therefore suggests no significant differences between the test conditions based on heart rate information, despite a trend towards the predicted pattern.

Symptoms of anxiety and depression. As noted previously, Allan's anxiety and depression scores placed him in the clinical range at initial assessment, with his self-esteem significantly below the norm. When reassessed during the experiment, all measures had increased, but

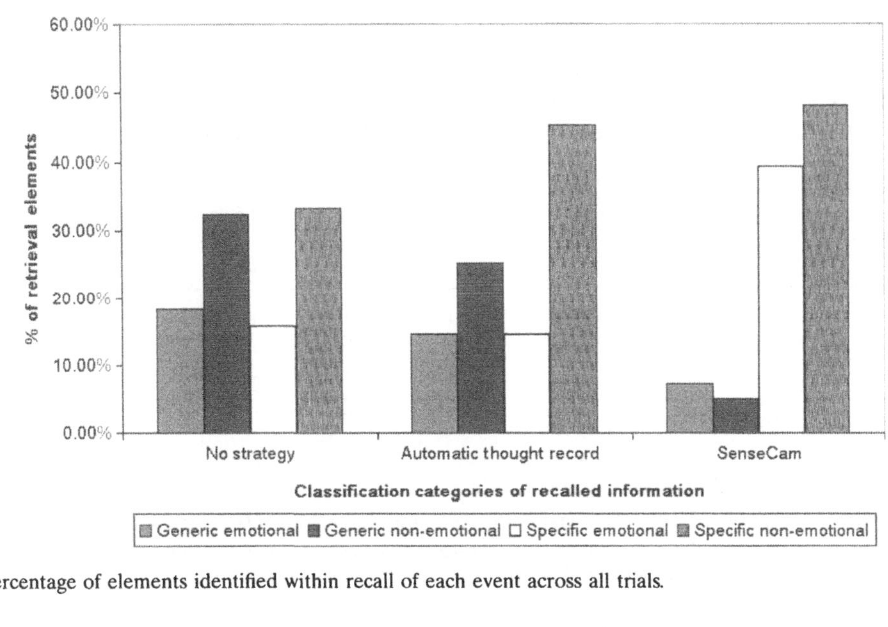

Figure 2. Percentage of elements identified within recall of each event across all trials.

TABLE 3
Comparison of mean heart rate (BPM: beats per minute) during a baseline session, each event, and during trial 1 and trial 7 recall of each event and condition

	Within event	*Trial 1*	*Trial 7*	*Average BPM across trials*
Baseline	73[1]	*89.25	*73.429	*81.239
Control	90.498	79.706	73.833	76.356
Thought record	71.395	77.640	71.438	75.336
SenseCam	74.553	82.396	75.529	75.901

[1]Baseline taken over an hour period during psychoeducation session with client.
*Baseline HR taken over 10–15-minute period immediately preceding testing sessions.

ratings returned to close to initial assessment levels after the experiment. This is summarised in Table 4.

Client reflections

Allan was asked to report on his experiences of using these strategies after each trial and more substantively at the end of testing, in order to examine the potential usefulness of these strategies and his motivation to use such strategies in CBT. Allan felt that both SenseCam and ATR strategies were useful additions to support his memory difficulties, but had very different qualities to bring to such work. He reported that thought records initially allowed him greater access to the experience of anxiety (e.g., thoughts and emotions) from during the event, but lacked the necessary context for these experiences and as time went on this connection with the experience became weaker, resulting in difficulty retrieving event details or personal experiences. Conversely, Allan argued that the SenseCam strategy allowed him to structure his memory, where he was able to associate actions and segments with particular events to place them in the correct order. Initially, watching the SenseCam movie did not support Allan to reflect on his experiences, but Allan felt as time went on he was able to recall detail not contained within the images and make connections to the felt experience of the event. Allan felt that both SenseCam and ATR strategies were complimentary to each other and that both might be useful within any further therapeutic work. Regarding Allan's emotional symptoms, he reflected that the experiment highlighted the potential for him to be able to improve his memory functioning, which he experienced as improving his sense of hope for the future.

DISCUSSION

This case study illustrates a number of potential benefits for the use of a wearable automatic camera with an individual experiencing memory difficulties resulting from an ABI. After seven trials of reviewing SenseCam images, Allan was able to recall approximately 94% of a personally salient anxiety-provoking event, compared with 39% and 22% for control and thought record conditions respectively. SenseCam-supported retrieval also resulted in specific emotional memory content,

TABLE 4
Assessment of symptoms of depression and anxiety prior to and following experiment

Questionnaire	*Initial assessment (prior to study)*	*Assessment 2 (prior to study)*	*Assessment 3 (following study)*
BAI	16	20	15
BDI-II	23	27	24
MIA avoid al	4.00	4.58	4.27
MIA avoid ac	2.37	2.40	1.96
MIA panic freq	3	3	3
MIA panic int	3	2	3
Robson SCQ	90	149	126

BAI = Beck Anxiety Inventory; BDI-II = Beck Depression Inventory 2nd edition; MIA = Mobility Inventory for Agoraphobia ratings of 0–5 for each subscale: avoid al = avoidance alone subscale; avoid ac = avoidance accompanied; panic freq = frequency of panic attacks; panic int = intensity of panic attacks (0 = low or minimal, 5 = maximum); Robson SCQ = Self Concept Questionnaire.

with internal states such as thoughts, emotions, physical sensations, and behaviours being identified. Conversely, the content of memories retrieved within ATR and no-strategy conditions were more general and made proportionally less reference to these internal states. This was supported by Allan's reflections, where he felt that SenseCam images initially allowed access to structuring the event, and then over time allowed greater access to the thoughts and feelings associated with the event. Allan also felt the reverse was true of the ATR strategy condition. The results are therefore clearly supportive of possible SenseCam use in CBT for this individual with memory impairment and an anxiety disorder. Theoretically, some support has been found for the hypothesis that SenseCam supported retrieval acts by building up an emotionally richer implicational representation of the event, as opposed to the more factual propositional representation. However, no significant differences were found between the strategy conditions in regards to heart rate information.

Although no specific prediction was made that ATR-supported retrieval would be superior to no-strategy, intuitively one would expect such an effect. However, this was not observed in this study. A number of explanations for this can be provided. First, while the favourable effect of SenseCam appears very strong, the less-clear difference in recall between ATR and no-strategy may be attributable to natural variability in recall across these two events. It is clear that the no-strategy condition event was recalled more effectively and to a similar level of detail as the SenseCam condition event when first assessed, by comparison to the ATR event, where baseline recall was already poor. Second, Allan noted ATRs to be helpful initially in supporting recall of internal state information. Attention to affective aspects of the memory may have interfered with encoding and consolidation of factual information that may serve to support structuring and therefore later recall of information. Third, if Allan had a tendency to suppress or avoid negative affect where possible, then a memory strategy highlighting negative emotional interpretations may be less effective than no-strategy, reducing recall to below what would be expected normally over time. This means that the interpretation of results regarding the relative efficacy of SenseCam versus no strategy can be made more robustly than interpretation of results relating to use of ATRs, which may still be a useful adjunct to CBT following ABI despite this study's results.

This study, while suggestive of efficacy of a strong effect for SenseCam-supported retrieval, is not without its limitations. Generalisation of conclusions about efficacy of SenseCam-supported retrieval in other cases of anxiety disorder in the context of memory impairment is not possible from this single case. The selection of the three examined events by Allan and his family, together with allocating a single event per experimental condition, raises issues around the comparability and generalisation of such events. However, these events were identified as areas of difficulty for Allan and as such would be appropriate foci for cognitive behavioural interventions with this individual. Also, the identified strategies were examined over a relatively short period of 4 weeks and so the long-term benefits or costs of these strategies were not ascertained.

Heart rate measurements across all conditions showed a similar pattern of response, irrespective of the order in which they were examined in each trial. Cognitive-behavioural models of anxiety disorders have suggested that presentation of threat stimuli results in physiological changes associated with arousal (e.g., increased heart rate) within specific-anxiety based disorders (Clark, 1999; Lewis & Drewett, 2005). A meta-review by Chida and Hamer (2008) suggested that anxiety and negative affect were associated with decreased reactivity to triggers and increased recovery of heart rate. However, studies involving participants with clinical diagnoses of anxiety disorders were excluded from the analysis, as the authors argued the medication associated with such disorders might dampen physiological response. Allan was prescribed antidepressants and epilepsy medication at the time of testing and such medication may have impacted on heart rate reactivity. Also, images were reviewed on an image-by-image basis and so this graded re-exposure to the recorded event may not have fully activated physiological responses. The loss of detail provided by averaging HR over event retrieval may have hidden specific physiological responses to individual pictures, and so more subtle analysis may be required in future studies.

Furthermore, it is difficult to draw any firm conclusions regarding the trend for reduction in heart rate response during the seven trials across the three conditions. One might expect an initial increase then decrease in affective response through exposure to the memory of the emotional trigger events, consistent with the behavioural model of anxiety. However, the trend for this to occur across trials regardless of amount of detail retrieved suggests that reduced affective response could also have occurred through either an implicit route to habituation (consistent with the fear conditioning model of LeDoux, 1995), or simply due to loss of detailed explicit memory of the event. Allan reported low confidence in his memory, as one would expect, so a further confound might be that for Allan, the retrieval trials themselves may have been emotional trigger events. Further investigation of arousal related to retrieval of emotional trigger events within the context of therapeutic interventions is needed in order to fully explore whether arousal information can provide any additional value or context to such approaches. Future studies of this type testing hypotheses about the mechanisms of exposure and habituation in the context of acquired memory impairment must address this problematic confounding of variables.

Overall, this study suggests that SenseCam-supported retrieval enabled an individual to develop an ability to recall event-specific elements with reference to internal states. Thought-record-supported retrieval and no-strategy zconditions elicited a significantly lower level of specific detail and emotional or internal state content. Within the ICS model, the increased references to internal states could be an indicator of development of implicational representation of the event, whereas the general non-emotional content would correspond to propositional elements. Given the notion that within CBT interventions should target the implicational level meaning (e.g., Bennett-Levy, 2003), this single-case study tentatively suggests that SenseCam-supported retrieval, by working to support development of implicational-level representations of events, may be of use in CBT to facilitate change in the context of memory impairment, and possibly also in non-impaired groups. While this study appears broadly supportive of an account of the process by which SenseCam may support retrieval in terms of the ICS model, further work is required to demonstrate that implicational and propositional representations can be reliably distinguished using the method of content analysis of generic versus specific and emotional versus non-emotional content.

The self memory system model (SMS: Conway, 2005) can also be considered to account for the differences in retrieved memories between conditions in this study. Conway suggests that autobiographical memory can be accessed at a number of levels within the conceptual self and episodic memory. The conceptual self contains multiple levels, moving from abstract ideas and values to those more closely related to specific events. At the most abstract level is the life story, where factual and evaluative information regarding an individual's life experience is held. This information is then separated into themes, and then split further into specific lifetime periods. The final level contains cumulative (and non-specific) information of repeated and/or categorical events, in categories of general events. In contrast, the episodic memory system is a single level sitting below the general event level. It contains a pool of specific memories, with each record representing the summation of the sensory, perceptual, conceptual, and affective aspects of a specific event. The organisation of episodic memory is governed by the goals and values held in the conceptual self. Episodic memory can therefore be seen as providing the building blocks of the conceptual self and autobiographical memory. The event-specific details and reference to internal states and felt experience in the SenseCam-supported condition would be consistent with retrieval of episodic memory as described by Conway, and would provide the basis for recalling or reflecting on material related to the conceptual self. However, in the other conditions, failure to recall specific event information at best provides a basis for development or maintenance of general themes, which might serve to maintain current conceptual-self representations, as they do not contain the detail to provide the basis on which the client could reflect on or update the conceptual self. Within therapy, access to memories with emotionally and/or personally salient content is required in order to engage with the change process. Again, however, these tentative hypotheses rest on the assumption that lack of detail in recall would lead to maintenance of generic level representations as described in Conway's model. Therefore, while the study is supportive of the clinical efficacy of SenseCam supported retrieval and added benefit of retrieving specific and emotional content, theoretical accounts of the underpinning processes are yet to be rigorously tested. We see this as an important next step in the systematic evaluation of potential mnemonic supports for CBT.

Conclusion

In this single-case experiment, SenseCam has been shown to be a useful memory aid in retrieving and consolidating both the felt experience and structure of an emotional trigger event compared with a more traditional diary technique and no strategy. Given methodological weaknesses to the current study, the apparent poor efficacy of ATRs should not be interpreted as lack of evidence for its use in CBT following ABI. Theoretical accounts of the findings have been tentatively suggested. Furthermore, these theoretical accounts provide the basis for further hypotheses regarding the more general use of SenseCam in supporting retrieval of emotional trigger events, and in potentially facilitating change by targeting processes thought to underpin the efficacy of so-called "third generation" CBT techniques such as mindfulness-based CBT, and the use of imagery. However, further investigation is needed to test more rigorously hypotheses about the processes by which SenseCam works and might influence change in self-related representations, and its potential role within therapeutic interventions.

REFERENCES

American Psychiatric Association. (2000). *Diagnostic and statistical manual of mental disorders* (4th ed.). Washington, DC: American Psychiatric Association.

Beck, A. T., Epstein, N., Brown, G., & Steer, R. A. (1988a). An inventory for measuring clinical anxiety: Psychometric properties. *Journal of Consulting and Clinical Psychology*, *56*(6), 893–897.

Beck, A. T., Steer, R. A., & Brown, G. K. (1996). *Manual for the Beck Depression Inventory-II*. San Antonio, TX: Psychological Corporation.

Beck, A. T., Steer, R. A., & Carbin, M. G. (1988b). Psychometric properties of the Beck Depression Inventory: Twenty-five years of evaluation. *Clinical Psychology Review*, *8*(1), 77–100.

Bennett, T. L., & Raymond, M. J. (1997). Emotional consequences and psychotherapy for individuals with mild brain injury. *Applied Neuropsychology*, *4*(1), 55–61.

Bennett-Levy, J. (2003). Mechanisms of change in cognitive therapy: The case of automatic thought records and behavioural experiments. *Behavioural and Cognitive Psychotherapy*, *31*, 261–277.

Berry, E., Kapur, N., Williams, L., Hodges, S., Watson, P., Smyth, G., et al. (2007). The use of a wearable camera, SenseCam, as a pictorial diary to improve autobiographical memory in a patient with limbic encephalitis: A preliminary report. *Neuropsychological Rehabilitation*, *17*(4/5), 582–601.

Bradbury, C. L., Christensen, B. K., Lau, M. A., Ruttan, L. A., Arundis, A. L., & Green, R. E. (2008). The efficacy of cognitive behavior therapy in the treatment of emotional distress after acquired brain injury. *Archives of Physical Medicine and Rehabilitation*, *89*(Suppl. 2), S61–S69.

Brage, S., Brage, N., Franks, P. W., Ekelund, U., & Wareham, N. J. (2005). Reliability and validity of the combined heart rate and movement sensor Acti-Heart. *European Journal of Clinical Nutrition*, *59*, 561–570.

Brown, S., Pinnington, L., & Ward, C. (2005). *Memory aids and techniques*. London: Medicines & Healthcare Products Regulatory Agency.

Chambless, D. L., Caputo, G. C., Jasin, S. E., Gracely, E. J., & Williams, C. (1985). The Mobility Inventory for Agoraphobia. *Behaviour Research & Therapy*, *23*(1), 35–44.

Chida, Y., & Hamer, M. (2008). Chronic psychosocial factors and acute physiological responses to laboratory-induced stress in healthy populations: A quantitative review of 30 years of investigations. *Psychological Bulletin*, *134*(6), 829–885.

Clark, D. M. (1999). Anxiety disorders: Why they persist and how to treat them. *Behaviour Research and Therapy*, *37*, S5–S27.

Coetzer, J. (2008). Holistic neuro-rehabilitation in the community: Is identity a key issue? *Neuropsychological Rehabilitation*, *18*(5), 766–783.

Conway, M. A. (2005). Memory and the self. *Journal of Memory and Language*, *53*(4), 594–628.

Conway, M. A., & Haque, S. (1999). Overshadowing the reminiscence bump: Memories of a struggle for independence. *Journal of Adult Development*, *6*(1), 35–44.

Epstein, R. S., & Ursano, R. J. (1994). Anxiety disorders. In J. M. Silver, S. C. Yudofsky, & R. E. Hales (Eds.), *Neuropsychiatry of traumatic brain injury*. Washington, DC: American Psychiatric Press.

Evans, J. J., Wilson, B. A., Needham, P., & Brentall, S. (2003). Who makes good use of memory aids? Results of a survey of people with acquired brain injury. *Journal of the International Neuropsychological Society*, *9*(6), 925–935.

Gracey, F., Evans, J. J., & Malley, D. (2009). Capturing process and outcome in complex rehabilitation interventions: A "Y-shaped" model. *Neuropsychological Rehabilitation*, *19*(6), 867–890.

Gracey, F., Palmer, S., Rous, B., Psaila, K., Shaw, K., O'Dell, J., et al. (2008). "Feeling part of things": Personal construction of self after brain injury. *Neuropsychological Rehabilitation*, *18*(5/6), 627–650.

Hibbard, M. R., Grober, S. E., Gordon, W. A., & Aletta, E. G. (1990). Modification of cognitive psychotherapy for the treatment of post-stroke depression. *Behaviour Therapist*, *13*(1), 15–17.

Judd, D., & Wilson, S. L. (2005). Psychotherapy with brain injury survivors: An investigation of the challenges encountered by clinicians and their modifications to therapeutic practice. *Brain Injury*, *19*(6), 437–449.

Kovarsky, D., Shaw, A., & Adingono-Smith, M. (2007). The construction of identity during group therapy among adults with traumatic brain injury. *Communication and Medicine*, *4*(1), 53–66.

LeDoux, J. E. (1995). Emotion: clues from the brain. *Annual Review of Psychology*, *46*, 209–235.

Lewis, L. E., & Drewett, R. F. (2005). Psychophysiological correlates of anxiety: A single-case study. *Journal of Anxiety Disorders*, *20*(6), 829–835.

Malec, J. (2005). The Mayo-Portland Adaptability Inventory. *The Center for Outcome Measurement in Brain Injury*. Retrieved from http://www.tbims.org/combi/mpai (accessed 30 March 2009).

Massimi, M., Berry, E., Browne, G., Smyth, G., Watson, P., & Baecker, R. M. (2008). An exploratory case study of the impact of ambient biographical displays on identity in a patient with Alzheimer's disease. *Neuropsychological Rehabilitation*, *18*(5), 742–765.

McGrath, J., & King, N. (2004). Acquired brain injury. In J. Bennett-Levy, G. Butler, M. Fennell, A. Hackman, M. Mueller, & D. Westbrook (Eds.), *Oxford guide to behavioural experiments in cognitive therapy*. Oxford, UK: Oxford University Press.

Nochi, M. (1998). "Loss of self" in the narratives of people with traumatic brain injuries: A qualitative analysis. *Social Science and Medicine*, *46*(7), 869–878.

Ownsworth, T. L., Turpin, M., Andrew, B., & Fleming, J. (2008). Participant perspectives on an individualised self-awareness intervention following stroke: A qualitative case study. *Neuropsychological Rehabilitation*, *18*(5), 692–712.

Riley, G. A., Brennan, A. J., & Powell, T. (2004). Threat appraisal and avoidance after traumatic brain injury: Why and how often are activities avoided? *Brain Injury*, *18*(9), 871–888.

Robson, P. (1989). Development of a new self-report questionnaire to measure self-esteem. *Psychological Medicine*, *19*(2), 513–518.

Soo, C., & Tate, R. (2007). Psychological treatment for anxiety in people with traumatic brain injury. *Cochrane Database of Systematic Reviews, 2007*(3), CD005239. doi: 10.1002/14651858.CD005239.pub2.

Story, T. J., & Craske, M. G. (2008). Responses to false physiological feedback in individuals with panic attacks and elevated anxiety sensitivity. *Behaviour Research and Therapy*, *46*, 1001–1008.

Teasdale, J., & Barnard, P. (1993). *Affect, cognition and change*. Hove, UK: Lawrence Erlbaum Associates Ltd.

Teasdale, T. W., & Engberg, A. W. (2001). Suicide after traumatic brain injury: A population study. *Journal of Neurology, Neurosurgery and Psychiatry*, *71*, 436–440.

Tiersky, L. A., Anselmi, V., Johnston, M. V., Kurtyka, J., Roosen, E., Schwartz, T., et al. (2005). A trial of neuropsychologic rehabilitation in mild-spectrum traumatic brain injury. *Archives of Physical Medicine and Rehabilitation*, *86*(8), 1565–1574.

Whitehouse, A. M. (1994). Applications of cognitive therapy with survivors of head injury. *Journal of Cognitive Psychotherapy: An International Quarterly*, *8*, 141–160.

Wilhelm, F. H., & Roth, W. T. (2001). The somatic symptom paradox in DSM-IV anxiety disorders: Suggestions for a clinical focus in psychophysiology. *Biological Psychology*, *57*, 105–140.

Williams, J. M. G. (1996). Depression and the specificity of autobiographical memory. In D. C. Rubin (Ed.), *Remembering our past: Studies in autobiographical memory* (pp. 244–267). Cambridge, UK: Cambridge University Press.

Williams, W. H., & Evans, J. J. (2003). Brain injury and emotion: An overview to a special issue on biopsychosocial approaches in neurorehabilitation. *Neuropsychological Rehabilitation*, *13*(1), 1–11.

Williams, W. H., Evans, J. J., & Fleminger, S. (2003). Neurorehabilitation and cognitive-behaviour therapy of anxiety disorders after brain injury: An overview and a case illustration of obsessive-compulsive disorder. *Neuropsychological Rehabilitation*, *13*(1), 133–148.

Williams, W. H., Evans, J. J., & Wilson, B. A. (2003). Neuro-rehabilitation for two cases of post-traumatic stress disorder following traumatic brain injury. *Cognitive Neuropsychiatry*, *8*(1), 1–18.

Williams, W. H., Williams, J. M. G., & Ghadiali, E. J. (1998). Autobiographical memory in traumatic brain injury: Neuropsychological and mood predictors of recall. *Neuropsychological Rehabilitation*, *8*(1), 43–60.

Wilson, B. A., Gracey, F., Evans, J. J., & Bateman, A. (2009). *Neuropsychological rehabilitation: Theory, models, therapy and outcome*. Cambridge, UK: Cambridge University Press.

Ylvisaker, M., & Feeney, T. (2000). Reconstruction of identity after brain injury. *Brain Impairment*, *1*(1), 12–28.

Psychology Press
Taylor & Francis Group

Exploring the basis and boundary conditions of SenseCam-facilitated recollection

Philip J. Barnard[1], Fionnuala C. Murphy[1], Maria Teresa Carthery-Goulart[1], Cristina Ramponi[1], and Linda Clare[2]

[1]MRC Cognition and Brain Sciences Unit, Cambridge, UK
[2]School of Psychology, Bangor University, Bangor, Gwynedd, UK

SenseCam review has been shown to promote and sustain subsequent access to memories that might otherwise remain inaccessible. While SenseCam review facilitates recollection for personally experienced events, we know little about the boundary conditions under which this operates and about how underlying processing mechanisms can be optimally recruited to offset memory impairments of the sort that occur in dementia. This paper considers some of these issues with a view to targeting future research that not only clarifies our evolving body of theory about how memory works, but also informs about how memory-assistive technologies for patients might be employed to maximal effect. We begin by outlining key factors that are known to influence recollection. We then examine variability in the decline of memory function both in normal ageing and in dementia. Attention is drawn to similarities in the recollection deficits associated with depression and dementia, and we suggest that this may reflect shared underlying mechanisms. We conclude by discussing how one particular theoretical rationale can be intersected with key SenseCam capabilities to define priorities for ongoing and future SenseCam research.

Keywords: SenseCam; Recollection; Dementia; Depression.

Healthy individuals who have had the opportunity to use SenseCam typically report similar intuitions when viewing a replay of a personally experienced event. As a sequence of discrete visual images sampled from the original event follow one another at a moderately rapid rate, memories of that event come flooding back. What is particularly striking about these memories is that they are not restricted to the actual content of these images. What comes to mind includes many hallmark elements of autonoetic consciousness and recollection of the episode (Tulving, 1983): thoughts, feelings, and impressions experienced at the time of encoding as well as other information not present in the replay, such as conversations that occurred at the time. Photograph albums or home videos can, of course, give rise to similar experiences but SenseCam-facilitated recollection seems to bring with it qualitative differences that include, among other things, reflecting on aspects of self-experience in new ways (Harper et al., 2007). Unlike video recordings, *the full event* is not re-experienced in real time, and unlike the often deliberately staged, framed, or otherwise contrived and *momentary* snapshots of photograph albums, SenseCam imagery captures sequential and relational aspects of how the real event unfolds in time from a first person or "field" perspective.

Address correspondence to: Philip J. Barnard, MRC Cognition and Brain Sciences Unit, 15 Chaucer Road, Cambridge, CB2 7EF, UK. E-mail: philip.barnard@mrc-cbu.cam.ac.uk
This research was funded by Microsoft Research Cambridge and the UK Medical Research Council under project code U.1055.02.003.00001.03 (Philip Barnard).

© 2011 Psychology Press, an imprint of the Taylor & Francis Group, an Informa business
http://www.psypress.com/memory http://dx.doi.org/10.1080/09658211.2010.533180

This informal testimony is now supported by behavioural and neuroscientific evidence. SenseCam review can facilitate recollection in normal healthy individuals (Sellen et al., 2007) and in patients with significant or mild memory impairments, with secondary benefits for confidence and well-being (Berry et al., 2007; Browne et al., 2011). An fMRI study of a patient with limbic encephalitis showed that successful recognition following SenseCam rehearsal, compared to unrehearsed and control conditions, activated cortical regions known to be involved in normal episodic memory (Berry et al., 2009). Healthy students also show increased activity in key brain regions supporting memory when viewing SenseCam traces (St. Jacques, Conway, Lowder, & Cabeza, 2011). Such evidence invites two relatively straightforward conclusions. First, SenseCam review promotes and sustains subsequent access to memories that might otherwise remain inaccessible. Second, at least some memory deficits may be partially counteracted by the informationally rich cues that life-logging devices such as SenseCam offer to support recollection (Lee & Dey, 2008).

While SenseCam review facilitates recollection for personally experienced events, we know little about the boundary conditions under which this operates and about how the underlying processing mechanisms can be optimally recruited to offset memory impairments of the sort that occur in dementia. Does SenseCam review promote recollection for only some types of material, such as special events, like trips out? Or does it also promote recollection for more ordinary events, like washing-up or shopping? An obvious attribute of SenseCam is that the pictures are taken automatically and without intention, enabling the wearer to document much more routine or ordinary activities than would typically be the case when still photography or video is used more selectively to capture perhaps rather more noteworthy material. We know little about how and when the content of SenseCam images promotes access to otherwise inaccessible material. Whether the kinds of mental activity that occur during the original experience and at the point of remembering contribute to the effectiveness of SenseCam review also remains unclear. There is also an acute lack of evidence directly comparing SenseCam to other memory-assistive technologies. This paper considers some of these issues with a view to targeting future research that not only clarifies our evolving body of theory about how memory works, but also informs how memory-assistive technologies for patients might be employed to maximal effect. Our strategy is straightforward. We first identify key factors from the literature that are known to influence recollection. Second, we examine variability in the decline of memory function in normal ageing and dementia. By drawing attention to similarities in the recollection deficits associated with depression and dementia, we then propose that these similarities could possibly reflect shared theoretical underpinnings. Finally, we discuss how these ideas might shape novel SenseCam interventions and assessments of their efficacy.

INFLUENCES ON RECOLLECTION

The literature on human recollection is extensive. It encompasses research conducted using tightly controlled but largely non-personally significant material such as pictures, words, and narratives (Baddeley, 1990) through to considerations of how autobiographical memory works on a lifelong scale (Conway, 1990; Conway & Pleydell-Pearce, 2000). This literature emphasises a number of core themes. Since the seminal work of Bartlett (1932) it has been recognised that memory for complex events is reconstructive rather than literal, depending on wider schemata for knowledge relevant to the topic in focus, as well as the detail of the experienced event. What happens at the time of the experienced event is equally important. Greater elaboration of meaning at the time of encoding leads to heightened recall of presented information (Craik & Lockhart, 1972). The cues used to frame access to information represented in memory are also important (Long, Prat, Johns, Morris, & Jonathan, 2008). In their classic study, Pichert and Anderson (1977) asked participants to recall a visit to an apartment, first from the perspective of someone wanting to buy the house and then from the perspective of a burglar. The body of material recollected from the second perspective differed with new information, not previously reported, being accessed.

Both generic and specific attributes of the experienced event and how these relate to the individual constitute other core themes. On a lifetime scale, recollection is not equally distributed. Reminiscence bumps of enhanced recollection have been reported for "public events" between the ages of 10 and 19 years and for more private events between 20 and 29 years (Conway & Holmes, 2004). Events coupled to emotional experience, whether extreme or mild, are typically better recollected than those not associated with affect (Anderson, Wais, & Gabrieli, 2006; Ochsner, 2000). For example, mildly emotional pictures, words, and narratives are better recollected than well-matched neutral ones (for a review, see Kensinger, 2009b). Recollections of events associated with extreme emotional experiences can be subject to distortions, such as in life-threatening situations that lead to post-traumatic stress disorder (Sotgiu & Mormont, 2008) and in scenes where emotionally arousing features are better recollected than peripheral details, termed the *weapon focus effect* (see Pickel, 2007).

Specific emotional attributes of stimuli modulate recollection. For example, whether a stimulus invokes a specific emotion (e.g., fear or disgust) or has positive or negative valence (Talarico, Bernsten, & Rubin, 2009) or is more or less arousing (Ochsner, 2000) can have powerful effects on recollection. Imageability is also a highly relevant attribute. Conway and Pleydell-Pearce (2000) noted that autobiographical recollection is often accompanied by visual or other forms of imagery. This is consistent with the finding that cue words of higher imageability give rise to greater specificity in autobiographical recollection (Williams, Healy, & Ellis, 1999). Much research has also emphasised the role of distinctiveness and related concepts (familiarity, incongruence, surprise) in modulating recollection (Hunt & Worthen, 2006; Schmidt, 2006). A key problem in unravelling the contribution of specific stimulus attributes to recollection is that the different attributes tend to intercorrelate. This has been shown in a large sample of pictures rated on 14 attributes, in which rated memorability correlated significantly with every other examined variable except valence (Libkuman, Otani, Kern, Viger, & Novak, 2007). An individual reviewing the recollection literature would thus find evidence to support many specific influences on recollection but little in the way of deeper theoretical consensus about underlying mechanisms.

Very similar considerations are relevant to the properties of individuals and tasks. It is well known that depressed individuals show characteristic memory impairments, and their recall patterns for positive and negative material exhibit systematic biases (Lloyd & Lishman, 1975). Recollection of a specific autobiographical episode in response to a cue is also compromised in depressed individuals, relative to normal healthy controls (Williams et al., 2007). Here evidence is accumulating that the mood state is not in itself causal, but rather that impaired recollection arises out of some intricate combination of properties of the underlying schemata relating to the self, world, and others, and how mental resources are deployed to process them in real time (Dalgleish et al., 2007; Ramponi, Barnard, & Nimmo-Smith, 2004; Williams et al., 2007). Likewise, in the context of recollecting everyday experiences in normal healthy individuals, generic properties of self-related schemata, other than valence, may play a key role in promoting access to memory. For example, Eldridge, Barnard, and Bekerian (1994) reported that people with more differentiated schemata for the activities that they undertake in their work report more information about what they were doing at work 1 week earlier than do those whose schemata are less differentiated. More widely, with complex materials like narratives, people recall the overall gist while disregarding minor detail (Kintsch & van Dijk, 1978); they also recall information relevant to the task at the focus of attention while omitting to report less-central detail (Frase, 1969; Gerrig & O'Brien, 2005). It is clear that recollection helps resolve specific "cognitive" tasks or problems, but it also serves wider communicative and social functions by allowing individuals to share experiences and explicitly or implicitly inform others about "who" they are (Conway, 2003; Horton & Gerrig, 2005; Nelson, 2003; Wilson & Ross, 2003; Woike, 2008).

As with the wider literature on recollection and autobiographical memory, the effects on memory of normal ageing and dementia are subject to a similar pattern of multiple determination. A substantial literature on memory functioning in normal ageing addresses such issues (Hess, 2005), and it is frequently emphasised that there is considerable variability in the pattern of decline (Luo & Craik, 2008). Some aspects of recollective capability are also better preserved than others. Of particular relevance are those that concern effort, context, and the offsetting role of specific attributes such as emotional content, categorical organisation, and the use of imagery. In a meta-analysis of 46 studies, Spencer and Raz (1995) concluded that age differences were reliably greater in memory for context than for content, but tasks requiring greater retrieval effort gave rise to larger age differences in memory for content relative to context. May, Rahhal, Berry, and Leighton (2005) showed that younger adults outperformed older adults in the recall of contextual information. However, when participants recalled emotional information concerning the context, age differences disappeared, suggesting that emotional information could well differentially engage older individuals (for a recent review see Kensinger, 2009a). In evaluating possible influences on recollection at encoding, Salthouse (1980) noted that older adults use imagery strategies less often and less effectively than younger adults (see also Dirkx & Craik, 1992). There is also evidence that cognitive support in the form of categorical organisation can offset age-related decline in recollective capability (Bunce, 2003).

Variable rates of decline are equally characteristic of patients with dementia. A recent study tracked 686 Alzheimer's disease (AD) patients on multiple measures over 2 years and reported that 12% of the cohort exhibited a very rapid decline, 25% exhibited relatively stable performance, and the remainder showed moderate but significant evolution of the disease (Cortes et al., 2008). It is generally agreed that there are discrepancies between neuropathology and clinical manifestation. Katzman and colleagues (1988) described patients with extensive AD pathology but little manifestation of the disease, arguing that these patients may have had greater "reserve" capacity to mitigate the underlying pathology of dementia (Boyle, Wilson, Schneider, Bienias, & Bennett, 2008). Ideas linked to both reserve properties of neural hardware and more "software-like" cognitive reserve have been discussed extensively, particularly in relation to a role for intelligence, education, and occupational attainment in offsetting decline. While the idea of generic "reserve" is easy to grasp, the evidence relating this to variability in rates of decline is unlikely to be fully accommodated without further differentiation of the neural and cognitive capabilities implicated in recollection. Indeed, studies of neuropsychological rehabilitation in dementia tend to support a multifaceted and holistic approach that includes targeted use of external memory aids (Clare, 2007).

MECHANISMS COMMON TO DEPRESSION AND DEMENTIA AND THEIR THEORETICAL UNDERPINNINGS

If memory-assistive technologies are to prove effective, we will unquestionably need a deeper understanding of the origins of the variable decline of recollective functions in dementia. Diagnostic challenges remain and emotional variables are frequently neglected in memory clinics. Dementia, mild cognitive impairment (MCI), and depression all involve memory impairments. Furthermore, depression is often reported to be comorbid with dementia and the links may run deeper (Saczynski et al., 2010). MCI is often thought to be a precursor to AD, but it progresses to AD in only some cases. Modrego and Ferrández (2004) conducted a prospective study of 114 patients with amnestic MCI over a 3-year period. Depression was observed in 36% of all the patients at baseline, and 59% of all the patients recruited subsequently went on to exhibit AD. Of those who were depressed at baseline, 85% went on to develop AD, compared to only 32% of the non-depressed patients. A more recent study has established depression as a *risk factor* for dementia, on the basis of a monotonic increase in risk for dementia and AD as a function of the number of episodes of depressive symptoms (Dotson, Beydoun, & Zonderman, 2010). These, and more recent findings concerning this relationship, are consistent with the hypothesis that mechanisms underlying depression, AD, and compromised recollective capabilities may have something in common.

It is possible that the memory deficits common to MCI, AD, and depression, together with evidence that links comorbid MCI and depression to the subsequent development of AD (Modrego & Ferrández, 2004), reflect common biological determinants. However, an alternative possibility is that the patterns of cognitive processing that determine poor recollection in depression may also occur in MCI, accelerating decline into AD irrespective of any underlying physical pathology. We refer to the interacting cognitive subsystems (ICS, Barnard & Teasdale, 1991; ICS, Teasdale & Barnard, 1993) architecture to explain impoverished recollection in depression and how similar mechanisms may help to explain rapid decline from MCI to AD.

The ICS architecture postulates two meaning systems. One type of meaning, propositional meaning, represents referentially specific content that lacks emotional charge (e.g., concepts, properties, and relationships); it is the kind of meaning that we think of as being expressed in sentences. The other, schematic meaning, is more holistic and can optionally carry emotional charge; it represents the deeper regularities of our experience as "schematic models" of the self, world, and others. The schematic level of representation is directly influenced by visual, auditory, and bodily inputs (hence the link to emotion), and these are combined with the products of processing propositional content. In contrast, propositional material captures just those subsets of referentially specific meanings activated to control verbal thoughts and vocal articulation, spatial imagery, and spatial-praxic interactions with the physical world. Propositional meanings are inherently narrower and more focused than schematic ones.

Each level of meaning has its own stored representations and human ideation is seen as an ongoing dialogue between the two levels: schematic representations are used to derive specific propositions, and the products of propositional elaboration feed back and update current schematic representations. This same internal dialogue, when augmented by access to stored representations, functions to support reconstructive retrieval. In this approach, retrieval and report of specific facts require activation of schematic models and the construction of specific propositions, not only to express the material recovered, but also to "validate" the content that is expressed as a recollection. This core account of memory and the data it accounts for is treated at some length in Teasdale and Barnard (1993) and Barnard (1999). The following paragraphs explore in more detail the arguments and evidence for a potential link between attributes of depressive thinking and rapid decline in those otherwise prone to dementia.

Depressive thoughts and feelings about the self, the world, and others are predominantly negative (Beck, 1979). These thoughts are characterised by over-simple generalisations and repetitive verbal rumination around restricted themes. We have argued elsewhere (Teasdale & Barnard, 1993) that depressed states are maintained by a toxic combination of three influences. First, individuals vulnerable to depression have over-simple and undifferentiated schematic models of the self, others, and the world that are associated with a characteristic pattern of "black-and-white" thinking. Second, attention in the mind is predominantly focused on the narrower content of propositional meanings and verbal thoughts with a corresponding neglect of attention to the broader content of schematic models and visuo-spatial imagery. Third, depressive thinking is guided by significant discrepancies and incongruities that are irresolvable in the context of currently activated self-models.

Given that an individual's schematic models capture regularities in experience and ultimately support adaptive responding, discrepancies between input and those schemas signal the need for further mental processing. In a wider evolutionary context, such discrepancies are highly significant as they implicitly index material that may require modification or the development and elaboration of new, more adaptive schemata (Barnard, Duke, Byrne, & Davidson, 2007). Elaborative processing of new information at or around the time of encounter or, for example, at the time of SenseCam review, could well be more focused on distinctive or incongruent features that lead to schema-discrepant states than on features that more readily fit existing models. Similarly, emotional charge associated with particular experiences can be understood as a marker to guide discrepancy reduction in the adaptive selection of actions towards appetitive ends and away from aversive ones (Oatley & Johnson-laird, 1987). These may be particularly salient in the context of SenseCam-facilitated recollection where incongruous or emotional images may act as triggers. To take an example, while looking through a set of images taken 8 months previously, a patient with memory impairment, Mrs W, had no recollection of the event until one particular image "jumped out" at her. The image was one of her dog jumping on a visitor. At this point, Mrs. W remarked "now I remember" and relayed the entire event to the researcher (Browne et al., 2011).

Recollection requires activation, reconstruction, elaboration, and evaluation of specific propositions about a target event in successive cycles of dialogue between the two levels of meaning, and verbal or visual imagery derived from those propositions. Depressive deficits in recollection are accounted for, partly because of low levels of differentiation in schematic model content which act to restrict access to the full range of information preserved in memory, and partly because attention in the mind is directed at propositional representations and their verbal realisations. There is evidence of a causal link between both low differentiation in schematic model content and a ruminative response style and compromised specificity of both autobiographical recollection and recollection of laboratory presentations of word lists (Barnard, Watkins, & Ramponi, 2006; Eldridge et al., 1994; Ramponi et al., 2004). This theoretical analysis suggests a number of ways in which more differentiated thinking should, in principle, bring about more differentiated thought patterns. It has been argued that increasing the attention paid to schematic model content allows *richer connections* to be made among domains of pre-existing knowledge of the self, others, and the world (Barnard, 2004; Teasdale & Barnard, 1993; Teasdale et al., 1999). This in turn facilitates the generation of more varied propositional content, greater elaborative processing, and more differentiated and richer cues, all of which should support access to information preserved in the memory substrates associated with both levels of meaning.

This theoretical reasoning provides a plausible basis for the observed links between depression and the rate of decline in AD. But in particular we suggest that this theoretical reasoning can provide a foundation from which future SenseCam research priorities and testable predictions can be drawn. While we await advances in drug interventions that will counteract the advance of neuropathology, much may be done to optimise the use of degrading neural capability. The conjectures derived from the ICS approach, though based on similarities between memory difficulties in depression and MCI and on evidence linking comorbid MCI and depression to the subsequent development of AD (Dotson et al., 2010; Modrego & Ferrández, 2004), give rise to testable predictions. Those patients who decline rapidly are predicted to be those with less-differentiated schematic models of the self, the world, and others and those who ruminate along negative lines of thought or who otherwise focus their thoughts around narrow themes less obviously coupled to negative ideation. Patients with these characteristics should be less likely to generate rich representations at the time of encoding or rich cues at a later point that promote reliable access to what is preserved in memory. While this reasoning maps onto the concepts of brain and cognitive reserve in dementia (Stern, 2009), it is more specific about the nature and inter-functioning of cognitive capabilities. This hypothesis has clearer implications for how SenseCam or similar technologies might best be deployed.

SenseCam differs from other forms of event recording such as videos or photos, as SenseCam imagery can usefully be thought of as providing a temporally scaled model of an event. Indeed, SenseCam can capture an 8-hour event structure in 960 images, many of which are effectively redundant. Although attempts to define the temporal extent of a "psychological moment" have remained controversial (Block, 1990), for the purposes of argument were we to assume that information is mentally "integrated" in 100-ms chunks, then a SenseCam trace of an event (with images captured every 30 s) would represent a 1/300 scale model of just the visual component of a far richer and multi-modal experience. It would be a temporal analogue of a hobbyist showing off a physical model of an Airbus A320 with a wingspan of just 5 inches.

Regularities underlying propositional and schematic representations act to support pattern completion in much the same way as occurs in visual and auditory perception (Kellman & Shipley, 1991; Warren, 1970; Warren, Wrightson & Puretz, 1988). Reconstructive retrieval involves a dialogue between the two proposed levels of meaning that involves pattern completion and testing whether any routine or event-specific content that emerges "feels right" in the context of either an explicit retrieval demand or an implicit product of current processing activity. Importantly, schematic meanings arise out of a blend of the products of information derived directly from sensation and those derived from propositional processing. The kind of temporally scaled visual input provided in SenseCam review would, in theory, massively augment the more selective, focused, and abstract cues for memory access derived from propositional meanings or more static pictures. Our current working hypothesis is that SenseCam review offers a very direct and rapid means of activating deeper schematic models related to the target event. This in turn provides the grounding from which specific retrieval cues can be elaborated to facilitate recollection.

We have so far examined a range of influences on recollection, the variation in rate of decline in ageing and dementia, and observed links between MCI, AD, and depression. For simplicity, this examination has been highly selective and has neglected to address definitional issues concerning different forms of memory. It nonetheless supports several key observations. First, while review of SenseCam traces of personally experienced events may well facilitate recollection, there are unlikely to be simple "univariate" answers to questions about the boundary conditions under which this process works. Recollection instead arises out of an intricate interaction between specific properties of not only the actual event experienced (e.g., distinctiveness) and mental processing activity at the time of encoding (e.g., elaborative processing), but also mental processing at the point of access (e.g., reconstructive effort). Second, this is true for healthy individuals, and even more so for patients with pathology of the brain regions that support human memory, in whom variable rates of decline have been reported. Third, observed links between depression and dementia suggest that priorities for patient research can be informed by intersecting theory-derived hypotheses with the novel features that SenseCam review enables us to exploit. When it comes to the potential benefits of using SenseCam or similar devices with such patients, isolation of the active ingredients that promote recollection and intersecting them with classes of memory deficits is a unique challenge.

INTERSECTING PRIOR EVIDENCE WITH PROPERTIES OF SENSECAM CAPTURE AND REVIEW

Faced with a progressive condition, a key aim of SenseCam research should be to maximise the potential use of available neural and cognitive capabilities. While SenseCam may facilitate recollection in all memory-impaired patients, our view is that benefits may be greatest for the 75% of patients who are vulnerable to more rapid rates of decline in cognitive function. If those prone to rapid decline do so because their mental functioning shares properties with depressed ideation, where there is a strong evidence base for the efficacy of cognitive interventions, then cognitive interventions with the "right" properties should also work to slow decline in dementia. While current evidence suggests that SenseCam review can lead to long-lasting effects for some events, the next research priority should be to establish whether SenseCam review can promote differentiation of skills in accessing memory that will then generalise to assist recollection in daily life. We will conclude here by giving an example of an application of the theoretical position outlined above to an intervention protocol that we are currently evaluating in a series of case studies with patients in the early stages of AD.

It was noted earlier that a restricted focus of attention to a narrow range of propositional meanings can be counteracted by drawing greater attention to schematic model content. This creates conditions where *richer connections* can be made within and among domains of pre-existing knowledge concerning the self, others, and the world. This in turn should lead to the generation of more varied propositional content, greater elaborative processing and more differentiated and richer cues to support access to information preserved in the memory substrates associated with both levels of meaning. Given the objective of developing generalisable cognitive skills, the focus was not on the review of "whole days" of experience, but rather on the review of patient-specific "montages" created by editing together a representative sample of traces of different activities undertaken in the course of daily life. The montage included the environments, tasks, contexts, and people they interact with in their social world. SenseCam traces of these activities are best seen not as a *solution* to the access problem but as a *vehicle* for enriching the generation of conceptual cues to facilitate access.

Five specific principles, justified on the basis of the research described above, guide the research protocol. First, schematic models of activities or states are open to hierarchical decomposition via description. Descriptions of activities can be more or less *elaborated* either in terms of the number of levels of decomposition or the number of elements decomposed at a level. Second, the elements of a schematic model are open to re-composition in which *new elements can be added* enabling alternative "paths" not currently captured in a particular description of an activity. Third, schematic models are composed of *multimodally derived sources of information*. When engaged in an activity, that activity will have an essence (e.g., a sequence of actions) but also projections into visual, auditory, bodily, verbal, and conceptual dimensions. If we think about the basic "schema" as abstracting just the essence of a routine event, then multimodal aspects may be more or less under-represented with the consequence that such information may not be readily available to cue memory access. Fourth, *conceptual links or associations* can bridge one idea to another in a variety of different ways. Many such associations are "latent" within conceptual networks and only a fraction of such associations are likely to be relevant in a particular context. Making these associations explicit has the potential to enrich the cues available for memory access. Fifth, *conceptual links can be processed in a range of different ways* – in most circumstances we can, for example highlight the similarities between two things or their differences. Awareness of alternative attributes of conceptual links relates to the role of perspective in memory access described earlier, and may facilitate elaboration of cues for the retrieval of schematic content.

A strategy for hierarchical decomposition capitalises on a key feature of SenseCam imagery: the ability to systematically vary rates of presentation. Exploratory work in our laboratory found that movies for specific days and more highly differentiated montages can be presented at up to 12 frames per second (fps). At this rate, the content of some frames masks information in preceding frames. Nonetheless, with appropriate editing, both our impressions and those of the patients we have recruited are that this enables the essence of the event to be grasped. The fleeting nature of an image sequence containing approximately 24 different basic activities, each lasting 4 seconds, naturally restricts elaborative processing of detail. Theoretically, however, this should function to activate or prime a wide range of schematic content in close temporal proximity, thereby rendering their respective contents more accessible in the immediate term. When the same montage is slowed to 6 fps (8 s per activity), less material is masked and more specific details of the decomposition of the montage become explicit. We introduce each intervention session by showing the patient his or her own montage at 12 fps, immediately followed by a 6-fps exposure, to prime the full range of schematic models encapsulated in the montage. The therapist or carer then presents only one or two of the 24 basic activities and the sequence can be paused to allow discussion of the detailed content of the activity. In this final phase, the patient is guided and encouraged to use concrete strategies based on decomposition and recomposition of schematic content; multimodal imagery; associations to bridge from one content area to another to render implicit links explicit; and cognitive tactics to explore similarities, differences, and use of alternative perspectives.

SUMMARY AND CONCLUSION

The ideas presented in this paper must, of course, be read and assessed for what they are: theoretically derived conjectures based on prior evidence concerning recollection in normal ageing, dementia, and depression. Evidence from divergent sources indicates that there are unlikely to be simple answers to deep theoretical questions about the underlying mechanisms of impaired recollection. Instead, variability in the decline of memory function is likely to arise from multiple factors. In particular, attention was drawn to similarities in the recollection deficits associated with depression and dementia, suggesting the possibility of shared underlying mechanisms. It is our view that future SenseCam research must pay careful attention to emotional and cognitive processes that are common to these disorders. Schemata or schematic representations were considered not only to be a key determinant of recollection but also to form a direct bridge to a key property of SenseCam imagery—the possibility for simulating a complete event schema in temporally compressed, but nonetheless contextualised form. This paper outlines a number of specific principles or strategies that may be usefully applied to enrich the generation of conceptual cues that may facilitate mnemonic access.

At a more practical level, only a firm evidence base for the efficacy of SenseCam-based interventions will justify the scale of commitment and effort required of users, carers, and therapists. That evidence base should include well-charted boundary conditions for effectiveness across patient samples and detailed information about SenseCam's "active ingredients". It should also demonstrate effect sizes that are not just "statistically" but also clinically and socially significant. Even for such an inherently engaging technology as SenseCam, these are tough challenges.

REFERENCES

Anderson, A. K., Wais, P. E., & Gabrieli, J. D. E. (2006). Emotion enhances remembrance of neutral events past. *Proceedings of the National Academy of Sciences of the United States of America, 103*(5), 1599–1604.

Baddeley, A. (1990). *Human memory: Theory and practice.* Hove, UK: Lawrence Erlbaum Associates.

Barnard, P. J. (1999). Interacting cognitive subsystems: Modelling working memory phenomena within a multi-processor architecture. In A. Miyake & P. Shah (Eds.), *Models of working memory: Mechanisms of active maintenance and executive control* (pp. 298–339). Cambridge, UK: Cambridge University Press.

Barnard, P. J. (2004). Bridging between basic theory and clinical practice. *Behaviour Research and Therapy, 42*, 977–1000.

Barnard, P. J., Duke, D. J., Byrne, R. W., & Davidson, I. (2007). Differentiation in cognitive and emotional meanings: An evolutionary analysis. *Cognition and Emotion, 21*(6), 1155–1183.

Barnard, P. J., & Teasdale, J. D. (1991). Interacting cognitive subsystems: A systemic approach to cognitive-affective interaction and change. *Cognition & Emotion, 5*, 1–39.

Barnard, P. J., Watkins, E. R., & Ramponi, C. (2006). Reducing specificity of autobiographical memory in nonclinical participants: The role of rumination and schematic models. *Cognition & Emotion, 20*, 328–350.

Bartlett, F. C. (1932). *Rembering: A study in experimental and social psychology.* Cambridge, UK: Cambridge University Press.

Beck, A. T. (1979). *Cognitive therapy of depression.* New York: Guilford Press.

Berry, E., Hampshire, A., Rowe, J., Hodges, S., Kapur, N., Watson, P., et al. (2009). The neural basis of effective memory therapy in a patient with limbic encephalitis. *Journal of Neurology Neurosurgery and Psychiatry, 80*(11), 1202–1205.

Berry, E., Kapur, N., Williams, L., Hodges, S., Watson, P., Smyth, G., et al. (2007). The use of a wearable camera, SenseCam, as a pictorial diary to improve autobiographical memory in a patient with limbic encephalitis: A preliminary report. *Neuropsychological Rehabilitation, 17*(4–5), 582–601.

Block, R. A. (1990). Models of psychological time. In R. A. Block (Ed.), *Cognitive models of psychological time.* Hove, UK: Lawrence Erlbaum Associates.

Boyle, P. A., Wilson, R. S., Schneider, J. A., Bienias, J. L., & Bennett, D. A. (2008). Processing resources reduce the effect of Alzheimer pathology on other cognitive systems. *Neurology, 70*(17), 1534–1542.

Browne, G., Berry, E., Kapur, N., Hodges, S., Smyth, G., Watson, P., & Wood, K. (2011). SenseCam improves memory for recent events and quality of life in a patient with memory retrieval difficulties. *Memory, 19*(7), 713–722.

Bunce, D. (2003). Cognitive support at encoding attenuates age differences in recollective experience among adults of lower frontal lobe function. *Neuropsychology, 17*(3), 353–361.

Clare, L. (2007). *Neuropsychological rehabilitation and people with dementia.* Hove, UK: Psychology Press.

Conway, M. A. (1990). *Autobiographical memory: An introduction.* Milton Keynes, UK: Open University Press.

Conway, M. A. (2003). Cognitive-affective mechanisms and processes in autobiographical memory. *Memory, 11*(2), 217–224.

Conway, M. A., & Holmes, A. (2004). Psychosocial stages and the accessibility of autobiographical memories across the life cycle. *Journal of Personality, 72*(3), 461–480.

Conway, M. A., & Pleydell-Pearce, C. W. (2000). The construction of autobiographical memories in the self-memory system. *Psychological Review, 107*(2), 261–288.

Cortes, F., Nourhashémi, F., Guérin, O., Cantet, C., Gillette-Guyonnet, S., Andrieu, S., et al. (2008). Prognosis of Alzheimer's disease today: A two-year prospective study in 686 patients from the REAL-FR Study. *Alzheimer's and Dementia, 4*(1), 22–29.

Craik, F. I. M., & Lockhart, R. S. (1972). Levels of processing: A framework for memory research. *Journal of Verbal Learning and Verbal Behavior, 11*(6), 671–684.

Dalgleish, T., Williams, J. M., Golden, A. M., Perkins, N., Barrett, L. F., Barnard, P. J., et al. (2007). Reduced specificity of autobiographical memory and depression: The role of executive control. *Journal of Experimental Psychology: General, 136*(1), 23–42.

Dirkx, E., & Craik, F. I. M. (1992). Age-related differences in memory as a function of imagery processing. *Psychology and Aging, 7*(3), 352–358.

Dotson, V. M., Beydoun, M. A., & Zonderman, A. B. (2010). Recurrent depressive symptoms and the incidence of dementia and mild cognitive impairment. *Neurology, 75*, 27–34.

Eldridge, M. A., Barnard, P. J., & Bekerian, D. A. (1994). Autobiographical memory and daily schemas at work. *Memory, 2*(1), 51–74.

Frase, L. T. (1969). Structural analysis of the knowledge that results from thinking about text. *Journal of Educational Psychology, 60*, 1–16.

Gerrig, R. J., & O'Brien, E. J. (2005). The scope of memory-based processing. *Discourse Processes, 39*(2–3), 225–242.

Harper, R., Randall, D., Smyth, N., Evans, C., Heledd, L., & Moore, R. (2007). Thanks for the memory. *Proceedings of the British HCI 2007*, September 3–7, 2007, Lancaster, UK.

Hess, T. M. (2005). Memory and aging in context. *Psychological Bulletin, 131*(3), 383–406.

Horton, W. S., & Gerrig, R. J. (2005). Conversational common ground and memory processes in language production. *Discourse Processes, 40*(1), 1–35.

Hunt, R. R., & Worthen, J. B. (2006). *Distinctiveness and memory.* Oxford, UK: Oxford University Press.

Katzman, R., Terry, R., DeTeresa, R., Brown, T., Davies, P., Fuld, P., et al. (1988). Clinical, pathological, and neurochemical changes in dementia: A subgroup with preserved mental status and numerous neocortical plaques. *Annals of Neurology, 23*(2), 138–144.

Kellman, P. J., & Shipley, T. F. (1991). A theory of visual interpolation in object perception. *Cognitive Psychology, 23*, 141–221.

Kensinger, E. A. (2009a). How emotion affects older adults' memories for event details. *Memory, 17*(2), 208–219.

Kensinger, E. A. (2009b). Remembering the details: Effects of emotion. *Emotion Review, 1*(2), 99–113.

Kintsch, W., & van Dijk, T. A. (1978). Toward a model of text comprehension and production. *Psychological Review*, *85*(5), 363–394.

Lee, M. L., & Dey, A. K. (2008). Lifelogging memory appliance for people with episodic memory impairment. *UbiComp*, *344*, 44–53.

Libkuman, T. M., Otani, H., Kern, R., Viger, S. G., & Novak, N. (2007). Multidimensional normative ratings for the International Affective Picture System. *Behavior Research Methods*, *39*(2), 326–334.

Lloyd, G. G., & Lishman, W. A. (1975). Effect of depression on the speed of recall of pleasant and unpleasant experiences. *Psychological Medicine*, *5*, 173–180.

Long, D. L., Prat, C., Johns, C., Morris, P., & Jonathan, E. (2008). The importance of knowledge in vivid text memory: An individual-differences investigation of recollection and familiarity. *Psychonomic Bulletin and Review*, *15*(3), 604–609.

Luo, L., & Craik, F. I. M. (2008). Aging and memory: A cognitive approach. *Canadian Journal of Psychiatry*, *53*(6), 346–353.

May, C. P., Rahhal, T., Berry, E. M., & Leighton, E. A. (2005). Aging, source memory, and emotion. *Psychology and Aging*, *20*(4), 571–578.

Modrego, P. J., & Ferrández, M. D. (2004). Depression in patients with mild cognitive impairment increases the risk of developing dementia of Alzheimer type: A prospective cohort study. *Archives of Neurology*, *61*, 1290–1293.

Nelson, K. (2003). Self and social functions: Individual autobiographical memory and collective narrative. *Memory*, *11*(2), 125–136.

Oatley, K., & Johnson-laird, P. N. (1987). Towards a cognitive theory of emotions. *Cognition & Emotion*, *1*(1), 29–50.

Ochsner, K. N. (2000). Are affective events richly recollected or simply familiar? The experience and process of recognizing feelings past. *Journal of Experimental Psychology: General*, *129*(2), 242–261.

Pichert, J. W., & Anderson, R. C. (1977). Taking different perspectives on a story. *Journal of Educational Psychology*, *69*, 309–315.

Pickel, K. L. (2007). Memory and eyewitness memory. In S. F. Davis & W. Buskist (Eds.), *21st century psychology: A reference handbook* (Vol. 1, pp. 441–449). Thousand Oaks, CA: Sage Publications.

Ramponi, C., Barnard, P. J., & Nimmo-Smith, I. (2004). Recollection deficits in dysphoric mood: An effect of schematic models and executive mode? *Memory*, *12*(5), 655–670.

Saczynski, J. S., Beiser, A., Seshadri, S., Auerbach, S., Wolf, P. A., & Au, R. (2010). Depressive symptoms and risk of dementia: The Framingham Heart Study. *Neurology*, *75*, 35–41.

Salthouse, T. A. (1980). Age and memory: Strategies for localizing the loss. In L. W. Poon, J. L. Fozard, L. Cermak, D. Arenberg, & L. W. Thompson (Eds.), *New directions in memory and aging* (pp. 47–65). Hillsdale, NJ: Lawrence Erlbaum Associates.

Schmidt, S. R. (2006). Emotion, significance, distinctiveness and memory. In R. R. Hunt & J. B. Worthen (Eds.), *Distinctiveness and memory*. Oxford, UK: Oxford University Press.

Sellen, A., Fogg, A., Aitken, M., Hodges, S., Rother, C., & Wood, K. (2007). Do life-logging technologies support memory for the past? An experimental study using SenseCam. *Conference on Human Factors in Computing Systems – Proceedings* (pp. 81–90). Microsoft Research Ltd.

Sotgiu, I., & Mormont, C. (2008). Similarities and differences between traumatic and emotional memories: Review and directions for future research. *The Journal of Psychology*, *142*(5), 449–469.

Spencer, W. D., & Raz, N. (1995). Differential effects of aging on memory for content and context: A meta-analysis. *Psychology and Aging*, *10*(4), 527–539.

St. Jacques, P. L., Conway, M. A., Lowder, M., & Cabeza, R. (2011). Watching my mind unfold versus yours: An fMRI study using a novel camera technology to examine neural differences in self-projection of self versus other perspectives. *Journal of Cognitive Neuroscience*, *23*(6), 1275–1284.

Stern, Y. (2009). Cognitive reserve. *Neuropsychologia*, *47*, 2015–2028.

Talarico, J. M., Bernsten, D., & Rubin, D. C. (2009). Positive emotions enhance recall of peripheral details. *Cognition & Emotion*, *23*(2), 380–398.

Teasdale, J. D., & Barnard, P. J. (1993). *Affect, cognition, and change: Remodelling depressive thought*. Hillsdale, NJ: Lawrence Erlbaum Associates.

Teasdale, J. D., Howard, R. J., Cox, S. G., Ha, Y., Brammer, M. J., Williams, S. C., et al. (1999). Functional MRI study of the cognitive generation of affect. *American Journal of Psychiatry*, *156*(2), 209–215.

Tulving, E. (1983). *Elements of episodic memory*. Oxford, UK: Clarendon Press.

Warren, R. M. (1970). Perceptual restoration of missing speech sounds. *Science*, *167*, 392–393.

Warren, R. M., Wrightson, J. M., & Puretz, J. (1988). Illusory continuity of tonal and infratonal periodic sounds. *Journal of the Acoustical Society of America*, *84*(4), 1338–1342.

Williams, J. M. G., Barnhofer, T., Crane, C., Herman, D., Raes, F., Watkins, E., et al. (2007). Autobiographical memory specificity and emotional disorder. *Psychological Bulletin*, *133*(1), 122–148.

Williams, J. M. G., Healy, H. G., & Ellis, N. C. (1999). The effect of imageability and predictability of cues in autobiographical memory. *The Quarterly Journal of Experimental Psychology*, *52A*(3), 555–579.

Wilson, A. E., & Ross, M. (2003). The identity function of autobiographical memory: Time is on our side. *Memory*, *11*(2), 137–149.

Woike, B. A. (2008). A functional framework for the influence of implicit and explicit motives on autobiographical memory. *Personality and Social Psychology Review*, *12*(2), 99–117.

MEMORY, 2011, 19 (7), 768–777

Psychology Press
Taylor & Francis Group

SenseCam, imagery and bias in memory for wellbeing

Fionnuala C. Murphy[1], Philip J. Barnard[1], Kayleigh A. M. Terry[2], Maria Teresa Carthery-Goulart[1], and Emily A. Holmes[2]

[1]MRC Cognition and Brain Sciences Unit, Cambridge, UK
[2]Department of Psychiatry, University of Oxford, Oxford, UK

Identifying and modifying the negative interpretation bias that characterises depression is central to successful treatment. While accumulating evidence indicates that mental imagery is particularly effective in the modification of emotional bias, this research typically incorporates static and unrelated ambiguous stimuli. SenseCam technology, and the resulting video-like footage, offers an opportunity to produce training stimuli that are dynamic and self-relevant. Here participants experienced several ambiguous tasks and subsequently viewed SenseCam footage of the same tasks, paired with negative or positive captions. Participants were trained to use mental imagery to inter-relate SenseCam footage and captions. Participants reported increased levels of happy mood, reduced levels of sad mood, and increased task enjoyment following SenseCam review with positive versus negative captions. This shift in emotional bias was also evident at 24-hour follow-up, as participants recollected greater task enjoyment for those tasks previously paired with positive captions. Mental imagery appears to play an important role in this process. These preliminary results indicate that in healthy volunteers, SenseCam can be used within a bias modification paradigm to shift mood and memory for wellbeing associated with performing everyday activities. Further refinements are necessary before similar methods can be applied to individuals suffering from subclinical and clinical depression.

Keywords: SenseCam; Cognitive bias modification; Emotion; Mental imagery.

Cognitive biases play a central role in the development and maintenance of depressed mood (Beck, 1979; Teasdale, 1988). Individuals suffering from depression tend to interpret information they encounter in their everyday physical and social worlds in a negative way. Targeting and modifying these maladaptive interpretations is central to successful treatments, such as cognitive therapy. Bias modification can reduce the propensity for a person's thoughts and negative interpretations of events to result in new depressive episodes or to relapse from recovered states (Segal, Williams, & Teasdale, 2002). More recently this idea has been developed in a variety of computerised "cognitive bias modification" (CBM) paradigms (MacLeod, Koster, & Fox, 2009).

Empirical research on computerised CBM has identified a range of strategies that offer the potential to modify or eliminate cognitive biases. Strategies that involve mental imagery have been a particular focus of research attention. For example, CBM training studies have shown that when healthy volunteers listen to auditory descriptions of emotional events, they report greater changes in self-reported mood when instructed to

Address correspondence to: Fionnuala C. Murphy, MRC Cognition and Brain Sciences Unit, 15 Chaucer Road, Cambridge, CB2 7EF, UK. E-mail: fionnuala.murphy@mrc-cbu.cam.ac.uk

This research was funded by Microsoft Research Cambridge, a Wellcome Trust Clinical Fellowship awarded to Emily A. Holmes (088217), and the UK Medical Research Council under project code A060_0022 (Philip Barnard). We would like to thank Leah Campbell for help with designing the tasks.

© 2011 Psychology Press, an imprint of the Taylor & Francis Group, an Informa business
http://www.psypress.com/memory
http://dx.doi.org/10.1080/09658211.2010.551130

form mental images than when instructed to verbally process the same events. This effect has been demonstrated for both negative (Holmes & Mathews, 2005) and positive (Holmes, Mathews, Dalgleish, & Mackintosh, 2006) resolutions of ambiguous verbal stimuli, and recent work has extended these findings to ambiguous pictorial stimuli (Holmes, Mathews, Mackintosh, & Dalgleish, 2008). Taken together, the results indicate that positive and negative emotional responses are significantly enhanced following training that relies specifically on mental imagery processes rather than verbal representations of ambiguous stimuli.

These findings have major implications for mood change and modification of cognitive bias in the context of psychological therapies. Indeed, research has already begun to explore the limits of positive and negative mental imagery in non-clinical samples, with an emphasis on depressed and anxious self-reported mood (Holmes, Lang, Moulds, & Steele, 2008; Stöber, 2000). Both studies reported a specific association between dysphoric mood and a reduced ability to vividly imagine positive but not negative future events. However, a potential limitation of the ambiguous training stimuli typically used in such CBM studies is that the verbal and pictorial stimuli are not only static and unrelated to one another, but also low in personal "relevance". Appraisal theorists have attempted to identify various criteria upon which the antecedent conditions of different emotional experiences and reactions are appraised, and a number of these emphasise the significance or relevance of an event to the individual (Scherer, 1999). A strong case can be made for using ambiguous training stimuli that exhibit higher levels of self-relevance and that are rich in dynamic visual content. Encouraging depressed individuals to use imagery-based processes to resolve these ambiguous stimuli in a positive way could facilitate engagement of attention and trigger recall of more positive autobiographical memories. This is because imagery is believed to be extremely important for the recall of specific episodes from autobiographical memory (Conway, 1990), as is evident in the term "sensory-perceptual episodic memory" (Conway, 2001). There is also evidence for overlapping mechanisms for remembering episodes from the past and imagining them in the future (D'Argembeau & Van Der Linden, 2006). Learning to use imagery-based processes to resolve ambiguous stimuli could thus have considerable training potential for the modification of maladaptive self-schemas and cognitive biases.

SenseCam is one of a class of devices that offers the opportunity to capture experiences with more dynamic, integrated, and realistic material that is self-relevant. SenseCam is an unobtrusive wearable camera that automatically captures sequences of images of activities and events undertaken by the wearer (Hodges et al., 2006). The wearer can subsequently review a SenseCam "movie" on his or her personal computer. Review of these SenseCam images has already been shown to improve autobiographical recollection in patients with severe memory impairment following limbic encephalitis (Berry et al., 2007) and also with mild cognitive impairment (Browne et al., 2011). In this latter study, SenseCam review was also found to have secondary benefits on the individual's confidence and quality of life. Given that depressed mood states and clinical depression are associated with difficulties in accessing specific autobiographical information (Moore, Watts, & Williams, 1988; Williams et al., 2007; Williams & Scott, 1988) and with reduced quality of life, guided SenseCam review could offer clinically useful application. In line with previous CBM studies, dynamic and integrated image sequences of personally experienced events could be paired with negative or positive captions in an effort to experimentally shift negative interpretations to more positive ones—were such shifts to be of useful magnitude, this approach could provide a platform for developing new interventions.

Here we report preliminary findings from a study that used SenseCam recordings of a range of simple structured tasks in a community sample. All performed these tasks, and then viewed the corresponding SenseCam footage with added captions to bias interpretation. Given evidence that mental imagery is important in the modification of individuals' interpretation bias, our participants were trained to produce a mental image to inter-relate SenseCam footage with positive and negatively valenced captions. The primary aim of the study was thus to assess the magnitude of any immediate and delayed effects on reported well-being of associating experienced events with positive and negative meanings. The secondary aim was to explore the extent to which any effects were dependent on participants' pre-existing mood and/or tendency to use mental imagery.

METHOD

Participants

A total of 13 women and 7 men participated for a small fee; 18 of the participants were students. The sample had a mean age of 19.8 years ($SD = 1.8$). The specific mood and individual difference measures used are described below. The Positive and Negative Affect Schedule (PANAS) (Watson, Clark, & Tellegen, 1988) and Stress-reactive Rumination Scale (SRRS-hopelessness) (Alloy et al., 2000) were also administered but are not reported here in the interests of brevity.

Materials

Beck Depression Inventory–second edition (BDI-II). Self-reported depression was measured using the 21-item BDI-II, known to have strong internal consistency (Beck, Steer, & Brown, 1996). Participants rated depression-related symptoms during the past 2 weeks on a scale with endpoints *0* to *3*. The mean self-reported depression score in our sample was 10.8 ($SD = 9.0$).

State Trait Anxiety Inventory–Trait (STAI-T). Trait anxiety was measured using the 20-item STAI-T (Spielberger, Gorsuch, Lushene, Vagg, & Jacobs, 1983). Each item was rated on a 4-point scale (*almost never* to *always*). Our sample had a mean trait anxiety score of 42.6 ($SD = 12.4$).

Spontaneous Use of Imagery Scale (SUIS). Tendency to use mental imagery was measured with the SUIS (Reisberg, Pearson, & Kosslyn, 2003). This questionnaire contains 12 items, for example, "When I think about a series of errands I must do, I visualise the stores I will visit". Each item is rated on a scale from 1 (*never*) to 5 (*always*). The mean score in our sample was 39.0 ($SD = 8.8$).

Tasks

All participants completed 12 "ambiguous" tasks. These included activities such as writing a shopping list, making a collage or greeting card from materials provided by the experimenter, finding a route on a map, spotting the differences between two almost identical pictures, selecting outfits from a clothing catalogue, and folding a pile of crumpled laundry. The 12 activities were selected on the basis that they were relevant beyond the laboratory setting, yet sufficiently ambiguous that participants' judgements of how enjoyable they were could potentially change following exposure to pairings of negative versus positive captions with SenseCam footage of someone else completing these tasks.

SenseCam and SenseCam Image Viewer

SenseCam is a small digital camera that takes photographs automatically without user intervention. It has a wide-angle fish-eye lens that maximises its field-of-view. There is also special SenseCam image viewing software that relies on rapid serial visual presentation to display images on a PC at the user's chosen speed up to approximately 10 images per second. Details of the operation of the most recent version of SenseCam hardware and software are reported in Hodges et al. (2006).

Although participants actually completed the tasks individually. In order to control for sequence content and allow prepared captioned versions to be in place, a standard SenseCam record was created for each task. SenseCam was worn by one of the researchers to capture image sequences for the 12 ambiguous tasks described above. During the task review phase participants viewed these standard sequences on a PC monitor using the SenseCam Image Viewer. Each task sequence included presentation of 113 photographic frames on average, presented at a rate of 1 frame per second. The footage for each task was simultaneously paired with presentation of a series of six consecutive negative or positive captions that were presented in the lower left corner of the SenseCam Image Viewer (see example below).

Procedure

On arrival participants completed the BDI-II, STAI-T, and SUIS. All participants then spent 3.5 minutes completing each of the 12 ambiguous tasks described above (performance phase). The order in which tasks were completed was randomly determined for each participant. Immediately following completion of each task participants completed 100-mm visual analogue scales, with end points "not at all" to "extremely", according to how they were feeling (sad, happy) and how enjoyable they had found the task. Completion of all 12 tasks was followed by a filler task that required participants to rate a number of classical music sound files.

Participants then received extensive mental imagery training (training phase). First, they completed a practice task in which they were asked to imagine cutting a lemon. This task has been used routinely in our studies to clarify what is meant by mental imagery and to provide a context for the intentional generation of a mental image (Holmes et al., 2006). Participants were also given a practice image that included presentation of a picture (e.g., a crowd) that was accompanied by a negative or positive caption (e.g., "get out of my way!" or "celebration time!"); participants were asked to close their eyes and form a mental image, in any sensory modality, of the caption and picture combined. An important distinction has been drawn between a "field" perspective, in which one imagines the situation from one's own perspective as though actively involved, and a "bystander" or "observer" perspective, in which one imagines the situation from a detached perspective as though looking at oneself from the outside (McIsaac & Eich, 2002). This distinction between field and bystander imagery was explained to participants and the experimenter emphasised that participants try to form mental images from a field, rather than a bystander, perspective (as in Holmes, Coughtrey, & Connor, 2008).

The performance and training phases were followed by the SenseCam review phase in which participants watched the standard SenseCam recordings of the 12 tasks they had themselves carried out in the performance phase described above. The 12 tasks were divided into two sets of 6 tasks each, such that these sets were as similar as possible. For half of the participants, six tasks (Set A) were paired with negative captions, while the remaining six tasks (Set B) were paired with positive captions. For the remaining participants, Set A tasks were paired with positive captions and Set B tasks with negative ones. So for example, while some participants viewed standardised SenseCam footage of the shopping list task paired with the captions "incapable", "disorganised", "inefficient", "overwhelmed", "unprepared", "daunting list" (negative captions), others viewed that same footage paired with the captions "capable", "organised", "efficient", "on top of it", "prepared", "thinking ahead" (positive captions). Participants were instructed to view the SenseCam footage and associated captions while at the same time producing a mental image that incorporated the combination of the footage and caption. It was emphasised that participants should imagine her/himself in the situation, as though present and actively involved. As for the performance phase, participants completed visual analogue scales following SenseCam review of each of the 12 tasks to indicate how they were feeling (sad, happy) and how enjoyable they found each task at that moment. To promote a field imagery focus, following SenseCam review of each task participants also rated the extent to which the mental image they had formed was through their own eyes (field imagery) or from a detached perspective (bystander imagery); this was done on 5-point scales with endpoints 1 (not at all) to 5 (extremely). Participants were given practice with additional SenseCam footage and negative/positive captions before completing the actual SenseCam review phase. Determination of which task set was paired with negative versus positive captions, and the order in which negative or positive captions were presented was done by random assignment.

Participants were contacted by telephone 24 hours later. They were asked to think back to their participation in the experiment and to rate each task for how vividly they could remember it and how enjoyable it had been on 100-point scales with endpoints 1 (not at all vividly/enjoyable) to 100 (extremely vividly/enjoyable). Participants were debriefed and thanked for their participation.

RESULTS

Unless specified otherwise, an alpha level of 0.05 was used for all statistical tests.

Effects of SenseCam captions on mood ratings

Mean mood ratings in the three phases of the study are presented in Table 1. To determine whether self-reported mood differed according to whether SenseCam task review was done with

TABLE 1
Mean (*SD*) mood visual analogue ratings in the three phases of the study: Performance, SenseCam review, and 24-hour follow-up

		SenseCam review		*24-hour follow-up*	
	Performance	*Positive captions*	*Negative captions*	*Positive captions*	*Negative captions*
Sad	25.5 (5.9)	25.2 (5.8)	39.4 (5.8)	–	–
Happy	56.8 (4.4)	54.6 (5.0)	36.8 (3.8)	–	–
Enjoyable	50.8 (2.9)	55.1 (4.6)	28.3 (2.9)	56.8 (3.1)	52.9 (3.3)
Vividly	–	–	–	68.5 (3.3)	69.0 (2.9)
Field imagery	–	3.65 (0.22)	3.54 (0.15)		
Bystander imagery	–	1.92 (0.77)	1.90 (0.55)		

For sad and happy mood, participants were asked to rate how they were feeling in the present moment, immediately following completion of each task in the performance phase, or immediately following SenseCam review of each task in the review phase. Participants were asked to rate how enjoyable they found each task in the same way. At follow-up, participants were asked to rate how enjoyable they had found each task during the performance phase and how vividly they could remember each task. Sad and happy mood, enjoyable ratings, and how vividly remembered were made on scales ranging from 1 (not at all) to 100 (extremely). Field and bystander imagery were rated on a 1 to 5 scale.

negative or positive captions, paired *t*-tests were used to analyse the effects of caption valence on sad mood, happy mood, and task enjoyment ratings. Following SenseCam review with negative, relative to positive, captions, sad mood ratings were significantly higher, $t(19) = 4.10$, $p = .001$, $d = 0.55$, happy mood ratings were significantly lower, $t(19) = 5.12$, $p < .001$, $d = 0.89$, and enjoyment ratings were significantly lower, $t(19) = 6.13$, $p < .001$, $d = 1.57$. These mood change results were in the expected direction in all three cases. However, relative to performance phase mood ratings, it was the negative, and not positive, captions that were producing these mood effects (see Figure 1). Thus, for sad mood, ratings following negative captions were significantly higher than performance phase ratings, $t(19) = 3.93$, $p = .001$, $d = 0.53$, whereas ratings following positive captions and baseline performance did not differ, $t(19) < 1$, *ns*. Similarly, for happy mood, ratings following review with negative captions were significantly lower than performance phase ratings, $t(19) = 7.51$, $p < .001$, $d = 1.08$, whereas ratings following review with positive captions and baseline performance did not differ, $t(19) < 1$, *ns*. Enjoyment mood ratings were also significantly lower following review with negative captions than following baseline performance, $t(19) = 8.67$, $p < .001$, $d = 1.74$, whereas enjoyment ratings following review with positive captions and baseline performance were not significantly different, $t(19) < 1$, *ns*.

To assess the part played by levels of depressed mood the data were re-analysed using a repeated measures analysis of variance (RMANOVA) with BDI-II scores as a covariate. The valence effects reported above remained significant in all three cases: sad mood, $F(1, 18) = 6.25$, $MSE = 126.6$, $p < .05$, $\eta_p^2 = 0.26$; happy mood, $F(1, 18) = 15.33$, $MSE = 123.0$, $p = .001$, $\eta_p^2 = 0.46$; task enjoyment, $F(1,18) = 20.34, MSE = 193.06, p < .001, \eta_p^2 = 0.53$. Similarly, to assess the role of imagery skills during SenseCam review we also analysed the data using RMANOVA with SUIS imagery scores as a covariate. The significant effect of caption valence on sad and happy mood ratings as well as task enjoyment were no longer significant after controlling for the trait measure of imagery, $F(1, 18) < 1$, *ns*, in all three cases. Trait imagery may thus be an important factor in determining the extent to which individuals report mood change following SenseCam review with negative or positive captions. Given that participants' reported changes in mood were no longer significant after controlling for trait imagery, experimenter demand is unlikely to provide a complete account of these effects.

Self-reported imagery following exposure to SenseCam captions

Participants were asked to rate the extent to which they adopted field and bystander forms of imagery following each task during performance and review phases of the study. As previous research has reported associations between different mood states and type of imagery, we sought

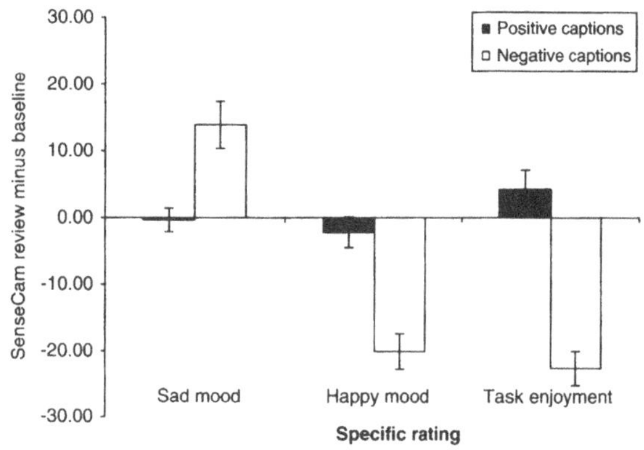

Figure 1. Change in sad mood, happy mood, and task enjoyment ratings following exposure to SenseCam review with positive versus negative captions. Change scores were calculated by subtracting baseline mood and task enjoyment ratings from the same ratings following task review. Thus a positive score indicates an increase in mood ratings from baseline to the review phase, whereas a negative score indicates a decrease in mood ratings. All ratings were made on visual analogue scales ranging from 1 (not at all) to 100 (extremely).

to establish whether field and bystander imagery ratings changed as a function of negative versus positive SenseCam review (Table 1, bottom two rows). Across all participants, field imagery ratings did not differ significantly following SenseCam review with negative versus positive captions, $t(19) < 1$, *ns*. The same was true for bystander imagery ratings, $t(19) < 1$, *ns*.

24-hour follow-up

From a clinical vantage, it is important to consider the extent to which any observed changes in mood or bias persist beyond the immediate experimental context. At 24-hour follow-up, participants were asked to rate the extent to which they enjoyed and how vividly they remembered each of the 12 tasks they had completed the day before. Even at follow-up, enjoyment ratings were significantly higher for tasks that had been paired with positive, relative to negative, captions, $t(19) = 2.1$, $p = .05$, $d = 0.27$ (see Table 1). Thus SenseCam review with both positive and negative captions produced the predicted effects on participants' recall of task enjoyment at 24-hour follow-up. However, the magnitude of this effect was reduced relative to the same effect immediately following SenseCam review, as indicated by the significant interaction term obtained in a 2 (caption: negative, positive) × 2 (phase: SenseCam review, follow-up) RMANOVA, $F(1, 19) = 22.2$, $p < .001$, $\eta_p^2 = .54$ Further, as for the review phase above, the effect of valence was no longer significant after controlling for the effect of trait imagery ability measured via the SUIS at baseline $F(1, 18) < 1$, *ns*.

It is noteworthy that, relative to task enjoyment ratings during the initial performance phase of the study prior to caption presentation, follow-up enjoyment ratings for those tasks that had been paired with positive captions were significantly higher, $t(19) = 1.8$, $p < .05$, one-tailed, $d = 0.45$, whereas follow-up enjoyment ratings for those tasks that had been paired with negative captions were not significantly different, $t(19) < 1$, *ns* (see Table 1). Vividness ratings were taken only at follow-up and did not differ for tasks paired with negative versus positive captions, $t(19) < 1$, *ns*. Thus, the increased enjoyment for those tasks paired with positive captions at SenseCam review cannot simply be explained in terms of how vividly participants remembered those same tasks.

Correlations

To further clarify the contributions of individual differences, Pearson correlations were computed between the mood ratings following negative or positive SenseCam review and individual difference measures (BDI-II, STAI-T, SUIS). As would be expected, the general pattern to emerge here was that strong associations were evident between self-reported mood on arrival at the lab and later ratings of sad mood, happy mood, and task enjoyment. For example, scores on the BDI-II correlated positively with sad mood ratings—$r(20) = .66$, $p < .001$, following both negative and positive SenseCam review—and negatively with happy mood ratings; $r(20) = -.59$, $p < .01$, following negative review, and $r(20) = -.60$, $p < .01$, following positive review. This association with BDI was in the same direction but did not achieve significance for enjoyment ratings at 24 hour follow-up; $r(20) = -.41$, $p = .07$. A very similar pattern of associations was found for STAI-T scores.

SUIS trait imagery scores also correlated positively with ratings of happy mood, $r(20) = .48$, $p < .05$, and task enjoyment, $r(20) = .44$, $p = .05$, following SenseCam review with positive captions, and importantly this association between SUIS scores and task enjoyment ratings following positive SenseCam review remained significant at 24-hour follow-up, $r(20) = .48$, $p < .05$. Associations between SUIS scores and mood ratings following negative review, on the other hand, did not approach significance ($p > .24$ in both cases).

Following SenseCam review with positive captions, sad mood also correlated positively with bystander imagery ratings, $r(20) = .50$, $p < .05$, whereas happy mood and task enjoyment correlated positively with field imagery ratings, $r(20) = .81$, $p < .001$ in both cases. Following review with negative captions, no correlations achieved significance (all $ps > .3$).

DISCUSSION

The present study sought to determine first whether SenseCam review with captions expressing positive and negative meanings could be used to bias mood and interpretation of ambiguous tasks performed by healthy volunteers; and second, to assess the contribution of individual differences. The results indicate that SenseCam review with captions does have significant potential to bias participants' mood and enjoyment experience of a set of ambiguous laboratory-based tasks—immediately afterwards *and* 24 hours later. These immediate and delayed effects are not simply related to memory, but are potentiated by an individual's mental imagery ability. The results are also asymmetric with respect to valence. Whereas negative captions gave rise to the larger component of mood effects immediately following SenseCam review, the valence effect on enjoyment at 24-hour follow-up was due to a shift to a generally positive assessment of experience of carrying out our 12 tasks.

With respect to the initial asymmetry evident in mood ratings following SenseCam review, several points must be considered. First, in contrast to clinically depressed samples, healthy participants generally show an overall positivity bias (Mezulis, Abramson, Hyde, & Hankin, 2004; Taylor & Brown, 1988). This is certainly true for the current sample, who reported higher baseline happy and enjoyable ratings than sad ratings in the initial performance phase of the study. Our positive captions could well have been consistent with that bias, leading at best to a modest additional mood shift. Negative captions, on the other hand, which are inherently "inconsistent" with that bias, may have been more noteworthy; this could have led to negative captions having larger effects on sad, happy, and enjoyable ratings. At 24-hour follow-up the demand characteristics of a less-formal assessment via telephone interview, that had greater distance between experience of our 12 tasks, meant that demand characteristics should have played a less-prominent role. Here, when participants were asked to recollect the extent to which they had enjoyed each of the tasks, enjoyment ratings for those tasks that had been paired with positive captions at review were found to be significantly higher than baseline, while those for negative captions were, at this point, no different from baseline and far less negative overall than immediately following SenseCam review. The data from the 24-hour follow-up are consistent with an interpretation that the shift in bias is primarily on the positive rather than negative pole of the valence dimension. It is not entirely clear why the positive captions produced more lasting changes at follow-up, though the results of an experiment by Ganzach and Mazursky (1995) are consistent with this observation. They demonstrated that immediately following information acquisition, when positive and negative information are vivid in memory, participants' judgements tend to be biased in a negative direction, whereas in the delayed stage, judgements become positively biased. Previous work has also shown that relative to negative CBM, positive CBM can be used to successfully manipulate appraisal bias in control participants, with fewer negative intrusions reported one week later (Lang, Moulds, & Holmes, 2009).

A second constraint on the interpretation of results following SenseCam review arises out of the patterning of effects in relation to individual differences. While the mood shift effects remained after covarying out Beck Depression Inventory scores, they were no longer significant when trait imagery scores were covaried out. Our sample size is modest for firm conclusions to follow; however, the results underline the importance of considering not just memory traces but also differences in the mental processing activity that is associated with laying down those traces and their recovery. During SenseCam review, participants were trained and encouraged to produce a mental image that incorporated the SenseCam footage together with the associated negative or positive captions. This aspect of the experimental design was based on previous evidence of a special role for imagery-based processing in the generation of emotional responses to ambiguous stimuli (Holmes & Mathews, 2005). In the present study participants' levels of trait imagery correlated positively with ratings of happy mood and task enjoyment following SenseCam review with positive captions, and importantly this latter association held at 24-hour follow-up. Associations between trait imagery and mood ratings following negative review, on the other hand, did not approach significance. In addition, following SenseCam review with positive (but not negative) captions, sad mood correlated positively with bystander imagery ratings, whereas happy mood and task enjoyment correlated positively with field imagery ratings. Previous investigations have manipulated whether participants use mental imagery or verbal elaboration to produce a combined percept of the verbal or pictorial stimulus and associated caption, whereas such strategies were not manipulated in the current study. Nevertheless, our data indicate that mental imagery processes, rather than mood, may be involved in the extent to which SenseCam review with positive captions influences ratings of task enjoyment. This latter finding reinforces our view that future research should target the relationship between imagery and more enduring effects on the positive pole rather than the larger short-term effect on the negative pole (Holmes, Lang, & Deeprose, 2009).

Overall our preliminary results offer some encouragement for further explorations on the value of integrating SenseCam technology into an emotional bias modification protocol by adding valenced captions. Of course, it could be argued that the current study demonstrates that SenseCam offers "just" another empirical means of inducing mood and that we already have a range of powerful enough mood induction techniques: Velten statements, emotional films, pictures, or music, and autobiographical memories (Coan & Allen, 2007). We would argue that SenseCam technology brings with it important new attributes. The present approach has the advantage not only of providing similar and standardised dynamic stimulus events, but also the content of the images generated are open to self-related, more systematic, and refined design than, say, the content of film clips or pictures. This element of the experimental design should enable future studies to eliminate potential confounds in the affective qualities of life experiences and the level of detail or differentiation in the recollection of an individual's experience.

While CBM paradigms started out using simple ambiguous words and pictures, as reviewed in our introduction, captioning self-experienced event types with richer content is now enabled by SenseCam recordings. Captioning offers the potential to re-model not just valence, but perhaps richer qualitative attributes linked to maladaptive self-models across a range of clinical conditions as well, such as imagery strategies (Holmes, Lang et al., 2008) and modes of attending to meanings (Teasdale et al., 1999). Both attributes are now established to be of clinical value. Further relevant to this idea is research by Ylvisaker and colleagues demonstrating that metaphors, rather than simple negative and positive assertions, are effective in helping to remodel self-identity in the context of disabilities that follow traumatic brain injury (Ylvisaker & Feeney, 2000). Their intervention procedures use metaphors to help individuals with traumatic brain injury reconstruct an organised and positive sense of personal identity. For example, one brain-injured patient, Jason, constructed a new model of self by using the metaphor of Jason-as-Clint-Eastwood. This was grounded in the insight that, like Clint Eastwood, he would have to take seriously his roles as actor *and* director with his success dependent on a blend of positive emotions (like strength and power over others) and restraint (by making effective use of support personnel).

Our preliminary results are naturally subject to a number of limitations and constraints on interpretation, including the possible role of demand characteristics. Our procedure invites replication with appropriate manipulation checks and implicit measures of change in cognitive bias after a delay (e.g., homograph interpretation task) (Hertel, Mathews, Peterson, & Kintner, 2003). Also of note, participants were encouraged to use mental imagery to inter-relate captions with SenseCam footage and trait levels of mental imagery were found to potentiate the observed mood effects. Whether training participants to use mental imagery to inter-relate SenseCam footage and captions is *necessary* cannot be determined in the present study as the use of SenseCam and mental imagery were confounded. Future research could refine the experimental methodology to include independent and combined comparisons of each factor. Furthermore, the present study did not profit fully from the valuable capabilities that SenseCam offers in terms of acquiring personalised and naturalistic footage. As the purpose of this preliminary study was to determine the feasibility of using SenseCam to modify cognitive bias, it was considered important to use well-controlled, standardised stimuli. A clear and important next step is for participants to collect their own SenseCam footage that can be used to generate corresponding and meaningful personalised positive and negative captions—an approach that can ultimately be applied to populations with subclinical and clinical variation in depressed mood. The extent to which mood and meaningful captions are integrated is also open to validation using fMRI. A paradigm developed by Teasdale and colleagues offers one route forward. They demonstrated that picture–caption combinations that cohered to create a meaningful "schematic model" (Teasdale & Barnard, 1993) gave rise to greater activation in frontal regions associated with cognitive-affective synthesis than did the same material when presented in non-coherent combinations (Teasdale et al., 1999).

While our conclusions must remain tentative at this stage, the evidence indicates that SenseCam technology, when combined with valenced meanings using mental imagery, has the potential to induce mood change in a community sample of healthy participants. The changes induced by combining SenseCam traces with captions persist on a 24-hour timescale, are asymmetric with respect to valence, and are modulated by trait differences in imagery. It will be the task of future empirical research to clarify with greater precision how SenseCam can best be integrated into a bias modification paradigm in clinical samples, and how imagery processing can be used to maximise the specific effects on emotional well-being, to promote a rose-tinted view of one's recently experienced past.

REFERENCES

Alloy, L. B., Abramson, L. Y., Hogan, M. E., Whitehouse, W. G., Rose, D. T., & Robinson, M. S. (2000). The Temple-Wisconsin Cognitive Vulnerability to Depression Project: Lifetime history of Axis I psychopathology in individuals at high and low cognitive risk for depression. *Journal of Abnormal Psychology, 109*, 403–418.

Beck, A. T. (1979). *Cognitive therapy of depression*. New York, NY: The Guilford Press.

Beck, A. T., Steer, R. A., & Brown, G. K. (1996). *Beck Depression Inventory—second edition manual*. San Antonio, TX: The Psychological Corporation.

Berry, E., Kapur, N., Williams, L., Hodges, S., Watson, P., Smyth, G., et al. (2007). The use of a wearable camera, SenseCam, as a pictorial diary to improve autobiographical memory in a patient with limbic encephalitis: A preliminary report. *Neuropsychological Rehabilitation, 17*(4–5), 582–601.

Browne, G., Berry, E., Kapur, N., Hodges, S., Smyth, G., Watson, P., & Wood, K. (2011). SenseCam improves memory for recent events and quality of life in a patient with memory retrieval difficulties. *Memory, 19*(7), 713–722.

Coan, J. A., & Allen, J. J. B. (Eds.). (2007). *Handbook of emotion elicitation and assessment*. Oxford, UK: Oxford University Press.

Conway, M. A. (1990). *Autobiographical memory: An introduction*. Milton Keynes, UK: Open University Press.

Conway, M. A. (2001). Sensory-perceptual episodic memory and its context: Autobiographical memory. *Philosophical Transactions of the Royal Society of London Series B: Biological Sciences, 356*, 1375–1384.

D'Argembeau, A., & Van Der Linden, M. (2006). Individual differences in the phenomenology of mental time travel: The effect of vivid visual imagery and emotion regulation strategies. *Consciousness and Cognition, 15*, 342–350.

Ganzach, Y., & Mazursky, D. (1995). Time dependent biases in consumer multi-attribute judgment. *Journal of Economic Psychology, 16*(2), 331–349.

Lang, T. J., Moulds, M. L., & Holmes, E. A. (2009). Reducing depressive intrusions via a computerized cognitive bias modification of appraisals task: Developing a cognitive vaccine. *Behaviour Research and Therapy, 47*(2), 139–145.

Hertel, P. T., Mathews, A., Peterson, S., & Kintner, K. (2003). Transfer of training emotionally biased interpretations. *Applied Cognitive Psychology, 17*, 775–784.

Hodges, S., Williams, L., Berry, E., Izadi, S., Srinivasan, I., Butler, A., et al. (2006). SenseCam: A retrospective memory aid. In P. Dourish & A. Friday (Eds.), *Ubicomp, LNCS 4206* (pp. 177–193). Berlin, Germany: Springer-Verlag.

Holmes, E. A., Coughtrey, A. E., & Connor, A. (2008). Looking at or through rose-tinted glasses? Imagery perspective and positive mood. *Emotion, 8*(6), 875–879.

Holmes, E. A., Lang, T. J., & Deeprose, C. (2009). Mental imagery and emotion in treatments across disorders: Using the example of depression. *Cognitive Behaviour Therapy, 38*, 21–28.

Holmes, E. A., Lang, T. J., Moulds, M. L., & Steele, A. M. (2008). Prospective and positive mental imagery deficits in dysphoria. *Behaviour Research and Therapy, 46*, 976–981.

Holmes, E. A., & Mathews, A. (2005). Mental imagery and emotion: A special relationship? *Emotion, 5*, 489–497.

Holmes, E. A., Mathews, A., Dalgleish, T., & Mackintosh, B. (2006). Positive interpretation training:

Effects of mental imagery versus verbal training on positive mood. *Behavior Therapy, 37*(3), 237–247.
Holmes, E. A., Mathews, A., Mackintosh, B., & Dalgleish, T. (2008). The causal effect of mental imagery on emotion assessed using picture-word cues. *Emotion, 8*(3), 395–409.
MacLeod, C., Koster, E. H. W., & Fox, E. (2009). Whither cognitive bias modification research? Commentary on the special section articles. *Journal of Abnormal Psychology, 118*(1), 89–99.
McIsaac, H. K., & Eich, E. (2002). Vantage point in episodic memory. *Psychonomic Bulletin and Review, 9*(1), 146–150.
Mezulis, A. H., Abramson, L. Y., Hyde, J. S., & Hankin, B. L. (2004). Is there a universal positivity bias in attributions? A meta-analytic review of individual, developmental, and cultural differences in the self-serving attributional bias. *Psychological Bulletin, 130*(5), 711–747.
Moore, R. G., Watts, F. N., & Williams, J. M. (1988). The specificity of personal memories in depression. *British Journal of Clinical Psychology, 27*(Pt 3), 275–276.
Reisberg, D., Pearson, D. G., & Kosslyn, S. M. (2003). Intuitions and introspections about imagery: The role of imagery experience in shaping an investigator's theoretical views. *Applied Cognitive Psychology, 17*(2), 147–160.
Scherer, K. R. (1999). Appraisal theories. In T. Dalgleish & M. Power (Eds.), *Handbook of cognition and emotion* (pp. 637–663). Chichester, UK: Wiley.
Segal, Z. V., Williams, J. M. G., & Teasdale, J. D. (2002). Cognition, mood, and the nature of depressive relapse. In Z. V. Segal, J. M. G. Williams, & J. D. Teasdale (Eds.), *Mindfulness-based cognitive therapy for depression: A new approach to preventing relapse.* New York, NY: The Guilford Press.
Spielberger, C. D., Gorsuch, R. L., Lushene, R., Vagg, P. R., & Jacobs, G. A. (1983). *Manual for the State-Trait Anxiety Inventory (STAI).* Palo Alto, CA: Consulting Psychologists Press.
Stöber, J. (2000). Prospective cognitions in anxiety and depression: Replication and methodological extension. *Cognition & Emotion, 14*, 725–729.
Taylor, S. E., & Brown, J. D. (1988). Illusion and wellbeing: A social psychological perspective on mental health. *Psychological Bulletin, 103*(2), 193–210.
Teasdale, J. D. (1988). Cognitive vulnerability to persistent depression. *Cognition & Emotion, 2*, 247–274.
Teasdale, J. D., & Barnard, P. J. (1993). *Affect, cognition, and change: Remodelling depressive thought.* Hove, UK: Lawrence Erlbaum Associates.
Teasdale, J. D., Howard, R. J., Cox, S. G., Ha, Y., Brammer, M. J., Williams, S. C., et al. (1999). Functional MRI study of the cognitive generation of affect. *American Journal of Psychiatry, 156*(2), 209–215.
Watson, D., Clark, L. A., & Tellegen, A. (1988). Development and validation of a brief measure of positive and negative affect. *Journal of Personality and Social Psychology, 54*(6), 1063–1070.
Williams, J. M. G., Barnhofer, T., Crane, C., Herman, D., Raes, F., Watkins, E., et al. (2007). Autobiographical memory specificity and emotional disorder. *Psychological Bulletin, 133*(1), 122–148.
Williams, J. M. G., & Scott, J. (1988). Autobiographical memory in depression. *Psychological Medicine, 18*(3), 689–695.
Ylvisaker, M., & Feeney, T. (2000). Reconstruction of identity after brain injury. *Brain Impairment, 1*(1), 12–28.

MEMORY, 2011, 19 (7), 778–784

Psychology Press
Taylor & Francis Group

Passive imaging technology in aphasia therapy

Kiernan Burke[1], Sue Franklin[2], and Olive Gowan[2]

[1]Department of Computer Science and Information Systems, Interaction Design Centre, University of Limerick, Limerick, Ireland
[2]Department of Speech and Language Therapy, University of Limerick, Limerick, Ireland

We describe a brief pilot study undertaken to investigate the potential benefit(s) of using a SenseCam in aphasia therapy. Five post-stroke persons with aphasia and their caregivers agreed to participate. Each person with aphasia wore the SenseCam for 1 day during the daytime. Slide shows and printed images were created from the images obtained and presented at a (videotaped) weekly group conversation session. Therapists' observations, reflections, and opinions were subsequently elicited in a group interview and online survey. Wearable, sensor-triggered automatic imaging devices offer potential advantages over both conventional cameras and generic pictures when used in aphasia therapy. We identified three advantages of a SenseCam over conventional imaging methods: Images can be acquired without the presence of the researcher, no action is required by the wearer for image acquisition and the continuous point of view is that of the wearer. Acquired images are of personal relevance to the wearer and may have greater efficacy for the person with aphasia in aiding conversation, and for the speech language therapist in setting functional language goals.

Keywords: Aphasia therapy; Speech and language therapy; Augmentative and alternative communication; SenseCam.

STROKE AND APHASIA

World Health Organisation statistics indicate that stroke is experienced by 15 million people worldwide (WHO, 2004). In the UK stroke is the leading cause of major disability (WHO, 2004). The worldwide number of strokes is expected to increase due to increasing life spans and consequent rise in elderly populations (Rothwell et al., 2005). Approximately one third of stroke victims will suffer aphasia—loss or impairment of language abilities. Estimates of actual percentages vary from 21% to 38% (Laska, Hellblom, Murray, Kahan, & Von Arbin, 2001) but no large-scale studies exist.

Language impairment impacts dramatically on the affected individual's quality of life in many areas; personal relationships, the ability to work, perceived self-efficacy, autonomy, access to services. The goal of speech and language therapy is to help maximise the individual's communicative potential by treating specific aspects of language directly, and by augmenting communication by alternative means; electronic or non-electronic aids, symbols (graphic, auditory, gestural, textured, tactile), and strategies and techniques for their

Address correspondence to: Kiernan Burke, Interaction Design Centre ER1, University of Limerick, Limerick, Ireland. E-mail: kiernan.burke@ul.ie

The authors gratefully acknowledge Professor Alan Smeaton, Daragh Byrne, and Aiden O'Doherty of Dublin City University's Centre for Digital Video Processing for access to, and assistance with, their event segmentation application, and to Steve Hodges and Emma Berry for their efforts in providing us with the loan of SenseCams. We would also like to thank the speech and language therapists and people with aphasia who took part in this study, and Dr Chris Exton for his comments and suggestions.

© 2011 Psychology Press, an imprint of the Taylor & Francis Group, an Informa business
http://www.psypress.com/memory http://dx.doi.org/10.1080/09658211.2010.551131

use (ASHA, 2004). Successful intervention requires appropriate goal setting, use of functionally appropriate vocabularies and materials, and the generalisation of abilities and strategies used in treatment to real-life situations.

SENSECAM IN APHASIA REHABILITATION

Goal setting

The majority of people with aphasia have multilevel language deficits. Thus, in discussion with the person with aphasia, a decision must be made regarding the therapeutic approach. Some areas of language processing will be more or less important depending on the individual's lifestyle; for example, an impairment of reading comprehension would be a serious impediment to an academic researcher.

In order to set useful treatment goals, therefore, it is important to know something of the person's lifestyle, social communication needs, and everyday activities. Paradoxically for a person with aphasia, the language impairment makes it difficult to report on these matters, especially in the case of severely disordered language. A therapist may ask a relative directly, or have the relative fill in a diary of the affected person's activities. These, however, fail to directly convey the perspective of the person with aphasia. And while direct communication can be achieved with photographs taken by the participant, this method is hampered by subjective selection and the technical difficulties of operation (Levin et al., 2007). While the SenseCam shares features with both conventional and digital still and film cameras, it is important from a research perspective to recognise its unique features. Images that are captured by passive means are independent of the device-bearer's action. Notwithstanding any decision on the bearer's part to position him or herself for the express purpose of recording a specific object, person, or place, captured images constitute an objective record of past events as triggered by sensor detection of physical phenomena. The passive acquisition of images stands in contrast to manually acquired, conventional photographs and film, which constitute subjective constructions of past events. We anticipate that one of the very real advantages of using the SenseCam with people with aphasia is that it is a way of recording all of a person's activities during a specified length of time, *irrespective of their salience*. The data are collected by the person with aphasia themselves. Once the result has been edited, the participant can easily indicate situations where the aphasia is causing difficulty and that most need to be worked on. As compared to a manually operated camera, the SenseCam requires minimal physical action, which is key when so much effort is being expended on communication, and where in many cases the individual may also have some degree of hemiplegia. For a person with aphasia who has severe comprehension disorders, the realistic materials that resonate in the individual's autobiographical memory are going to make it more likely that the individual understands the communication areas that are being alluded to in the goal setting discussion.

Therapeutic use

Another potentially significant use of the SenseCam in aphasia is its use as a source of therapy materials. The most prevalent symptom in aphasia is a word-finding difficulty, and naming treatment will very often include picture-naming therapy. Many images recorded by the SenseCam will be content rich and useful therefore in this therapeutic exercise. Using such autobiographical information should be both motivating and provide a semantically rich context, which will maximise naming performance. The obtained images are also an excellent resource for supported communication and the development of low-tech aids such as communication books. These books are generally used by people with severe aphasia, which means comprehension will also be impaired. SenseCam would suggest to the therapist what the content of such a book should be, and the familiarity of the items will facilitate residual comprehension.

The range of information about the person's life allows the therapist to see the whole person, improving empathy and mutual respect. The information is also important with respect to helping negotiate the new self-image that must be mediated post stroke (Brumfitt, 1999).

Therapy generalisation

Therapeutic interventions may successfully increase communicative ability in the clinical situation with the speech and language therapist, but this will be of little value unless this improvement can be carried over to the life of the person with aphasia. Ideally the speech and language therapist would accompany the person with aphasia in vivo, but in practice this is rarely possible. The SenseCam offers the opportunity for the person with aphasia to use new communication strategies in planned communicative situations. Particularly for the person with a severe communication impairment, using the SenseCam post-therapy can demonstrate to the patient and their therapist that they have achieved agreed goals with respect to generalisation (i.e., having small group conversations in the local pub) and can also highlight any difficulties with these communicative attempts (e.g., not being able to order a drink at the bar). It could also be used as an outcome measure, allowing the therapist to compare the number of communicative contexts experienced by the person with aphasia before and after intervention.

In this paper we describe the first pilot study attempting to use the SenseCam with people with aphasia. There were three objectives to this study. First it was important to establish whether people with severe aphasia were able to use this technology given potential motor and comprehension impairments. Second it was of interest to see whether the participants found the resultant images engaging and motivating. Finally we were interested to get feedback from the speech and language therapists working with these individuals to establish whether they thought the SenseCam was likely to be of use with this client group.

METHOD

Participants

Five people with aphasia and their communication partners (Kagan, 1998; Kagan et al., 2001; Lyon et al., 1997) agreed to participate in the study. Four of the participants were male, one was female. All of the participants worked with trained communication partners to assist with their rehabilitation. The male participants' communication partners were their female spouses; the female participant's partner was a neighbour. All participants lived at home. We first met with participants and their partners individually and explained SenseCam operation, confidentiality and privacy issues, the participant's right to withdraw from the study, and what we would do with the acquired images. We provided information sheets that explained the operation of the SenseCam. We took the participant's impairment into consideration in the design of the information sheet by placing pictographic and photographic symbols in the left-hand margin adjacent to the relevant paragraph(s) of text. Beneath each symbol we summarised the adjacent text in a single sentence. Participants received group and individual therapy. As the five participants met for weekly group conversation in the hospital's clinic, the study authors agreed to conduct a group session to present slides and prints selected from the acquired images. Prior to this each participant wore the SenseCam for one day. We decided to film the session for later review. We subsequently conducted a group interview with the participating therapists, made the participant images and a DVD of the group session available for review, and conducted an online survey of their impressions.

Procedure

The SenseCam was delivered to each participant's home in the morning, and retrieved in the evening. At the time of delivery, caregivers were shown the location of a pause button on the SenseCam (when privacy was desired). No other technical instruction or instruction for participant activity was given. After retrieving the SenseCam in the evening, images were transferred to a laptop computer with a software program supplied with the SenseCam. Transferred images on the laptop were then processed with an event-detection program provided to us by the Centre for Digital Video Processing at Dublin City University.

The following materials were prepared from selected images:

A computer-based slide show containing four slides of different activities that each participant was engaged in.

Printed pages of 8 or 12 images (depending on the amount of participant activity) of each participant's activity.

Narrative slide shows of two participants engaged in an extended period of continuous activity.

The images were chosen both to reflect non-sedentary activity and extra-ordinary activities that would reflect an aspect of each participant's unique identity. Presentation of the slide shows and printed images took place 1 week following the image collection. We set up a projector connected to a laptop containing the slide shows, and placed a video camera at the back of the room to record the session.

Therapists interview and online survey

Two days after the group session, a group interview was convened with the therapists and session facilitator and the principal investigator. This was a loosely structured interview with questioning directed to elicit the therapists' impressions of the impact of the images in the group session, and the potential of passive imaging technology in therapy. The session was recorded and transcribed. The following week an online survey was posted to elicit responses and suggestions from the therapists.

RESULTS

In the description of the participants' group conversation we have used fictitious names. Information about the participants is shown in Table 1. All participants are severely aphasic, and more than 1 year post-onset.

TABLE 1
Patient statistics (names are fictitious)

Name	*Age*	*Type of aphasia*	*Speech production*	*Motor difficulty*
Darragh	56	Non-fluent	Severely non-fluent	L weakness
Hugh	69	Fluent, word deafness	Jargon	No impairment
Liam	57	Non-fluent	Severely non-fluent	R weakness
Sean	46	Global	No verbal output	Generalised weakness
Catherine	69	Conduction	Fluent, phonological impairment	No impairment

Participants' group conversation

We began by showing two narrative episodes. During the presentation of these episodes the facilitator commented and asked questions of Catherine and Daragh. During the viewing the therapist asks Catherine questions about the location and people in the slides. Catherine is able to communicate that it is her daughter's house, and to spontaneously name the town where her daughter lives. The second episode takes place in Daragh's back garden. During the viewing Daragh appears enthusiastic. He gestures frequently while searching for words to describe places and people. Next we presented the slide show depicting four events (in chronological sequence) from each participant's day. Lastly, we presented each participant with pages of printed images. Therapists then engaged in one-on-one conversation with participants, asking them questions about the images and discussing topics that the images gave rise to.

Therapists' group interview

A week following the participants' group conversation, we conducted a 30-minute interview with the participating therapists. Reflection on the usefulness of the SenseCam ("Did you find the camera to be of use?") elicited unanimous and enthusiastic positive comments. The view was expressed by all participants that the SenseCam offered insights into participants' personal lives that were previously not possible, that this was a motivating factor for participants, and helpful for therapists getting to know their participants better. Therapists also expressed the view that in comparison to previous sessions their patients displayed greater animation, and increased motivation to communicate. This was particularly evident in the one-to-one conversations that took place (between therapists and their clients) when printed images were distributed. However we cannot claim that this was due to the introduction of the SenseCam images, as observed reactions may be attributable wholly or in part to novel experience.

The desire to continue to use the device and images in therapy was also expressed. We list several key observations with comments:

1. The SenseCam was useful because it allowed therapists to see the participant's own environment.
   "... significantly useful. You can actually see where the clients are living and the reality of what's around their house and everything."
   "And it was lovely to hear, you know, them talking about their families. It was something that we never really got to do. I don't think I've ever got to do it with a client, really talk about their family and see them."
   "We can see where they live and who the family are so then we can relate to it a bit better and it's easier to talk."
2. Pictures of participants' real lives were more effective in eliciting participant conversation than pictographs or generic photographs.
   "... The communication folder we had before was kind of cartoon pictures and you know pictures that weren't of their real life and this really gets them to talk about their real life. ... It would help them to practice at home as well you know when they're meeting other people."
3. Printed images were more effective than projected images in eliciting conversation.
   "And the moment the focus went off them and the confrontation naming stopped and they were handed the pictures the volume in the room increased tenfold. They just started chatting to each other, describing pictures to us."
4. The SenseCam images were effective in eliciting spontaneous word naming.
   "It cued her into saying the name of where she lived and that was an issue that... so yeah, areas that they wouldn't have been able to recruit spontaneously. Using the pictures then cued them in."
5. Images of the participant's environment can be helpful in tailoring naming exercises.
   "And for example if you wanted to do naming or work on functional nouns and verbs that you would mostly find in the home anyway, you know, by opening the kitchen cupboard you see exactly what cereal they eat so you can devise the whole program around their life."
6. The addition of sound recording would not be beneficial.
   "I think just having the pictures is a good basis for all sorts of therapy."
   "... but then some people would be put off by it and wouldn't want to be recorded especially if they're having difficulty getting something across and it's going to come up on the camera."
   "And then there's the real issue then of consent and what if you picked up a very uncomfortable conversation that you ... there's a huge ethical issue and reporting of same and then there's losing confidence and respect."

Mini-survey results

All therapists (five) who were present at the participant group session responded to the survey. The survey was designed to (a) elicit opinion on the usefulness of the SenseCam in needs assessment and supported communication as compared to existing methods, (b) elicit opinion on the level of participant involvement when compared to group sessions without a camera, (c) solicit suggestions for any methods or devices that the therapist deemed more beneficial either for needs assessment or supported communication (see Table 2).

TABLE 2
Therapist mini-survey responses

Question	*Strongly disagree*	*Disagree*	*Neither*	*Agree*	*Strongly agree*
The passive digital camera offers no advantages in needs assessment over existing methods that you have used.	3	2			
The passive digital camera offers no advantages in supported communication over existing methods that you have used.	4	1			
Question	*Much less*	*Less*	*Neither*	*More*	*Much more*
We looked at slides and printed images taken by the camera in the patient group. Indicate the level of participant involvement that you experienced compared to previous group sessions without a camera.			1	4	

Responding to suggested methods or devices (existing or potential) that would be as or more beneficial for needs assessment, one therapist stated that the use of a digital camera and discussion with client and family would be more effective; a second that home visits would be as effective. Likewise, there were two responses to suggestions for improvement in supported communication. One respondent maintained that a camera would be as effective; the second stated that using pictures in an organised communication folder would be more effective.

DISCUSSION

Our intention in undertaking this study was to determine if a SenseCam might be useful for people with aphasia. Specifically, we wanted to determine the potential of images taken from real life for engagement and motivation and usefulness in supported conversation, and to garner the opinions and impressions of the participating speech language therapists. All participants were able to use the SenseCam. Usable images were obtained in every case. This is a significant finding, given that several of the participants have motor impairments which would preclude them from using a conventional camera (Levin et al., 2007), none would be able to write a diary themselves, and speech was in every case too impaired to allow the participants to describe the events of the day to their therapist.

As we observed in the group session and in later re-viewings of the video, participants were engaged with both the projected and printed images. We noticed that the group as a whole was more engaged when looking at printed images. The one-to-one communication between the participants and their therapists may account for this.

One fact that we noticed only in a later re-viewing was the noticeably greater engagement and motivation of those participants who used the SenseCam on extra-ordinary versus ordinary days. We judged extra-ordinary to mean time spent away from home and local environs: a day out, as it were. This accords with the finding reported in the Berry et al. (2007) paper where the SenseCam was used to enhance recall in a case of amnesia, where non-salient events showed a lesser effect. However, while for our population highly salient images may be particularly motivating, we would argue that for people with aphasia the SenseCam's ability to record even the most humdrum, repeating events of life may be crucial. This is so because vocabulary used in everyday situations will be most useful. These are exactly the type of events that may not enter long-term memory (Conway, 2005).

Therapists expressed unanimous agreement that images drawn from participants' real lives were more relevant in supported conversation and offered greater insight and understanding for assessing functional language requirements than generic images. We did not determine if passively acquired images could be useful in goal setting, and whether their use in therapy might aid in generalisation. These will be the topics of future studies.

REFERENCES

ASHA. (2004). *Roles and responsibilities of speech-language pathologists With respect to augmentative and alternative communication: Technical report.* Retrieved from http://www.asha.org/docs/pdf/TR2004-00262.pdf.

Berry, E., Kapur, N., Williams, L., Hodges, S., Watson, P., Smyth, G., et al. (2007). The use of a wearable camera, SenseCam, as a pictorial diary to improve autobiographical memory in a patient with limbic encephalitis: A preliminary report. *Neuropsychological Rehabilitation*, *17*(4–5), 582–601.

Brumfitt, S. (1999). *The social psychology of communication impairment.* London, UK: Whurr.

Conway, M. A. (2005). Memory and the self. *Journal of Memory and Language*, *53*(4), 594–628.

Kagan, A. (1998). Supported conversation for adults with aphasia: Methods and resources for training conversation partners. *Aphasiology*, *12*(9), 816–830.

Kagan, A., Black, S., Duchan, J. F., Simmons-Mackie, N., & Square, P. (2001). Training volunteers as conversation partners using 'supported conversation for adults with aphasia' (SCA): A controlled trial. *Journal of Speech, Language & Hearing research*, *44*(3), 624–639.

Laska, A., Hellblom, A., Murray, V., Kahan, T., & Von Arbin, M. (2001). Aphasia in acute stroke and relation to outcome. *Journal of Internal Medicine*, *249*, 413–422.

Levin, T., Scott, B., Borders, B., Hart, K., Lee, J., & Decanini, A. (2007). Aphasia talks: Photography as a means of communication, self-expression, and empowerment in persons with aphasia. *Topics in Stroke Rehabilitation*, *14*(1), 72–84.

Lyon, J., Cariski, D., Keisler, L., Rosenbek, J., Levine, R., Kumpula, J., et al. (1997). Communication partners: Enhancing participation in life and communication for adults with aphasia in natural settings. *Aphasiology*, *11*(7), 693–708.

Rothwell, P., Coull, A., Howard, S., Silver, L., Bull, L., Gutnikov, S., et al. (2005). Change in stroke incidence, mortality, case-fatality, severity, and risk factors in Oxfordshire, UK from 1981 to 2004 (Oxford Vascular Study). *Lancet*, *363*(9425), 1925–1933.

World Health Organisation. (2004). Global burden of stroke. Retrieved from http://www.who.int/cardiovascular_diseases/en/cvd_atlas_15_burden_stroke.pdf.

Psychology Press
Taylor & Francis Group

Automatically assisting human memory: A SenseCam browser

Aiden R. Doherty[1], Chris J. A. Moulin[2], and Alan F. Smeaton[1]

[1]CLARITY: Centre for Sensor Web Technologies, Dublin City University, Ireland
[2]Institute of Psychological Science, University of Leeds, UK

SenseCams have many potential applications as tools for lifelogging, including the possibility of use as a memory rehabilitation tool. Given that a SenseCam can log hundreds of thousands of images per year, it is critical that these be presented to the viewer in a manner that supports the aims of memory rehabilitation. In this article we report a software browser constructed with the aim of using the characteristics of memory to organise SenseCam images into a form that makes the wealth of information stored on SenseCam more accessible. To enable a large amount of visual information to be easily and quickly assimilated by a user, we apply a series of automatic content analysis techniques to structure the images into "events", suggest their relative importance, and select representative images for each. This minimises effort when browsing and searching. We provide anecdotes on use of such a system and emphasise the need for SenseCam images to be meaningfully sorted using such a browser.

Keywords: SenseCam; Lifelogging.

... If we remembered everything, we should on most occasions be as ill off as if we remembered nothing. It would take as long for us to recall a space of time as it took the original time to elapse, and we should never get ahead with our thinking ...

(James, 1890)

The SenseCam, developed by Microsoft Research in Cambridge, UK, is a wearable camera worn via a lanyard around one's neck (Hodges et al., 2006). On average this device captures an image every 22 seconds, and temperature, accelerometer (read motion), light, and passive infrared readings on average every 1.5 seconds. This device provides individuals with a visual record of their day, which may provide powerful autobiographical retrieval cues (Berry et al., 2009).

Work from our laboratories suggests that between 2000 and 5000 SenseCam images can be generated in the typical day. As an example of the large amount of data generated by the "lifelogging" that SenseCam facilitates, one person who wears the device on a daily basis has produced approximately 3,125,000 images in the last 38 months. For the SenseCam to be a useful rehabilitation tool in memory-impaired groups in any ongoing sense, we believe it is important to

Address correspondence to: Dr Aiden R. Doherty, CLARITY: Centre for Sensor Web Technologies, Dublin City University, Glasnevin, Dublin 9, Ireland. E-mail: aiden.doherty@dcu.ie

This material is based on works supported by the Science Foundation Ireland under Grant No. 07/CE/I1147. The authors also wish to acknowledge the support of Microsoft Research (grant number 2007-056). We would also like to extend our gratitude to our friends in Tampere, Utrecht, and Duke Universities for their feedback. In addition to this we very much appreciate the insightful feedback comments from our reviewers. An open source version of the browser described here is available at: http://sensecambrowser.codeplex.com/

© 2011 Psychology Press, an imprint of the Taylor & Francis Group, an Informa business
http://www.psypress.com/memory http://dx.doi.org/10.1080/09658211.2010.509732

facilitate researchers, caregivers, and participants in finding the images they wish to identify in this vast collection of images. One strategy to achieve this has been to suggest to caregivers that participants only use the device for significant events, thus reducing the total amount of images to sift through. In short, the instruction is to wear the device only for periods that the caregiver anticipates will be memorable (e.g., Berry et al., 2009). This, too, has been the most pragmatic means of assessing the quality of the device: where people are tested on their memory for particular events (Berry et al., 2007)

We feel it is more desirable to use the SenseCam in a way in which one does not have to predict the later memorability of a prospective event, nor risk missing important and novel occurrences by using it selectively. By crude analogy with the human system, it seems desirable to ensure that material is encoded continuously, but that retrieval is selective and organised. That is, all SenseCam images should be available, but not necessarily accessible (Tulving & Pearlstone, 1966). In this paper we present a technological solution for dealing with the large amount of information generated by SenseCam.

Earlier visualisation methods for reviewing SenseCam images include a clustered time view of query results (Gemmell, Bell, Lueder, Drucker, & Wong, 2002) and a geographical map with the wearer's route highlighted and images popping up along the route (although this requires the user to carry a GPS[1] data-logging device in addition to the SenseCam), and an interactive story-authoring interface that results in a slide show (Gemmell, Aris, & Lueder, 2005). The dominant presentation paradigm for these methods is a conventional "replay" or fast-forwarding of the images sequentially, more formally known as rapid serial visual presentation (RSVP) (Spence, 2002). This method provides the reviewer of images with a sense of what happened during the day as if looking at a movie of the day from the user's own perspective; but given the large number of images taken, fast-forwarding at 10 images per second would still take 5 minutes to review just 1 day.[2] Fast-forwarding of temporally ordered images of a day's events can be an engaging experience, but at the same time it causes problems of cognitive overload as trying to absorb a fast sequence for over 5 minutes can be tiresome, especially in someone with cognitive impairment. A momentary distraction could miss an important image, and even with a pace controller such as pause/rewind, intense concentration is required for the duration of the reviewing. In addition, transitions from one event to another or from one location to another are difficult to notice without a more distinctive indication of where the event boundaries are.

The problem of sequential playback or fast-forward is also found in playing video sequences and has been the driving factor for many video browsing tools that have been developed (Smeaton, 2004), most notably the extraction of thumbnail-size keyframes for spatial browsing which removes some usability problems with the sequential fast-forwarding/fast-rewinding method. In this article we outline two implemented applications that leverage an automated structuring process to turn the linear and sequential nature of the original SenseCam image set (incorporating various sensor values too) into an interactive, spatially oriented (image-driven) experience in which the user can more easily review days' worth of images likely requiring a lower cognitive load (Sweller, Van Merrienboer, & Paas, 1998).

In this paper we describe computing systems that we built to automatically structure and organise SenseCam data and later facilitate quick retrieval of desired events with a lower cognitive load on the user, through returning them fewer candidate events that are more relevant to the information they seek. We believe that research into understanding how the human mind works is useful in guiding the development of these automated computing systems. The main considerations are: (1) as the human mind thinks in terms of events, SenseCam data should be stored as event; (2) as distinct events are encoded more strongly, we automatically attempt to identify those events; (3) as the human mind works by association, similar SenseCam events to a given event should be easy to find.

METHOD

In this section we first discuss how the above goals are realised. Second we describe two implemented systems to gain feedback on the usefulness of our automated techniques. Finally in

[1] GPS (global positioning system) is a mechanism to automatically locate a person's location anywhere on earth.

[2] One week would take 35 minutes to review, with 1 year taking over 30 hours to look back on using RSVP alone!

this section we detail a group of participants who provided us with feedback on using the systems we built.

Automatic structuring and interactive retrieval of SenseCam images

> *... Digital memories surpass biological memories by enabling people to directly see and interact with captured information. This powerful capability can help people manage their personal information ...*
>
> (Barreau et al., 2007)

We have developed a suite of functions applied to SenseCam data that automatically provide digital memory retrieval cues. We structure our processing into a number of logical steps that exploit various characteristics of human memory (See Figure 1).

Event segmentation

Memory perspective. Human memory segments a *continuously experienced present* into a series of discrete events (Williams, Conway, & Baddeley, 2008). Zacks and colleagues elaborate on this, stating that "... *segmenting ongoing activity into distinct events is important for later memory of those activities* ..." (Zacks, Speer, Vettel, & Jacoby, 2006, p. 466).

Computing solution. We segment sequences of images into distinct events, such as having breakfast, working on a computer, etc. This is achieved very quickly using the SenseCam's on-board motion sensors to recognise changes in activity (see Doherty & Smeaton, 2008a, for further detail). This event segmentation process typically results in a day's images yielding 20–30 events, and presenting these units of information significantly reduces the potential information overload associated with presenting so many images.

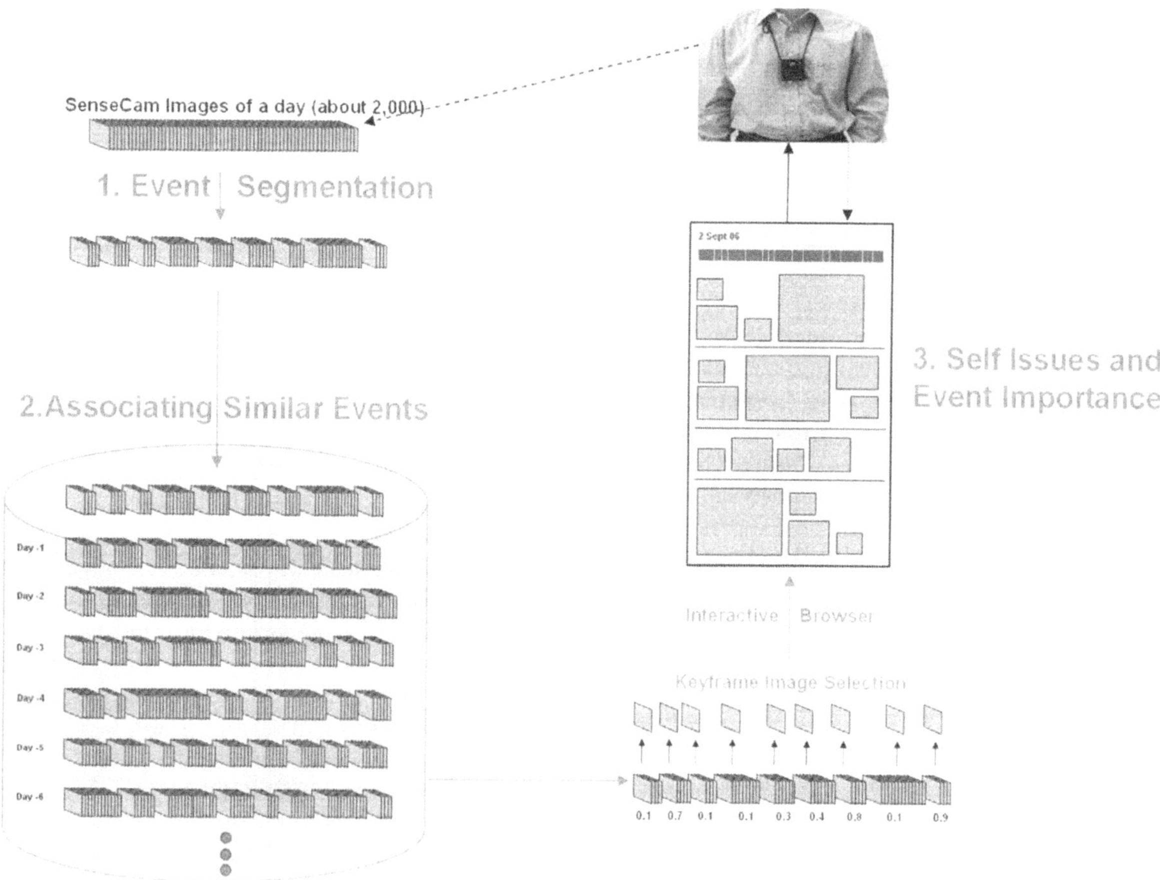

Figure 1. Our model of automatically structuring SenseCam images. To view this figure in colour, please see the online issue of the journal.

The most representative image in an event is also determined, which aids the visual browser aesthetics by summarising the event in just one image.[3] Similar to keyframe selection in a video sequences, the image that best represents the set of images in an event is selected as the representative image of that event (see "Keyframe Image Selection" in Figure 1). We select the highest-quality image near the midpoint of the event (Doherty, Byrne, Smeaton, Jones, & Hughes, 2008).[4]

Associating similar events

Memory perspective. Human memories are stored within a conceptual framework, which means that related events and locations are associated in memory (e.g., Conway, 2005).

Computing solution. We provide users with automated search functions to find events similar to a given event, e.g., "show me other times when I was at the park". By intelligently representing events through the fusion of MPEG-7 image descriptions and the on-board sensor values, we found that users can find events related to any given "query event", with three out of the top five returned results generally being relevant. The technical description is not repeated here (but see Doherty, O'Conaire, Blighe, Smeaton, & O'Connor, 2008, for detailed information).

Self issues and event importance

Memory perspective. Memory is organised by self-relevant structures and goals (e.g., Conway, 2005). Considering that more-distinctive events are better remembered (Brewer, 1988), it follows that we should suggest events to a user in a cued manner that may be more interesting. This notion of distinctiveness is very important, and we believe that those events that are most interesting for users to review from their own lives are the events that were most distinct to them, e.g., talking to a new person, going to a new place, etc.

Computing solution. It is computationally difficult to automatically gauge personal significance of images stored in a visual lifelog. This is due to the well-known computational problem of the "semantic gap", where computers fail to translate bytes into real semantic meaning (Smeulders, Worring, Santini, Gupta, & Jain, 2000). We believe an effective approach is to combine the automated detection of faces (to indicate social engagement) with detecting how visually novel each event is. To obtain the novelty score, each event in a day is visually compared, using MPEG-7 colour and edge descriptors, to see how dissimilar it is to every other event occurring at the same time of day within the previous fortnight (Doherty & Smeaton, 2008b).

Implementation of SenseCam browser

Due to development time constraints in implementing image analysis extraction features that could be distributed to and easily used by participants, we developed two distinct systems. One was an event-based browser that we distributed to international research groups, and another incorporates all facets of our visual lifelog processing cycle.

Event-based browser. This browser first automatically segments sequences of collected images into distinct events or activities, based on the sensor values alone. These events are then visualised as displayed in Figure 2. The top left corner of the screen is a daily calendar, which allows a user to browse to a desired day. The currently selected day in the calendar is highlighted by a different background colour (the 19th of October 2006 in Figure 2). The middle column of the browser displays a single keyframe image of every event present in the selected day. The middle image in each event is selected as the keyframe image, meaning that processing is very quick. The events for the morning, afternoon, and evening have different background colours, to allow the user to navigate to the section of the day in question that they are most interested in reviewing. Events that are selected to be browsed in detail are highlighted with a red border and arrow as illustrated with the first "Afternoon" event in Figure 2. The right-hand side of the browser then displays all the individual images present in a selected event. Above the event's images, other details are given about the event, e.g., the start/end times, the duration of the event, and also any associated comments. Users can add

[3] Users still have access to all the images in the given event. For display purposes a single keyframe image is displayed to the user to summarise all the (broadly similar) images in the given event.

[4] In the cited work the keyframe was based on the most visually representative event image. A worthwhile future investigation would see if this technique selects the most powerful memory trigger too.

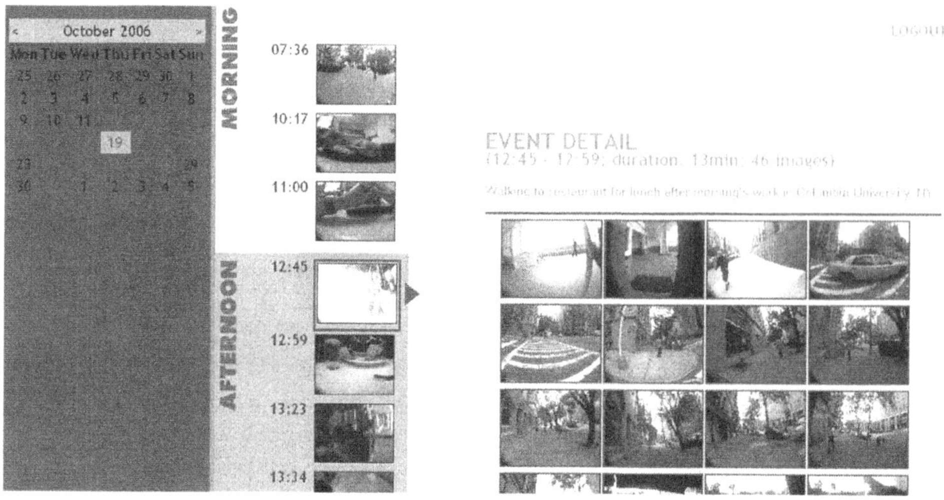

Figure 2. A cropped screenshot of the "event-based" browser.

textual comments to an event. Finally, if the user is interested in any particular image within the event they can click on it to display it in full size.

Advanced browser. Figure 3 provides an overview of the more advanced browser that was used by members of our research team. The top left region of the browser provides the user with calendar functionality where the user can select any desired day to show. Again, as with the event-based browser, this exploits the fact that people can estimate or infer the approximate time that events take place (Dumais et al., 2003). Days available for selection are highlighted in bright white text, with the current day on view highlighted via yellow font. The predominant focus of the browser is on the middle of the screen where numerous images of the day are displayed. These images were segmented into distinct events/activities, and on the browser each image is an event keyframe image, i.e., the image with the highest quality score. As can be seen, some images are larger than others, and those images that are larger correspond to events with a high importance score, suggesting more interesting events to review, which parallels the finding that distinct

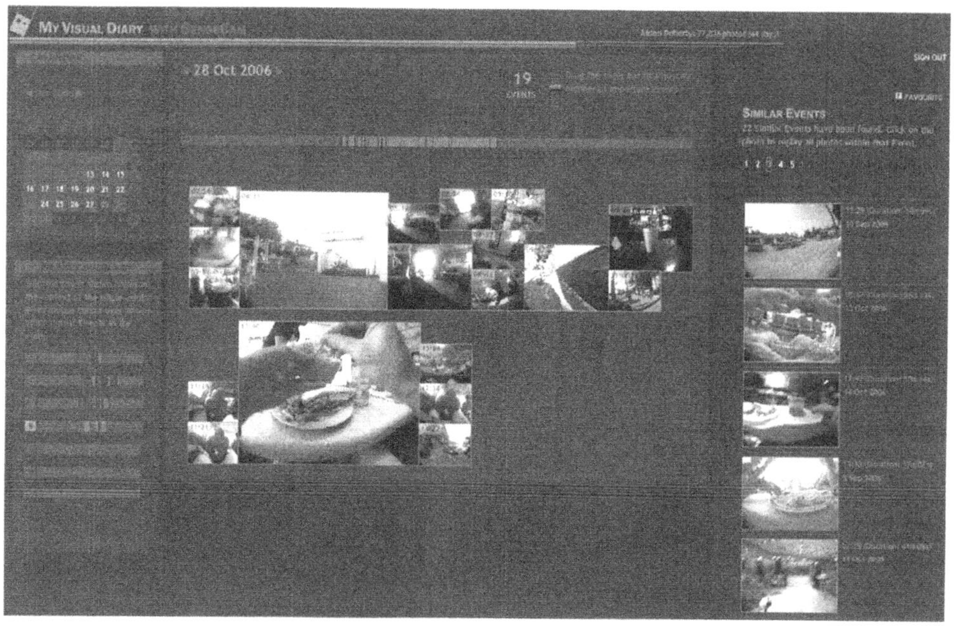

Figure 3. Our "advanced" browser; with event segmentation/interestingness/searching. To view this figure in colour, please see the online issue of the journal.

events tend to be better recalled. In the top left corner of each image its starting time is displayed. The information at the top centre of the browser details the day being displayed and also the number of events being displayed. The slider bar can adjust the number of events being displayed, and in the case of Figure 3 the 19 most important events, as determined by the system, are displayed to the user. Below the slider bar there is a timeline visualising when events started, and also their duration. The panel to the left of the browser titled "Weekly Summary", just below the calendar section, provides a timeline of other events in the days surrounding the day being displayed. Only those events that are similar to any of the events in the displayed day are visualised in the weekly timeline, taking advantage of the fact that the human mind stores items associatively and thus is curious to see other related events. When the user puts the mouse cursor over any event in the centre of the screen, the images are displayed at full size and played back at a rate of ten frames per second. The playback is stopped when the user exits the mouse cursor from the event. The other events are still visible and transparent in the background. The event is also highlighted in red in the daily timeline above, and the weekly timeline to the left too. Any events that are similar are highlighted in amber on the daily and weekly timelines.

Thus far we have displayed aspects of the application that highlight the usefulness of event segmentation in terms of detecting the different events, of automated event importance calculations to emphasise more interesting events, and of selecting a good keyframe for visual display. However, there are other capabilities that are useful to provide to the user. We provide the user with a menu of options anytime that they click on any event being displayed. This then empowers the user with much extra functionality. The user can add/amend a textual comment to any event via selecting an "Add Caption" option on the menu. The user can also add an event to their list of favourite events via selecting an "Add To Fave" option on the menu. Events can also be removed from the favourite list too.

The user is also provided with the important capability of searching for other potentially relevant events in their lifelog to a given event, by selecting a "Find Similar" option on the menu. A list of other potentially relevant events to the event in question are displayed on the "Similar Events" panel to the right-hand side of the browser, as illustrated in Figure 2, where keyframe images from the list of potentially relevant events to a given event are displayed. Other information regarding the date, time, and duration of the potentially relevant events is displayed too. The top of the panel also gives the user feedback on how many potentially relevant results were returned (22 in the case of Figure 3). As the event playback rate is at ten frames per second, it is excellent at giving the user the gist of what an event is about. However, if the user is interested in viewing a certain image in any given event, we provide the opportunity to view such images in a new tab of the browser. This new tab is opened when the user selects an "Event Images" option from the floating event menu bar. Once the tab is open, the user is presented with thumbnails of all the images in a given event, and they can then select any image to view it in full size.

Evaluation of the browsers

Participants. We presented nine participants, who wore SenseCams for varying periods over a 2-year period (May 2006 to August 2008), with one of the two different systems to review their own data (see Table 1). The "event-based browser" was distributed to five people in four collaborating SenseCam universities: the University of Tampere, Finland; Duke University, USA; University of Toronto, Canada; and Utrecht University, in the Netherlands. The "advanced browser" was used by four participants among our own research team.

The event-based browser was used in Utrecht by a participant who collected 102,113 images over a period of 55 days, which were segmented into 1290 events. It was also used in Tampere where one participant reviewed images received from six molecular medical workers, which amounted to approximately 72,000 images over a period of 52 days that were segmented into approximately 800 events (Byrne et al., 2008; Kumpulainen et al., 2009). At the University of Toronto two people have used this browser, one collecting 5524 SenseCam images over a period of 5 days, which were segmented into approximately 67 events. The other participant collected a much larger dataset. One person in Duke University has used this browser too and our evaluation section will focus on how useful our event-based browser was for these participants.

TABLE 1
Overview of participants using systems implementing our lifelog browsing model

Participant	*Place (M/F, age)*	*Browser*	*Number of days*	*Number of images*	*Number of events*
1	Dublin (M, 35)	Advanced	614	1,686,424	19,995
2[a]	Dublin (M, 24)	Advanced	60	92,837	1182
3	Dublin (M, 35)	Advanced	21	44,173	443
4	Dublin (M, 28)	Advanced	23	40,715	505
5	Utrecht (M, 35)	Event-Based	55	102,113	1290
6	Tampere (F, 30)	Event-Based	52	~72,000	~800
7	Toronto (M, 28)	Event-Based	5	5524	~67
8	Toronto (M, 28)	Event-Based	Unavailable	Unavailable	Unavailable
9	Duke (F, 26)	Event-Based	Unavailable	Unavailable	Unavailable
TOTAL	*9 users*		*830 days*	*1,971,786 images*	*23,415 events*

[a]It should be noted that participant 2 is one of the authors of this article.

The advanced browser was used by four participants at Dublin City University. They used the system to review their own SenseCam images to view past days/events. In total the participants collected 1,864,149 images over a period of 23 months, which were segmented into 22,125 events (Table 1). We realise that Participant 1 may appear to skew the dataset but we include him for two reasons: (1) to illustrate the volumes of data that can be gathered by enthusiastic lifeloggers; and (2) to provide an accurate reflection on the effectiveness of the model in dealing with scaled-up datasets.

RESULTS

Anecdotes received from participants

This section focuses on how effectively participants' images were segmented into distinct events/activities, how effective the event importance determination was, the usefulness of the selected keyframe, and the relevance of other retrieved events to a queried event. As the "event-based" browser was used in a number of remote locations, feedback on the event segmentation aspect of our model was elicited via an e-mail questionnaire. Feedback obtained via our four participants using the "advanced browser" was obtained in a one-on-one session monitoring their usage of the system on a particular day and prompting them for feedback on various aspects of the system. Note that this was work carried out within a computer science paradigm, with the goal of evaluating the device more generally, but we believe that they illustrate the benefit of the system more generally.

Event segmentation: Used by 9 participants (5 × event browser, 4 × advanced browser). Participants found the "event-based" browser to be very easy to use, given that it segmented images into events, and had no additional functionality that might have introduced an element of confusion. Our participant in Utrecht, commented:

> *... initially I was not sure if a pure time-based segmentation would have been sufficient already (e.g., new segment every 30 min). However, after using it, I think the one provided by your system is much better ... In Cape Town, I made a tour to the Cape of Good Hope. When browsing the pictures, I was interested in finding the ones that actually show the Cape. I remembered which day it was and given the segmentation, it was easy to find the related segments ...*

One of the Toronto participants commented:

> *... the calendar feature allows for easy recall of the events experienced in different days and gives an overall theme for each day. On certain events, I felt like the computer actually understood the photos and their sequence, segmenting them into appropriate events with sharp boundaries separating them ...*

Our participant in Duke University noted that the segmentation process sometimes wrongly "... *created several 'events' while that person was driving in her car* ...".

While pointing out some examples where the events were over-segmented, in general the researchers in Utrecht, Toronto, and Duke Universities found our process of segmenting images into events to be effective. While participants of our in-house "advanced browser" were able to identify certain instances where the segmentation algorithm incorrectly identified event boundaries, the event segmentation was recognised as an important and useful facet.

Our participant in Tampere was not so concerned about extra events being incorrectly proposed by the system; however she did want to make sure that all semantic boundaries were detected, to find out about every small event/activity in which the medical researchers were involved. To accommodate the wishes of this participant, we were simply able to lower a thresholding parameter so as to present more segmented events.

Participants made very few remarks on the keyframe selection choice in the advanced system. When prompted for a comment, participants made very general comments such as the keyframes selected are "*good*". In fact, when participant 3 was asked to make a more detailed comment, he responded:

> *... the performance overall is good, when I see each keyframe I know what the event is about, however given the fact that they're my events I have a good knowledge what the event is about regardless of the image given ...*

Participants did not seem very enthusiastic or appreciative about this aspect of the system, only commenting on the few cases where it incorrectly selected a representative keyframe image. This perhaps suggests that this is a less-striking feature for potential users of a SenseCam browser.

Associating similar events: Used by 4 participants (4 × advanced browser). All participants found the retrieval facility very useful in the "advanced browser". Participant 2 noted that "*... sifting through the query results I am reminded of many other interesting events and days that I want to review ...*"

Participant 4 also found the retrieval facet of the system "*very useful*". While this feature is useful, all participants also highlighted the need for better accuracy. This mirrors the findings of previous experiments where we found that the retrieval performance of some topics was excellent, but for other topics the performance was not (Doherty, O'Conaire, et al., 2008). Participant 3 was satisfied with his results for a query of walking in the centre of the city he was living in, commenting that "*... the first rank was wrong, but all the other results returned on the first page were relevant and also interesting ...*"

Participant 4 commented that "*... when trying to find other presentations I gave, I could only find one other relevant event. The search facility is useful, but needs better accuracy ...*"

Participant 1 had a desire to search for events by time and location, in a fashion quite similar to that carried out in the domain of organising traditional photographs (O'Hare et al., 2007). These features were not integrated into the application presented to the participants in this study, but could be integrated into future lifelogging systems. However, this participant was satisfied with the actual results returned for each query he requested, as the results were amusing and set the participant off on different browsing trails, which he enjoyed very much.

Self issues and event importance: Used by 4 participants (4 × advanced browser). Overall, participants found that emphasising more important/interesting events was very helpful. Participant 2 noted that "*... I like events being highlighted as they gave me a focus or trail to start browsing with ...*"

Participant 4 noted that he was "*... happy that the mundane events of working on my computer are either very small or hidden. I find the top two most important events proposed by the system pleasurable to review, and all the other events aren't interesting to look at, so the system is correct ...*"

However, participant 3 felt there was little benefit to the event importance, as he commented on being unable to trust the system to consistently identify the most important events; but against this he still felt it is a useful feature and noted that "*... I like the fact that events I manually marked as 'favourites' are then highlighted as important events ...*"

While all participants were agreed on the usefulness of highlighting important events, given these comments by participant 3 it is evident that not everyone was completely satisfied with the actual performance of the algorithm. Interestingly participant 1 noted that, while the most important events presented by the system were "*quite good*", some of his events of social interaction recurred quite regularly, e.g., having coffee with a work colleague. Participant 1 felt that these events, even though they contain a high element of social interaction, should not be weighted as strongly due to the fact that they are not highly novel.

Figure 4. Our open-source released browser. To view this figure in colour, please see the online issue of the journal.

DISCUSSION

Until recently lifelogging was still a new area with no commercial devices or tools to support people to start recording their lives, yet the SenseCam device allowed us to explore issues related to this emerging field. We experienced and discovered several issues with constant visual recording and subsequent access to one's lifelog. However, we believe the tools we are developing to provide effective retrieval mechanisms, based on neuropsychological principles, are moving in the right direction. The model we have built is particularly timely given the commercial release of SenseCams in the form of the Vicon Revue.[5]

In this article we have shown that various aspects of our computational model (i.e., event segmentation, associating similar events, and self issues and event importance) were all anecdotally found to be helpful. It remains to be seen whether memory-impaired groups will likewise benefit from this tool for accessing SenseCam images, and we believe this is a worthwhile future area of collaborative investigations.

While event retrieval is a very useful function, we feel that in future it will be interesting to provide "free text" or multi-faceted retrieval functionality, where people can easily search not only via "query-by-example" but also for events in a certain location, or for events of a certain temperature condition, or for events taken on a certain day of the week, etc. It would be a worthwhile future area of research to work with many participants to determine how this functionality should be most effectively offered. Most notably, if memory rehabilitation is to be furthered through devices such as SenseCam, it seems that browsers such as those described here are critical, and also the collaboration of computer scientists and neuropsychologists. Indeed our model can be further improved by incorporating the idea that retrieval is another form of encoding, and this may help in determining those events that score highly in the "self issues and event importance" facet of our model.

Since carrying out the study detailed in this article, our "event-based" browser has been used to manage 40 users' data by 19 institutions across eight countries, from backgrounds including: computing science, information science, epidemiology and public health promotion, neuropsychology, clinical practices, etc. An updated and easier-to-use version of our "event-based" browser (see Figure 4) has been released on the codeplex website.[6] This is an open-source release, meaning that the software is free to be used by anyone, and also meaning that it can be modified and extended by interested parties. Already in the first 4 months there have been

[5] http://www.omg3d.com/html/IPLicenseagreement.html

[6] http://sensecambrowser.codeplex.com/

over 200 downloads of this software, which we will continue to improve and update.

In summary, the SenseCam has displayed much potential as a device that may help improve the quality of life of those with memory impairments. Much research up to now has been carried out on selected events, as memory researchers have been overwhelmed by the sheer volume of SenseCam images produced. However, to build up a more complete picture of people's lives, to make better informed decisions, and to have the chance to capture those unexpected moments, we strongly believe that individuals should be encouraged to wear their SenseCams as much as possible. This will require an effort on the part of information researchers to manage this large amount of visual SenseCam images. We have released a SenseCam browser and our research efforts are ongoing to build more intelligent and easy-to-use systems, which will be of benefit to the numerous communities who now are building on the lifelogging platform.

REFERENCES

Barreau, D., Crystal, A., Greenberg, J., Sharma, A., Conway, M., Oberlin, J., et al. (2007). Augmenting memory for student learning: Designing a context-aware capture system for biology education. *Proceedings of the American Society for Information Science and Technology, 43*, 251–251.

Berry, E., Hampshire, A., Rowe, J., Hodges, S., Kapur, N., Watson, P., et al. (2009). The neural basis of effective memory therapy in a patient with limbic encephalitis. *Neurology, Neurosurgery, and Psychiatry with Practical Neurology, 80*(3), 582–601.

Berry, E., Kapur, N., Williams, L., Hodges, S., Watson, P., Smyth, G., et al. (2007). The use of a wearable camera, SenseCam, as a pictorial diary to improve autobiographical memory in a patient with limbic encephalitis. *Neuropsychological Rehabilitation, 17*(4), 582–601.

Brewer, W. F. (1988). Memory for randomly sampled autobiographical events. In U. Neisser & E. Winograd (Eds.), *Remembering reconsidered: Ecological and traditional approaches to the study of memory. Emory symposia in cognition* (pp. 21 90). New York, NY: Cambridge University Press.

Byrne, D., Doherty, A. R., Smeaton, A. F., Jones, G. J., Kumpulainen, S., & Jarvelin, K. (2008). *The SenseCam as a tool for task observation.* Presented at HCI 2008-22nd BCS HCI Group Conference, Lancaster, UK.

Conway, M. A. (2005). Memory and the self. *Memory and Language, 53*(4), 594–628.

Doherty, A. R., Byrne, D., Smeaton, A. F., Jones, G. J., & Hughes, M. (2008). Investigating keyframe selection methods in the novel domain of passively captured visual lifelogs. In *CIVR '08: Proceedings of the 2008 international conference on content-based image and video retrieval* (pp. 259–268). New York, NY: ACM Press.

Doherty, A. R., O'Conaire, C., Blighe, M., Smeaton, A. F., & O'Connor, N. E. (2008). Combining image descriptors to effectively retrieve events from visual lifelogs. In *MIR '08: Proceeding of the 1st ACM international conference on multimedia information retrieval* (pp. 10–17). New York, NY: ACM Press.

Doherty, A. R., & Smeaton, A. F. (2008a). Automatically segmenting lifelog data into events. In *WIAMIS: 9th international workshop on image analysis for multimedia interactive services* (pp. 20–23). Washington, DC: IEEE Computer Society.

Doherty, A. R., & Smeaton, A. F. (2008b). Combining face detection and novelty to identify important events in a visual lifelog. In *CIT: 8th international conference on computer and information technology, workshop on image- and video-based pattern analysis and applications.* Washington, DC: IEEE Computer Society.

Dumais, S., Cutrell, E., Cadiz, J., Jancke, G., Sarin, R., & Robbins, D. C.(2003). Stuff I've seen: A system for personal information retrieval and re-use. In *SIGIR '03: Proceedings of the 26th annual international ACM SIGIR conference on Research and Development in information retrieval* (pp. 72–79). New York, NY: ACM Press.

Gemmell, J., Aris, A., & Lueder, R. (2005). Telling stories with MyLifeBits. In *IEEE international conference on multimedia and expo* (pp. 1536–1539). July 6–9, Amsterdam, The Netherlands.

Gemmell, J., Bell, G., Lueder, R., Drucker, S., & Wong, C. (2002). MyLifeBits: Fulfilling the Memex vision. In *Multimedia '02: Proceedings of the tenth ACM international conference on multimedia* (pp. 235–238). New York, NY: ACM Press.

Hodges, S., Williams, L., Berry, E., Izadi, S., Srinivasan, J., Butler, A. et al. (2006). SenseCam: A retrospective memory aid. In *UbiComp: 8th International Conference on Ubiquitous Computing, Vol. 4602 LNCS* (pp. 177–193). New York, NY: Springer.

James, W. (1890). *The principles of psychology.* New York, NY: Henry Holt.

Kumpulainen, S., Jarvelin, K., Serola, S., Doherty, A. R., Byrne, D., Smeaton, A. F., et al. (2009). Data collection methods for analyzing task-based information access in molecular medicine. In *MobiHealthInf 2009 – 1st international workshop on mobilizing health information to support healthcare-related knowledge work.* Porto, Portugal.

O'Hare, N., Gurrin, C., Jones, G. J. F., Lee, H., O'Connor, N. E., & Smeaton, A. F. (2007). Using text search for personal photo collections with the Mediassist system. In *SAC '07: Proceedings of the 2007 ACM symposium on applied computing* (pp. 880–881). New York, NY: ACM Press.

Smeaton, A. F. (2004). Indexing, browsing and searching of digital video. *ARIST – Annual Review of Information Science and Technology, 38*(8), 371–407.

Smeulders, A. W., Worring, M., Santini, S., Gupta, A., & Jain, R. (2000). Content-based image retrieval at the end of the early years. *IEEE Transactions on*

Pattern Analysis and Machine Intelligence, 22, 1349–1380.

Spence, R. (2002). Rapid, serial and visual: A presentation technique with potential. *Information Visualization, 1*(1), 13–19.

Sweller, J., van Merrienboer, J. J. G., & Paas, F. G. W. C. (1998). Cognitive architecture and instructional design. *Educational Psychology Review, 10*(3), 251–296.

Tulving, E., & Pearlstone, Z. (1966). Availability versus accessibility of information in memory for words. *Journal of Verbal Learning and Verbal Behavior, 5*, 381–391.

Williams, H. L., Conway, M. A., & Baddeley, A. D. (2008). The boundaries of episodic memories. In T. F. Shipley & J. M. Zacks (Eds.), *Understanding events: From perception to action*. Oxford, UK: Oxford University Press.

Zacks, J. M., Speer, N. K., Vettel, J. M., & Jacoby, L. L. (2006). Event understanding and memory in healthy aging and dementia of the Alzheimer type. *Psychology and Aging, 21*, 466–482.

MEMORY, 2011, 19 (7), 796–807

Psychology Press
Taylor & Francis Group

The effects of end-of-day picture review and a sensor-based picture capture procedure on autobiographical memory using SenseCam

Jason R. Finley, William F. Brewer, and Aaron S. Benjamin

Department of Psychology, University of Illinois at Urbana-Champaign, Champaign, IL, USA

Emerging "life-logging" technologies have tremendous potential to augment human autobiographical memory by recording and processing vast amounts of information from an individual's experiences. In this experiment undergraduate participants wore a SenseCam, a small, sensor-equipped digital camera, as they went about their normal daily activities for five consecutive days. Pictures were captured either at fixed intervals or as triggered by SenseCam's sensors. On two of five nights, participants watched an end-of-day review of a random subset of pictures captured that day. Participants were tested with a variety of memory measures at intervals of 1, 3, and 8 weeks. The most fruitful of six measures were recognition rating (on a 1–7 scale) and picture-cued recall length. On these tests, end-of-day review enhanced performance relative to no review, while pictures triggered by SenseCam's sensors showed little difference in performance compared to those taken at fixed time intervals. We discuss the promise of SenseCam as a tool for research and for improving autobiographical memory.

Keywords: Autobiographical memory; Experiences; Events; Life-logging; SenseCam; Photographs.

The study of human cognition has much to gain from advances in technology. Increasingly compact and powerful devices—such as SenseCam, a wearable, sensor-equipped digital camera—enable the automated chronicling, or "life-logging", of many aspects of a person's daily experience (see Bell & Gemmell, 2007, 2009). One research domain in which such technology has great potential is the study of autobiographical memory: "memory for information related to the self" (Brewer, 1986, p. 26). Such research explores the ways in which humans maintain and remember personal experiences, and how those memories serve to "support a coherent and effective self" (Conway, 2005, p. 596).

Serious methodological challenges are posed by the study of autobiographical memory, as people's everyday experiences are not experimentally controlled, can span decades, and are largely unknowable to others (Brewer, 1986, 1996; Conway, 1990). Galton (1879a, 1879b) created a technique for the study of autobiographical memory (later modified by Crovitz & Schiffman, 1974) that used experimenter-chosen probe words to elicit participants' associated memories. This method suffers from potentially unrepresentative sampling of memory and inconsistency in retrieval and response strategies across participants. Another approach to the study of

Address correspondence to: Jason R. Finley, Department of Psychology, University of Illinois, 603 E. Daniel St., Champaign, Illinois 61820, USA. E-mail: jrfinley@illinois.edu

This research was supported by a grant from Microsoft Research, Ltd., Cambridge, UK (grant # 2007-066), and from the National Institute of Health to ASB (grant # R01 AG026263). We thank Ellen Brewer for comments on an earlier version of this manuscript. Special thanks to James Scott, Gavin Smyth, Alex Butler, and Steve Hodges for superb technical support.

© 2011 Psychology Press, an imprint of the Taylor & Francis Group, an Informa business
http://www.psypress.com/memory
http://dx.doi.org/10.1080/09658211.2010.532807

autobiographical memory used the contents of long-running daily diaries to cue and assess memory (Linton, 1975; Wagenaar, 1986), but this method suffers from biased selection of experiences by the participants themselves. Advances in technology enabled the advent of experience sampling methods (Conner, Barrett, Tugade, & Tennen, 2007), such as Brewer's (1988) experiments in which participants carried small electronic devices that prompted them at random intervals to record certain aspects of their current experience on paper response cards. Portions of these cards were later used to test memory. This method suffers the disadvantage of frequently and actively involving participants in the capture of information, potentially altering the very memories it sets out to measure. SenseCam can unobtrusively capture a pictorial record from the lives of individuals, thus opening a new route to the investigation of autobiographical memory.

SenseCam also has potential for augmenting human cognition: as a cognitive prosthetic for people with memory impairments (Berry et al., 2007) or a memory aid for those with unimpaired memory (Sellen, Fogg, Hodges, & Wood, 2007). In this paper we consider how the capabilities of the device and the nature of its use can serve to investigate and enhance autobiographical memory. Specifically, we evaluate whether end-of-day review of SenseCam pictures enhances memory for the day's events, and also whether the sensors built into SenseCam capture more memorable pictures than those captured using a simple interval timer.One way in which SenseCam can augment memory is by providing pictures with which one can easily review a day's experiences. It has long been known that repeated presentation of stimuli improves memory (Ebbinghaus, 1885/1913). More specifically, prior work has shown that reviewing still pictures from a previously viewed movie of everyday events enhances performance on subsequent free recall and recognition (Koutstaal, Schacter, Johnson, Angell, & Gross, 1998; Schacter, Koutstaal, Johnson, Gross, & Angell, 1997). Koutstaal, Schacter, Johnson, and Galluccio (1999) found similar effects on free recall (Experiment 1) and recognition combined with cued recall (Experiment 2) when participants performed a variety of activities in the laboratory and then reviewed photographs of actors performing those same activities. The current experiment sought to extend these findings to the investigation of unconstrained personal activities, review of first-person pictures, and longer retention intervals. We predicted that an end-of-day review of SenseCam pictures would improve memory.

Life-logging technologies like SenseCam can produce a wealth of durable external personal memory; however, this raises new problems of information management, organisation, and searching (Jones & Ross, 2007). One way to ameliorate these problems is to strategically filter which data are captured. SenseCam can do so by using sensors (white light, passive infrared, and accelerometer) to capture pictures potentially relevant for future memory needs. If there is a systematic relationship between objectively measurable physical characteristics of experience (e.g., incidence of white light) and psychological characteristics of experience (e.g., memory for an event), and if SenseCam's sensors and triggering algorithm are well calibrated to this relationship, then we would expect sensor-triggered pictures to elicit memory better than pictures simply captured at regular intervals throughout the day.

The goal of the present experiment was to gather data that would allow us (a) to evaluate a variety of potential memory measures, (b) to compare memory for days that had been reviewed with memory for days that had not been reviewed, (c) to compare memory for a set of pictures triggered by SenseCam's sensors with a set taken at regular time intervals, and (d) to examine the course of forgetting under each of these conditions.

METHOD

Participants

There were 12 undergraduates who participated for payment of $50 each. There were 4 males and 8 females, ages 18 to 21.

Recruitment and selection

Participants were recruited via posters and web notices. Of the 24 undergraduates interviewed and who returned completed questionnaires, 12 participants were selected on the basis of their punctuality, ability to follow directions precisely, self-rated responsibility in caring for electronic devices, and having living situations and daily activities that would least interfere with wearing a SenseCam for a considerable portion of each day.

Privacy

Several aspects of the experimental procedure were designed to safeguard the rights and privacy of participants and others. Potential participants were told to complete the initial questionnaire only if they were comfortable with the full procedure as described in the interview. Each participant's data were identified only by a unique code number assigned to each individual. Pictures from an individual participant's acquisition period were never seen by anyone except the experimenters and that participant.

Participants could deactivate the SenseCam (using the on/off button or the privacy button) at any time that they chose to avoid the possibility of pictures being captured. Pressing the privacy button deactivates picture capture for 7 minutes, with a warning beep sounding 15 seconds before reactivation. Participants were further instructed to deactivate the SenseCam in several specific situations: restroom, changing/locker room, doctor's office, ATM or bank, and any time someone else requested that it be deactivated. Furthermore, when entering their workplace or a private residence, participants were instructed to deactivate the camera until they received permission to reactivate it. Finally, participants could note time periods for deletion in the small notepad they carried (e.g., if they suddenly realised they had left the SenseCam on while using the restroom). All pictures falling in such time periods were deleted at the end of each day without having been seen by anyone.

Apparatus

SenseCam is a small, wearable, sensor-equipped digital camera developed by the Microsoft Research lab in Cambridge, UK. The SenseCams used in this experiment were hardware version 2.3b and firmware version 2.6.7. A built-in adjustable lanyard allows SenseCam to be worn around the neck at upper chest height. Pictures are captured using a fisheye lens with a wide angle of view (119° diagonal) and stored with time-stamps on a 1Gb SD flash memory card. The pictures are saved as JPEG files with display size 640×480 pixels, resolution 72 dots per inch, colour depth 32-bit (16.7 million colours), and file size approximately 30 kilobytes. The maximum rate of picture capture is approximately once every 5 seconds. Capture may be triggered by three different methods, each of which can be independently enabled or disabled by experimenters: (a) manually (by pressing the manual trigger button); (b) by timer; (c) by sensors. The device gives no audible or visible indication of picture capture due to timer or sensor triggering, although it beeps upon manual triggering.

SenseCam sensors

SenseCam has sensors for measuring: (a) temperature (in units of .5° C); (b) white light intensity (on a scale of 0 to 10,000); (c) change in infrared radiation (e.g., from a moving warm body) as either presently occurring (1) or not (0) within a range of approximately 2.5 m for a human-sized object; and (d) acceleration in three dimensions (in units of 1/819th g). Data from these sensors are recorded, along with date and time, approximately every 1.5 seconds. Pictures and sensor data are transferred to a computer via a USB interface, which is also used for recharging the battery.

Sensor-triggering algorithm

The default algorithm and threshold values for sensor triggering of picture capture were established by Microsoft Research through informal testing. The algorithm compares current sensor values to the set of values most recently measured (typically about 1.5 seconds prior). If a picture is not already currently being captured and saved, a new capture will be triggered if either (a) there is a change in white light level greater than 4500 units as measured by the detector, or (b) the change in accelerometer value on all three axes is no greater than 500 units as measured by the detector (indicating that the device is probably stationary) *and* the passive infrared value is 1 (indicating change in infrared, typically due to nearby human movement). More detailed specifications can be found in Hodges et al. (2006).

Design

The experiment used a $3 \times 2 \times 2$ within-participants factorial design with three retention intervals (1, 3, 8 weeks); two types of trigger condition (sensor-triggered, timer-triggered); and two types of review condition (no review, review). The order in which participants received each trigger and review condition was counterbalanced using a balanced Latin Square.

Acquisition period

Participants wore a SenseCam as they went about their normal daily activities for five consecutive weekdays (i.e., Monday through Friday). The first day was treated as practice, and pictures from that day were not reviewed or tested. SenseCam operated automatically throughout the day, capturing pictures according to the trigger condition for that day (described below).

The starting and ending time of acquisition for each day were determined by each individual participant, and thus varied by participant and by day. For the four experimental days, the mean starting time was 09:55 ($SD = 1$ hr 11 min), the mean ending time was 19:17 ($SD = 1$ hr), and the mean duration of acquisition per day was 9 hours and 22 min ($SD = 1$ hr 37 min, range = 5 hr 13 min to 12 hr 43 min).

Participants were informed before the acquisition period that their memory for that period would later be tested, and were told the general nature of the questions they would be asked (e.g., "You may be asked to write down details about the events that occurred during the days on which you wore the SenseCam, either cued by images from those days or with no such cues").

At the end of each day participants returned to the lab. The experimenter transferred all of the day's pictures from the SenseCam onto a computer, deleted any pictures falling in a time period marked for deletion by the participants in their notepads, and updated the SenseCam's trigger setting for the following day. Participants then received a review of that day's pictures (described in detail below), if the day had been assigned to be a review day. This entire procedure was repeated for 5 days.

Trigger condition. Manual triggering of picture capture was disabled for the experiment. On any given day, the SenseCam captured pictures either as triggered by its sensors (see Apparatus), or as triggered by its fixed-interval timer. The measured mean timer interval for the timer-triggered condition was 10.6 seconds ($SD = 1.3$). Note that because timer-triggered pictures were not triggered by any external criteria, and because pictures were randomly selected for review and for testing, this condition provides a de facto random sampling of experience and thus serves as a logical control condition against which to test sensor triggering.

End-of-day review. The end-of-day review was a movie composed of a sequence of randomly selected pictures captured by the SenseCam on that day for that participant. The review was shown on a computer monitor with pictures presented one-at-a-time for 1 second each in chronological order. Participants were told that they would be watching a movie composed of a sequence of pictures taken throughout that day; they were given no special instructions on how to process the review. Each participant received two end-of-day reviews, one on a sensor-triggered day and one on a timer-triggered day.

The number of pictures used to create the review movie was half of the number of pictures captured on the practice day for that participant (which was always the first day and used sensor-mode without review). We could not use the same number of pictures for all participants because it was not known ahead of time how many pictures would be captured for each participant on each day. Our main concern was to ensure that, for each individual participant, the same number of images was used for both end-of-day reviews. A participant's first day of SenseCam use provided an estimate of the number of daily pictures we could expect to be captured for that individual. To account for the possibility of fewer pictures being captured on subsequent days, we conservatively set the number of pictures to be used for review as half of the number captured on each participant's first day ($M = 1{,}022$, $SD = 235$). The mean duration of the reviews was 17 min 2 s ($SD = 3$ min 55 s).

Memory measures

Memory for events that occurred during the acquisition period was tested with six different test procedures:

Recollection Judgement. Participants were shown a picture and made a *yes/no* judgement in response to the following instructions: "Recollective memory is when you are able to recall a specific episode or moment from your life. It is almost like reliving or re-experiencing the past event. Please indicate whether you have a recollective memory for this picture."

Recognition Rating. Participants were shown a picture accompanied by the following instructions: "Please rate the strength of your memory for the scene(s) and/or event(s) depicted by this picture." Participants responded using a 1–7 scale, with 1 labelled as "no memory" and 7 labelled as "extremely strong memory". In contrast to the standard old–new recognition method used in laboratory experiments, no lures were presented. Since lures could be made arbitrarily easy or difficult to correctly reject (e.g., a picture taken on the Moon vs a picture taken from 10 cm to the participant's right), we saw no value in including them.

Picture-Cued Recall. Participants were shown a picture accompanied by the following instructions: "Please describe in detail the visual scene(s)/event(s) as they would appear to the SenseCam in the one minute following this picture. If you can't remember anything for this picture, you may type a question mark to continue to the next picture." There was a maximum of 1 minute to respond to each item, with no minimum time requirement.

Time-Cued Recall. Participants were shown a date and time from their acquisition period (e.g., "Tuesday 11:09 am") accompanied by the following instructions: "Please describe in detail the visual scene(s)/event(s) as they appeared to the SenseCam at the above day and time. If you can't remember anything for this day and time, you may type a question mark to continue to the next trial." There was a maximum of 1 minute to respond to each item, with no minimum time requirement.

Recall of Time. Participants were shown a picture and asked to give the day and time it was taken. They made a forced choice on *day* from among the days they wore SenseCam (e.g., Monday, Tuesday, Wednesday, Thursday, Friday), and a forced choice on *time of day* (12:00 am to 11:55 pm in intervals of 5 minutes). A response was required for each field, and participants were instructed to give their best guess if they were not sure.

Temporal Order Judgement. Participants were shown two pictures arranged vertically on the screen and they made a forced-choice judgement about which was captured first. Paired pictures were selected from the same acquisition day (and thus from the same review condition), with acquisition order counterbalanced.

Memory test procedures

Tests were administered individually on computers with instructions presented entirely via onscreen text. Pictures were selected randomly (without replacement) from each participant's total set of captured pictures for inclusion on the tests for that participant. Pictures were never tested more than once. For a given test session each participant completed the following number of items: Recollection Judgement (192); Recognition Rating (192); Picture-Cued Recall (48); Time-Cued Recall (8); Recall of Time (96); Temporal Order Judgement (192). Fewer trials were given for the more time-consuming memory measures in order to reduce the total duration of the testing sessions.

Counterbalancing ensured equal representation in each phase of each test for each participant for all manipulated variables, as well as whether or not the picture had been included in the review if it came from a review day. Participants were only shown and tested on pictures from their own acquisition periods. They had been informed about this aspect of the experiment, so they knew that all of the pictures were ones from their lives.

Each test consisted of four phases, with participants allowed to take 5-minute breaks between phases. Each of the first three phases included five blocks, with each block consisting of only one type of item (all but the Time-Cued Recall items). Block order was determined randomly. The fourth phase consisted of the Time-Cued Recall items.

Memory test intervals

Participants returned to the lab for testing sessions at retention intervals of approximately 1, 3, and 8 weeks. The mean number of days that the testing sessions occurred after the final acquisition day are as follows: Test 1: 5.67 days ($SD = 2.01$, $range = 4–10$); Test 2: 29.50 days ($SD = 1.12$, $range = 27–31$); Test 3: 57.50 days ($SD = 2.43$, $range = 52–62$).

Payment schedule

Participants were each paid $50 in cash in four instalments: $15 at the end of the acquisition period, $10 upon arriving for the first and the second test sessions, and $15 upon arriving for the third (final) test session.

RESULTS AND DISCUSSION

For all tests reported below, an alpha level of .05 was used to indicate statistical significance. Effect sizes for ANOVAs are reported as estimated partial ω^2 calculated using the formulae provided by Maxwell and Delaney (2004).

Pictures captured

For the four experimental days, the mean number of pictures captured per day was 2390 ($SD = 566$, *range* = 1358–3479) in the timer-triggered condition and 2031 ($SD = 565$, *range* = 721–3200) in the sensor-triggered condition. The mean number of pictures captured per hour was reliably greater for the timer-triggered condition ($M = 272$, $SD = 60$) versus the sensor-triggered condition ($M = 209$, $SD = 60$), $t(11) = 3.37$.

Of pictures captured in the sensor-triggered condition, 95% were triggered by passive infrared (which can only be triggered when the camera is stationary), 4% were triggered by white light level, and 1% were triggered by both. Thus, for the types of events in the weekday lives of American undergraduates, the sensor algorithm was most often triggered by the passive infrared sensor. This may reflect the sedentary nature of common activities in undergraduates' daytime weekday lives (e.g., sitting in classrooms, working at computers, watching television) along with their interactions with sources of infrared (e.g., motion of other people or of the participant's hands in front of the device).

Memory measures: Scoring criteria

The six memory measures were scored as follows: (a) Recollection Judgements: 0 for "no" and 1 for "yes," (b) Recognition Rating: 1 to 7, where 7 was "extremely strong memory," (c) Picture-Cued Recall and Time-Cued Recall: amount recalled as response length in number of characters (length = 0 for "?" responses), (d) Recall of Time: 0 to 2, with one point each for correct day and correct time to within one hour, and (e) Temporal Order Judgement: 0 for incorrect and 1 for correct.

Overall data

In the results and discussion section we focus on those aspects of the data that let us answer the questions we set out to study. However, for completeness we give the entire data set for all six memory measures as a function of retention interval, review condition, and trigger condition in the Appendix.

Evaluating the memory measures

We assumed that over 8 weeks there would be substantial forgetting, enabling a rough comparison of the sensitivity of our various memory measures. We reasoned that the greater the decline in performance across tests for a particular measure, the greater the degree to which actual retrieval of episodic details was required for that measure, and thus the more sensitive it is as a measure of autobiographical memory. The values for each memory measure were first standardised within participants, to account for individual differences in absolute levels of performance and to allow direct comparison of memory measures. The mean of the participant means of these standardised values, across retention interval, is shown in Table 1. The right-most column shows the difference from the first test to the third test.

The *Picture-Cued Recall* measure showed the largest amount of forgetting. One would expect a standard probed recall measure for the content of experienced events to be a good response measure. It appears to work well using just the amount written down without scoring for accuracy. The *Recognition Rating (1–7 scale)* for the pictures was the next most sensitive measure. This is consistent with previous studies of autobiographical memory that found this type of measure to be effective (e.g., Brewer, 1988). The data for the *Time-Cued Recall* task suggest that time was not as good a probe for recall as were the pictures of the actual events. This is somewhat analogous to the findings reported in Brewer (1988) that time was a relatively poor

TABLE 1
Memory measures: Means of participant means of scores standardised within participants

Memory measure	*Retention interval*			
	1 week	*3 weeks*	*8 weeks*	*1 week − 8 weeks*
Picture-Cued Recall	.37	−.10	−.28	.65
Recognition Rating	.29	−.07	−.22	.50
Time-Cued Recall	.30	−.10	−.20	.49
Recollection Judgement	.18	−.07	−.11	.29
Temporal Order Judgement	.02	.03	−.05	.06
Recall of Time	.00	.05	−.05	.05

probe cue in autobiographical memory. Furthermore, we think that when given a time and a day of the week, participants could have used knowledge of their weekly schedules during that semester to infer where they would have been and what the visual scene would have been, without necessarily having any specific episodic memory for that time. The simple binary *Recollection Judgement* shows some modest memory sensitivity. Note that in some ways this measure can be thought of as a binary version of the more sensitive 1–7 recognition scale. The *Temporal Order Judgement* and *Recall of Time* measure show little sensitivity to forgetting. Friedman (1993) has made powerful arguments that much time information in autobiographical memory is reconstructed from knowledge of script-based information. We think it is likely that these two measures reflect this type of reconstruction and thus do not show episodic forgetting over the time intervals studied. For example, it would have been trivial for participants to correctly order a daytime and a night-time picture from the same day, without any recourse to episodic memory. Similarly, the approximate time of day could be inferred from information in the picture along with participants' knowledge of their schedules.

On the basis of the above analysis, and for the sake of brevity, we have chosen to focus on Recognition Rating and Picture-Cued Recall as the memory measures for the rest of the analyses. They are the top two measures in terms of forgetting effect size, and the use of two different measures (one recognition and one recall) allows us to see how consistent our findings are across different indexes of memory.

Overall ANOVA for Recognition Ratings

A three-way ANOVA was conducted to evaluate the effect of retention interval (three levels), review condition (two levels), and trigger condition (two levels) on Recognition Rating. Mauchly's test indicated that the assumption of sphericity was met for all main effects and interactions. There was a statistically significant main effect of retention interval, $F(2, 22) = 11.19$, $MSE = 1.07$, $\omega^2 = .170$, and of review condition, $F(1, 11) = 5.02$, $MSE = 0.65$, $\omega^2 = .028$, but not of trigger condition, $F(1, 11) = 0.54$, $MSE = 0.69$, $p = .476$, $\omega^2 = -.004$. No interactions were statistically significant. Follow-up analyses are presented in separate sections below.

Overall ANOVA for Picture-Cued Recall

A three-way ANOVA was conducted to evaluate the effect of retention interval (three levels), review condition (two levels), and trigger condition (two levels) on Picture-Cued Recall. Mauchly's test indicated that the assumption of sphericity was violated for the interaction of retention interval with trigger condition, $\chi^2(2) = 8.08$, $p = .018$, and nearly violated for the main effect of retention interval, $\chi^2(2) = 5.41$, $p = .067$. Analyses were conducted using Greenhouse-Geisser adjusted degrees of freedom for these two effects, but because the results did not differ importantly from analyses assuming sphericity, we present the latter here for the sake of consistency. There was a statistically significant main effect of retention interval, $F(2, 22) = 7.09$, $MSE = 1{,}017.54$, $\omega^2 = .129$, and of review condition, $F(1, 11) = 5.24$, $MSE = 175.18$, $\omega^2 = .012$, but not of trigger condition, $F(1, 11) = 3.62$, $MSE = 324.45$, $p = .083$, $\omega^2 = .013$. No interactions were statistically significant.

Forgetting function

Figure 1 shows the decline in memory performance across the three time intervals for both Recognition Rating and Picture-Cued Recall.

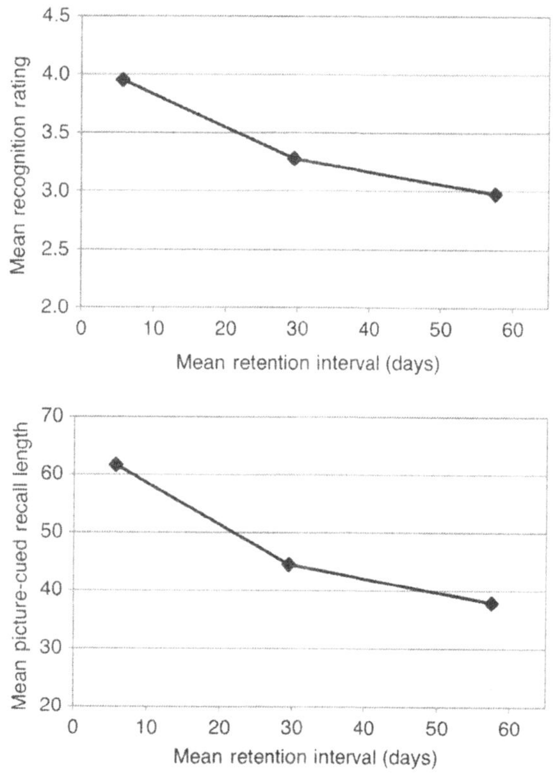

Figure 1. Mean recognition rating (top) and mean picture-cued recall length (bottom) as a function of mean retention interval for the three testing sessions.

Mean performance on both measures decreased reliably across the three retention intervals, as confirmed by separate least-square fittings of a power function ($P = at^b$, where P is performance and t is time) for each participant for Recognition Rating (mean standardized $b = -0.22$, $t(11) = -4.12$, one-tailed), and for Picture-Cued Recall (mean standardized $b = -0.19$, $t(11) = -2.44$, one-tailed). One-tailed tests were used based on the strong theoretical prediction that memory declines over time.

End-of-day review

Figure 2 shows that an end-of-day review improved performance for both Recognition Rating and Picture-Cued Recall. Recognition Ratings were reliably higher for reviewed days ($M = 3.55$, $SD = 0.69$) versus non-reviewed days ($M = 3.25$, $SD = 0.80$). Picture-Cued Recall lengths were reliably higher when there had been an end-of-day review ($M = 50.55$, $SD = 20.85$) versus no such review ($M = 45.51$, $SD = 18.49$).

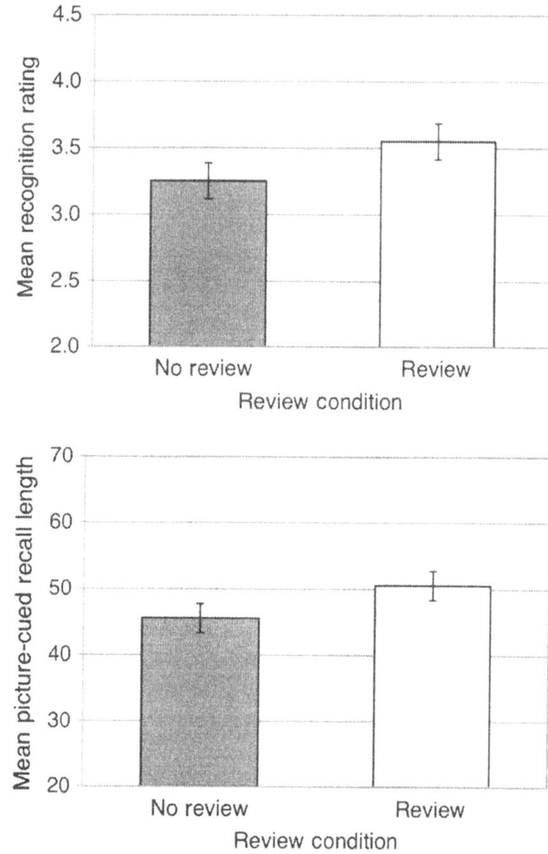

Figure 2. Mean recognition rating (top) and mean picture-cued recall length (bottom) as a function of review condition. Error bars represent standard error of the difference between conditions.

Trigger condition

Figure 3 shows that the default SenseCam sensor settings provide little improvement in selecting items yielding higher memory performance compared to randomly selected items for both Recognition Rating and Picture-Cued Recall. Recognition Ratings were not reliably different for pictures captured as triggered by the sensors ($M = 3.45$, $SD = 0.75$) versus the timer ($M = 3.35$, $SD = 0.75$). Picture-Cued Recall lengths were not reliably different for pictures captured as triggered by the sensors ($M = 50.89$, $SD = 20.05$) versus the timer ($M = 45.17$, $SD = 19.94$). Recognition Ratings were reliably greater for pictures triggered by the passive infrared sensor ($M = 3.47$, $SD = 0.76$) versus the white light level sensor ($M = 2.92$, $SD = 1.13$), $t(11) = 2.83$. There were not enough data to conduct the same comparison for Picture-Cued Recall.

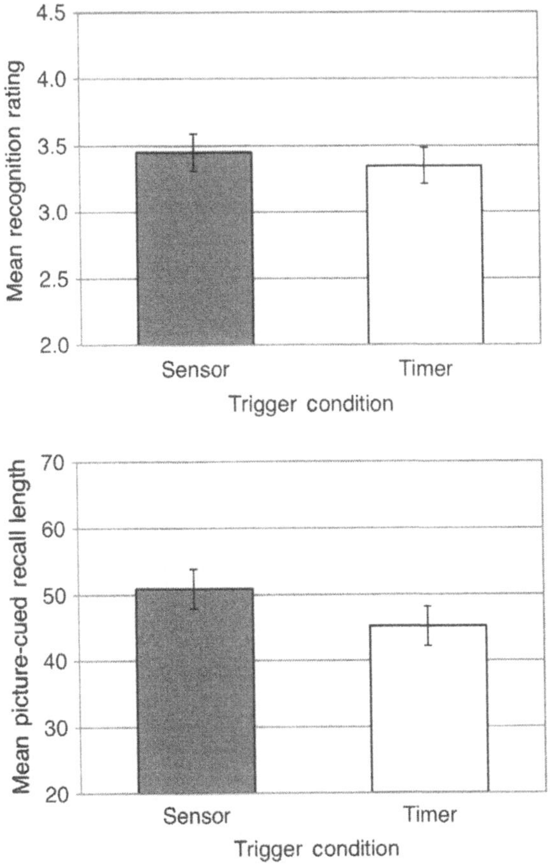

Figure 3. Mean recognition rating (top) and mean picture-cued recall length (bottom) as a function of trigger condition. Error bars represent standard error of the difference between conditions.

GENERAL DISCUSSION

The results showed substantial forgetting across retention intervals, and also revealed that certain memory measures were better indicators of episodic memory than others (i.e., they were more sensitive to forgetting), as shown in Table 1. Performance was greater for reviewed days than for non-reviewed days, but did not reliably differ for sensor-triggered versus timer-triggered pictures.

Our data suggest that an end-of-day review of an individual's activities (via pictures captured by SenseCam) increases performance on several memory measures for that day. However, we need a deeper understanding of the factors involved in the review process. Such factors include (a) types of pictures chosen for review, (b) presentation order (e.g., non-chronological ordering might actually enhance memory), (c) presentation speed, (d) self-paced versus experimenter-paced review, and (e) spacing (e.g., the number and scheduling of review presentations). Furthermore, picture review needs to be compared to other forms of review. For example, Koutstaal et al. (1998) found that reviewing a verbal description of events enhanced memory to the same extent as reviewing photographs of the events. Picture review should also be compared to unaided mental review.

As a research tool for autobiographical memory, SenseCam has two important attributes: it can unobtrusively capture a pictorial record of an individual's experiences, and it has sensors that can be set to automatically select the pictures to be taken (as well as providing sensor data). In the present study the current sensor-based trigger algorithm showed little success at selecting the more memorable events. That is, the sensor-triggered picture capture strategy did not have an impact on participants' memory as we measured it when compared to a strategy of capturing pictures at regular intervals and randomly sampling for review and testing. The question of whether a sensor-driven approach to input filtering is appropriate depends on the user's goals and on the extent to which the measured physical environment is systematically related to those goals. Ongoing analyses of the rich data collected here have begun to uncover systematic relationships between sensor values and improved memory performance, and have also begun to demonstrate ways to devise more effective thresholds and selection algorithms (Finley, Brewer, & Benjamin, 2009).

The variability in memory performance that can be accounted for by physical characteristics of the environment almost certainly varies by the structure of peoples' lives, the nature of their activities, their cognitive functioning, and their particular memory goals. Any of these may differ between individuals, and may particularly differ for memory rehabilitation patients versus the healthy young adults in the present study. Thus, adaptive calibration of sensor thresholds and triggering algorithms may be necessary on the individual user level in order to implement effective sensor-based strategies of picture capture.

SenseCam constitutes a new tool for autobiographical memory research that has different capabilities and different disadvantages from those previously available. For example, although SenseCam does provide a veridical visual record which should be useful for evaluating recall accuracy, there are several issues that will have to be resolved: (a) Script-based responses. It is often difficult to differentiate between information in participants' responses that was genuinely recalled versus information that was provided in the picture itself or inferred from the picture and participants' general knowledge of the structure of their own lives (e.g., "I am walking to Spanish or German class. I know this because the tree angle is very dramatic and it wouldn't be at noon, which is when I'd normally leave this area."). (b) Narrative summarisation. It seems likely that participants often did not provide as much detail as they actually had in memory (e.g., "Dinner with friends"). (c) Non-picture information. Many recall responses contain specific details that cannot easily be verified by the picture alone, such as: thoughts or emotions, the topic of a lecture or conversation, the identities of other people, the name of a building (e.g., "I was in design class being bored out of my mind at this point ... ", "telling my boyfriend on aim [AOL Instant Messenger] that all the rum is gone on Friday ... ", "I am showing off bad paint brushes that no one washed off so they were useless. I am behind the front desk at [X] Hall ... ").

Making maximum use of the picture information will require addressing these difficulties. For example the occurrence of script-based responses could be studied by seeing how much the experimenters (acting as control participants) might themselves be able to describe the visual scene or infer what would be pictured next. The issue of narrative summarisation could be addressed by more elaborate instructions or by adjustments in the scoring procedures. The occurrence of non-picture information could be studied using additional experience sampling methods (e.g., Brewer, 1988), or using other information sources (e.g., course lecture notes). Additional research possibilities will continue to arise as additional sensor information becomes available (e.g., audio, location, physiological data).

In this paper we have focused on the use of an end-of-day review of SenseCam pictures to fortify autobiographical memory, and on their effectiveness as memory cues. However, as with any form of external memory, SenseCam pictures could be used for a variety of other purposes (cf. Bush, 1945), such as a tool for reminiscing about the past, for evaluating allocation of activities during a day, to complement human memory by revealing what may not have been noticed or encoded upon initial experience, for back-up reference in case human memory fails, or even to supplant human memory for certain purposes. Proliferation of such technology should continue to transform not just research, but the way we live.

REFERENCES

Bell, G., & Gemmell, J. (2007, March). A digital life. *Scientific American*, *296*(3), 58–65.

Bell, G., & Gemmell, J. (2009). *Total recall: How the e-memory revolution will change everything*. New York, NY: Dutton.

Berry, E., Kapur, N., Williams, L., Hodges, S., Watson, P., Smyth, G., et al. (2007). The use of a wearable camera, SenseCam, as a pictorial diary to improve autobiographical memory in a patient with limbic encephalitis: A preliminary report. *Neuropsychological Rehabilitation*, *17*(4–5), 582–681.

Brewer, W. F. (1986). What is autobiographical memory? In D. Rubin (Ed.), *Autobiographical memory* (pp. 25–49). Cambridge, UK: Cambridge University Press.

Brewer, W. F. (1988). Memory for randomly sampled autobiographical events. In U. Neisser & E. Winograd (Eds.), *Remembering reconsidered: Ecological and traditional approaches to the study of memory* (pp. 21–90). Cambridge, UK: Cambridge University Press.

Brewer, W. F. (1996). What is recollective memory? In D. C. Rubin (Ed.), *Remembering our past: Studies in autobiographical memory* (pp. 19–66). Cambridge, UK: Cambridge University Press.

Bush, V. (1945). As we may think. *Atlantic Monthly*.

Conner, T. S., Barrett, L. F., Tugade, M. M., & Tennen, H. (2007). Idiographic personality: The theory and practice of experience sampling. In R. W. Robins, R. C. Fraley, & R. Kreuger (Eds.), *Handbook of research methods in personality psychology* (pp. 79–98). New York, NY: The Guilford Press.

Conway, M. A. (1990). *Autobiographical memory: An introduction*. Buckingham, UK: University Press.

Conway, M. A. (2005). Memory and the self. *Journal of Memory and Language*, *53*, 594–628.

Crovitz, H. F., & Schiffman, H. (1974). Frequency of episodic memories as a function of their age. *Bulletin of the Psychonomic Society*, *4*(5b), 517–518.

Ebbinghaus, H. (1885). Retention as a function of the number of repetitions. In *Memory: A contribution to experimental psychology* (Ch 6). Translated by Henry A. Ruger & Clara E. Bussenius (1913). New York, NY: Teachers College, Columbia University.

Finley, J. R., Brewer, W. F., & Benjamin, A. S. (2009, October). *Reflections of memory in the environment: Improving the use of physical sensor data to predict memorability of SenseCam pictures from everyday life*. Presentation given at SenseCam 2009 Symposium, Chicago, IL.

Friedman, W. J. (1993). Memory for the time of past events. *Psychological Bulletin*, *113*, 44–66.

Galton, F. (1879a). Psychometric experiments. *Brain*, *2*, 149–162.

Galton, F. (1879b). Psychometric facts. *The Nineteenth Century, 5*, 425–433.

Hodges, S., Williams, L., Berry, E., Izadi, S., Srinivasan, J., Bulter, A., et al. (2006). SenseCam: A retrospective memory aid. In P. Dourish & A. Friday (Eds.), *Ubicomp 2006, LNCS 4206* (pp. 177–193). Berlin, Germany: Springer Verlag.

Jones, W., & Ross B. H. (2007). Personal information management. In F. Durso (Ed.), *Handbook of applied cognition: Second edition* (pp. 471–495). Chichester, UK: John Wiley & Sons, Inc.

Koutstaal, W., Schacter, D. L., Johnson, M. K., Angell, K. E., & Gross, M. S. (1998). Post-event review in older and younger adults: Improving memory accessibility of complex everyday events. *Psychology and Aging, 13*, 277–296.

Koutstaal, W., Schacter, D. L., Johnson, M. K., & Galluccio, L. (1999). Facilitation and impairment of event memory produced by photograph review. *Memory & Cognition, 27*, 478–493.

Linton, M. (1975). Memory for real-world events. In D. A. Norman & D. E. Rumelhart (Eds.), *Explorations in cognition* (pp. 376–404). San Francisco, CA: W. H. Freeman.

Maxwell, S. E., & Delaney, H. D. (2004). *Designing experiments and analyzing data: A model comparison perspective* (2nd ed.). Mahwah, NJ: Lawrence Erlbaum Associates.

Schacter, D. L., Koutstaal, W., Johnson, M. K., Gross, M. S., & Angell, K. E. (1997). False recollection induced by photographs: A comparison of older and younger adults. *Psychology and Aging, 12*, 203–215.

Sellen, A., Fogg, A., Hodges, S., & Wood, K. (2007). Do life-logging technologies support memory for the past? An experimental study using SenseCam. *Conference on Human Factors in Computing Systems, CHI*, Irvine, CA, 81–90.

Wagenaar, W. A. (1986). My memory: A study of autobiographical memory over six years. *Cognitive Psychology, 18*(2), 225–252.

APPENDIX A

Mean and *SD* of participant means of six memory measures by retention interval, review, and trigger condition

	1 week		*3 weeks*		*8 weeks*	
Memory measure	*No review*	*Review*	*No review*	*Review*	*No review*	*Review*
Recollection Judgement						
Sensor	0.41	0.54	0.35	0.38	0.36	0.37
	(0.18)	(0.19)	(0.19)	(0.19)	(0.16)	(0.19)
Timer	0.44	0.52	0.31	0.39	0.28	0.36
	(0.19)	(0.19)	(0.21)	(0.19)	(0.19)	(0.15)
Recognition Rating						
Sensor	3.89	4.14	3.28	3.37	2.97	3.07
	(0.94)	(0.60)	(0.94)	(0.89)	(1.06)	(1.17)
Timer	3.61	4.17	3.11	3.34	2.65	3.22
	(0.86)	(0.78)	(1.02)	(0.95)	(1.03)	(0.92)
Picture-Cued Recall						
Sensor	64.18	68.33	46.25	47.54	38.57	40.44
	(26.52)	(29.21)	(26.33)	(24.27)	(22.03)	(25.88)
Timer	51.56	62.53	38.94	45.42	33.53	39.05
	(24.71)	(24.12)	(23.23)	(25.42)	(22.41)	(26.05)
Time-Cued Recall						
Sensor	78.17	76.38	46.00	55.08	41.29	54.83
	(50.35)	(54.06)	(23.16)	(31.30)	(19.63)	(32.89)
Timer	60.17	84.04	46.96	69.88	55.67	48.00
	(50.02)	(47.40)	(29.25)	(31.79)	(27.08)	(26.32)
Temporal Order Judgement						
Sensor	0.62	0.63	0.63	0.65	0.57	0.64
	(0.09)	(0.09)	(0.08)	(0.08)	(0.11)	(0.09)
Timer	0.63	0.65	0.64	0.64	0.58	0.61
	(0.07)	(0.09)	(0.07)	(0.08)	(0.11)	(0.09)
Recall of Time						
Sensor	1.23	1.27	1.15	1.39	1.11	1.26
	(0.31)	(0.24)	(0.34)	(0.21)	(0.42)	(0.21)
Timer	1.03	1.20	1.10	1.24	1.11	1.08
	(0.26)	(0.29)	(0.30)	(0.32)	(0.39)	(0.33)

MANUSCRIPT SUBMISSION

The journal welcomes all forms of original work of a high quality on memory. In addition to full reports of research, we also publish short reports, provided that they are of significant empirical or theoretical impact. Short reports should consist of single experiments or comments on other papers, with a limit of 4000 words, 1 figure and/or table. Alternative forms of manuscript, such as theoretical papers or reviews, are also welcome if they are of a high standard of scholarship and originality.

New manuscripts should be submitted in either Word or PDF files to http://mc.manuscriptcentral.com/pmem

List the following information in the body of your covering letter: full contact details, the title of your article, the abstract, and whether you wish to submit the manuscript for publication as a regular article or as a short report.

All manuscripts must be accompanied by a statement confirming that it has not been previously published elsewhere and that it has not been submitted simultaneously for publication elsewhere. Submission of a paper is taken as acceptance by the author that it contains nothing libellous or infringes copyright. When a paper is accepted for publication the copyright will belong to the publisher.

FORMAT

Papers should be prepared in the format prescribed by the *American Psychological Association*. For full details of this format, please see the *Publication Manual of the APA* (6th edition).

Title. This should be as concise as possible, and typed on a separate page, together with the name(s) of the author(s) and the full postal address(es) of their institution(s). Proofs and requests for offprints will be sent to the first author unless otherwise indicated. A short running title of not more than 40 characters (including spaces) should also be indicated if the title is longer than this. Please provide up to 5 Keywords.

Abstract. An abstract of 100–150 words should follow the title page on a separate page.

Acknowledgements. These should be as brief as possible and typed on a separate page.

Permission to quote. Any direct quotation, regardless of length, must be accompanied by a reference citation that includes a page number. Any quote over six manuscript lines should have formal written permission to quote from the copyright owner. It is the author's responsibility to determine whether permission is required from the copyright owner and, if so, to obtain it.

Footnotes. These should be avoided unless absolutely necessary. Essential footnotes should be indicated by superscript figures in the text and collected on a separate page at the end of the manuscript.

Figures. Artwork should be saved (preferably as tiffs or jpegs) at a resolution of at least 300 dpi.

Reference citations within the text. Use authors' last names, with the year of publication in parentheses after the last author's name, e.g.: "Jones and Smith (1987)"; alternatively: "(Brown, 1989; Jones & Smith, 1987; White, Johnson, & Thomas, 1990)". On first citation of references with three, four, or five authors, give all names in full, thereafter use first author "et al.". If more than one article by the same author(s) in the same year is cited, the letters a, b, c, etc., should follow the year.

Reference list. A full list of references quoted in the text should be given at the end of the paper in alphabetical order of authors' surnames (or chronologically for a group of references by the same authors), commencing as a new page, typed double spaced. Titles of journals and books should be given in full, e.g.:

Books:

Cronbach, L. J., & Gleser, G. C. (1965). *Psychological tests and personnel decisions* (2nd ed.). Urbana, IL: Glencoe Press.

Chapter in edited book:

Jones, R. R., Reid, J. B., & Patterson, G. R. (1975). Naturalistic observation in clinical assessment. In P. McReynolds (Ed.), *Advances in psychological assessment* (Vol. 3, pp. 234–297). San Francisco, CA: Jossey-Bass.

Journal article:

Ellis, H. D., Lewis, M. B., Moselhy, H. F., & Young, A. W. (2000). Automatic without autonomic responses to familiar faces: Capgras delusion differentiates components of face recognition. *Cognitive Neuropsychiatry*, *5*, 255–269. doi:10.1080/13546800050199711

If a paper is in preparation, submitted, or under review, the reference should include the authors, the title, and the year of the draft (the paper should also be cited throughout using the year of the draft). Manuscripts that are in press should also include the publisher or journal, and should substitute "in press" for the date (and should be cited as "in press").

This publication has been produced with acid-free paper manufactured to strict environmental standards and with pulp derived fr

For Product Safety Concerns and Information please contact our EU representative GPSR@taylorandfrancis.com Taylor & Francis Verlag GmbH, Kaufingerstraße 24, 80331 München, Germany